# ONE WEEK LOAN

1 0 l  ᵞ 2010

D0279833

# MANAGING
# DIVERSITY
## *in the* Global
# Organization

## CREATING NEW BUSINESS VALUES

**CELIA DE ANCA**

*and*

**ANTONIO VAZQUEZ**

translation by Andy Goodall

palgrave
macmillan

First published in Spanish in 2005 by Pearson Educación, S.A.
This edition published 2007 by
PALGRAVE MACMILLAN
Houndmills, Basingstoke, Hampshire RG21 6XS and
175 Fifth Avenue, New York, N.Y. 10010
Companies and representatives throughout the world

PALGRAVE MACMILLAN is the global academic imprint of the Palgrave Macmillan division of St. Martin's Press, LLC and of Palgrave Macmillan Ltd. Macmillan® is a registered trademark in the United States, United Kingdom and other countries. Palgrave is a registered trademark in the European Union and other countries.

ISBN-13: 978–0–230–01882–2
ISBN-10: 0–230–01882–3

This book is printed on paper suitable for recycling and made from fully managed and sustained forest sources.

A catalogue record for this book is available from the British Library.

A catalog record for this book is available from the Library of Congress.

10  9  8  7  6  5  4  3  2  1
16  15  14  13  12  11  10  09  08  07

Printed and bound in China

*To Arpad, teacher, mentor, advisor
and, above all, a friend*
Celia


*To my wife, who has taught me the
true richness of diversity*
Antonio

# Contents

# List of Figures and Tables

## Figures

## Tables

# Prologue

Diversity is the reverse of globalization. It is not a paradox, in the sense that the globalization of many business sectors over the last few decades has brought with it an increased awareness of diversity of culture, gender and, at a more focussed micro-level, individuals and their personalities. This book, which I have the honor of writing the Prologue to, has the basic aim of analyzing the phenomena of diversity, its implications for business management and to propose a range of models that will allow us to take advantage of the opportunities it provides for organizational development and improvements in management systems.

The debate about cultural diversity has become increasingly relevant in management science in recent years. Both academic literature and business practice have incorporated relevant aspects, and diversity now forms part of competitiveness strategy in an increasing number of companies. In this sense, the fundamental hypothesis of this book is that diversity, when it is well managed, can be a source of competitive advantage for all types of company, whether small, medium or large.

Curiously, the analysis of cultural diversity in the field of sociology and business science has found an echo in other disciplines such as political philosophy and ethics. This development has led to confrontation between the recognition of cultural diversity as a fact, and efforts to construct a cosmopolitan moral philosophy, a minimum common denominator of respect for basic principles and human rights, as Immanuel Kant foresaw in his brief essay "Perpetual peace." This debate has on occasion led to the rejection of diversity, on the assumption that it could be an obstacle to achieving a fairer, more cosmopolitan society that respects the rights of individuals, and has led to the condemnation of various undesirable practices in several countries that were justified on the grounds of a mistaken principle of normative diversity. Nevertheless, we should clarify one fundamental point so as to avoid ill-informed arguments, both from the speculative point of view and the point of view of political and social action; the recognition of cultural diversity as a given does not imply accepting moral relativism.

Moral relativism is a normative position, which arises from debateable meta-ethical arguments that, in my opinion, can be rejected. The acceptance of cultural diversity as an object of study, on the other hand, is a methodological attitude that is both necessary and unavoidable. Confusing the study of cultural diversity and respect for the phenomena with moral relativism would result in falling into the naturalist fallacy, a classical logical error recognized by David Hume. The British philosopher explained that it is not possible to leap the logical abyss that separates descriptive propositions, aimed at conceptualizing reality, with formulating normative propositions about how things should be or should be done.

Certainly, respect for diversity is at the core of modernism and has been central to the struggle for individual rights over the last few centuries. This recognition of diversity is a consequence of the right to individual freedom, and it is connected to freedom of opinion and conscience, religious freedom and, of course, the principle of equality and the prohibition of discrimination on unjustified grounds.

A further common mistake is to study diversity with a presumption of cultural superiority. If diversity is accepted as a fact, scientific analysis and the development of proposals for action that will allow this diversity to be exploited as a pillar in the construction of a cosmopolitan society need to be undertaken with an attitude of humility and respect toward diversity in all its forms. The history of culture and European integration provides valid models that can be used as examples in many other spheres, including business. It is impressive, in this sense, that the majority of European Union citizens consider themselves to be European, whilst at the same time having a sense of national and regional identity.

In a similar way, the study of gender differences and the integration of women into all levels of professional life provide an outstanding opportunity for both social development and improvements in the management and results of companies. This book provides information about the current situation and about what remains to be achieved. A positive attitude to change and the implementation of imaginative proposals that allow integration and the promotion of women to the highest levels, on equal terms to men, should be on the agenda of senior managers in all companies.

It is also an honor to write the Prologue to this book, given the personal and intellectual qualities of the authors. Since meeting Professor Celia de Anca, I have been impressed by the depth of her cultural and intellectual background, her capacity for hard work, and her commitment to achieving change through her academic activity, which is, without doubt, the most genuine and valuable quality of all true academics. Celia has been the director of the Instituto de Empresa's Center for Diversity in Global Management since it was created two years ago. The

Center's mission is to promote the management of gender, cultural, age and competence diversity as a source of competitive advantage in the business world, through study, knowledge creation and the diffusion of know-how. During the two years it has been in existence, the Center has been incredibly busy investigating and disseminating best practice, both in Spain and abroad, with a special focus on the training of management and providing training courses on diversity for companies.

I have also known Antonio Vazquez Vega for a long time, and have seen how his abilities as both a manager and a thinker have borne fruit throughout his career. The work that Antonio has undertaken for Universia, the most important consortium of universities in the Spanish-speaking world, is to be highly commended. And it is also a source of pride that Antonio was a student of the Instituto de Empresa's Master in Legal Practice.

Finally, I would also like to praise the work of Jose Luis Silvestre, who has also helped with the creation of case studies and practical examples for this book. Jose Luis holds an MBA from the Instituto de Empresa, and has worked closely with the Center for Diversity in Global Management; his laudable work is included here as it is both necessary and useful for business practice.

I hope the reader will find this book easy to read, interesting and, fundamentally, relevant to business management. I would like to congratulate the authors on their highly necessary and timely contribution, which meets a theoretical and practical need in a field of study that is still in its infancy.

SANTIAGO IÑIGUEZ DE ONZOÑO
*Dean, Instituto de Empresa Business School*

# Initial Reflections: Reinventing Yourself in Diversity

The ability to reinvent yourself, to change your career path to realign your environment with who you really are, is an element of business theory that is considered essential in achieving professional success today. In a similar way, the company, as a living organism, finds itself today facing the need to reinvent itself to harmonize with its environment. The hypothesis put forward in this book is that diversity, when accepted as a natural element in a flexible environment, can provide the necessary instruments to acquire the values and characteristics that, in increasing measure, the company needs in the 21st century, to adapt to the environment in which it finds itself.

The economic and business environment in which the majority of companies move has changed radically over the last decade. This has resulted in significant change in the way that companies are managed, and in the way that new skills and competences are managed. Some of these changes have had profound effects on society, and on the way in which roles are perceived; roles that often implied specific abilities and skills.

One of the most significant factors has been the incorporation of women into the workplace, which has transformed the roles that society traditionally ascribed to each of the genders. The so-called "feminization" of the workplace has, among other things, resulted in the acceptance in the professional environment of things that were previously relegated to private life, such as achieving a better work–life balance, both for men and women.

Globalization, and its concomitant of companies that over time are becoming more and more multicultural, is another factor affecting companies today. In the 1970s we got used to the idea of thinking globally and acting locally, but, without wanting to negate the value of this concept today, it is becoming increasingly difficult to differentiate between the global and the local, when increasingly teams represent a wide range of cultures, and when multinational markets coincide in the same geographic environment. This multiculturalism, if it is managed, enables the company to grow by assimilating concepts and ways of working that are culturally different but complementary at the same time.

The integration of disabled people, made possible by developments in new technology, is another factor that is affecting companies, making them focus on new areas that enrich them from all points of view. Increasingly, the company today is allowing contributions from different perspectives that are increasing the capacity for innovation. Personal development provides an exponential increase in the innovatory and creative capacity of the individual and, as a result, of the company, if it is capable of incorporating the advantages of creativity that flow from the different forms of diversity.

This is not about proposing major changes or new theories. We are highlighting a fact that over recent years has been present in most multinational companies that have developed policies aimed at promoting and integrating diversity. We are aiming to fit these policies into a practical reference framework that will allow us to monitor them efficiently.

Theories of business management usually emphasize the importance of action, even before having cleared the new model that is being aimed at. Learning by doing has become one of the key elements in adapting to change. When it comes to diversity and inclusion policies, companies have been able to act quickly, and as a result we can observe how the majority of large companies, far in advance of what is required by legislation in the countries where they are based, have initiated a series of policies aimed at improving the quality and the quantity of diversity management. These policies fit into a new strategy from senior management, which is made concrete in a number of human resource policies that improve hiring and promotion policies and the flexibility of the career paths of their employees. These policies are supplemented by training programs and internal and external communication strategies aimed at increasing sensitivity to these issues.

Some management theorists[1] highlight the importance in any individual professional reorientation process of beginning with a phase of experimentation and change followed by a period of reflection to make sense of the process that began in an almost intuitive way. Making sense of the process once it has begun allows us to complete the equation. And making sense of the process is, as we understand it, the modest contribution that we academics can make at the moment to the management of corporate diversity, by understanding the policy framework that companies have been developing, fitting this into the current international and social framework and measuring how it affects business efficiency.

In this book we aim to develop a new frame of reference that encompasses these policies, and to understand how it has evolved in order to achieve the efficiency necessary to compete in a changing world; which in itself is a demonstration of the effectiveness of these policies and how they have evolved. Our aim in this book is, through theoretical analysis complemented by practical application and validation in business contexts, to find a reference point; the past and present that lead naturally to a future of increasing harmonization of the company with its environment. In other words, to create a vision of the company as a flexible organism that grows and innovates to the extent that its members can grow and innovate.

We are not aiming to change, but rather to enlarge the field of vision, to expand the values and traditional concepts within a wider frame of reference, where these values not only exist side by side with new values, but where they complement them, allowing the company not only to compete in a traditional environment, but also to compete in the much wider world in which we operate today.

Therefore the book leads to in-depth reflection on how the company can grow, to the extent that its human potential is allowed to grow and develop. This can of course lead to great complexity, as managing diversity requires openness to a wide range of ways of thinking and acting, some of which are radically opposed to each other. We intend to reflect on how to solve the paradox of these opposites and how to resolve the common human way of thinking that everything will work better if only everyone else would think as one, instead of accepting that the others are not worthless but complementary.

Finally, there is one further consideration. As you can see, this book does not have just one author, but two. Perhaps this was the only way for us to see and understand that, from the very beginning, we do everything together. Whatever the case may be, it came about by chance and perhaps both authors having to agree on everything is one of the sources of the riches, however few or many there may be, that you will find in these pages. As with everything, at various times we each had to give way on something or be adamant about something else. And perhaps this is an example of the extraordinary game of diversity in which at different times some move and others wait, and in the end we all win.

# Structure of the Book

This book has two fundamental objectives:

1. To provide a review of the existing theoretical framework by analyzing the historical perspective of diversity, while incorporating some of the new ideas developed in recent decades about gender, culture and personality and how they apply to the company.
2. To create a new framework for analysis that will allow us to understand the different management policies that are taking root in companies, and how to refine the tools available to the desired objectives.

In order to achieve this we have divided the book into two main sections.

Part One: Understanding Diversity undertakes an analysis of the environment of diversity, of organizational change and the role that diversity now plays within companies. At the same time, it also analyzes the content of diversity: culture, gender and personality as fundamental components of diversity within organizations, concluding with a correlation of the values supplied by diversity with those emerging in companies in the 21st century.

Part Two: Managing Diversity has a more practical purpose as it aims to develop a new framework for analysis to help understand current business policies related to diversity, together with the most appropriate tools to achieve specific objectives, taken from the practices of today's companies. We also look at some case studies that illustrate these policies.

Finally, by way of an epilogue, we present the testimony of various experts and practitioners who, over the last decade, have influenced society to help it take greater advantage of a dimension that is changing the way in which we understand the company. To give a diversity flavor in this last part of the book, a decision has been taken to leave the section in the original languages of the experts.

# Acknowledgements

This book has been possible thanks to the support we have received from various people and institutions, who we would like to take this opportunity to thank and to recognize.

In the first place, we must recognize the contribution made by Jose Luís Silvestre of the Instituto de Empresa Business School's Center for Diversity in Global Management, who we wish to thank for his help in preparing the case studies. We also appreciated his enthusiasm and valuable supply of facts and ideas that are reflected throughout the book.

We would also like to thank Luiza Helena Trajano, Rachid Slimi, Arpad von Lazar, Marianne Toldalagi, Amparo Moraleda and Gracia Cardador who provided their ideas in the answers to the questionnaire in the Epilogue, which give the reader important ideas to reflect upon, and a valuable cultural richness that enables us to dig deeper into our understanding of diversity. We would also like to highlight the support received from JP Morgan Chase, Ford and SCH, all of whom provide valuable examples of the ways in which diversity can be harnessed for the greater good of an organization.

Finally we would like to thank the Instituto de Empresa Business School and Universia for providing us with the platform to begin this work, without whose support we would not have been able to complete this book.

# Part One

## *Understanding Diversity*

# Introduction to Part One

It is 10:25 at night. I just managed to get the last flight, but only because it was delayed. As always, the flight was full and I ended up sitting at the back. We took off 10 minutes ago and, even though there must be more than 200 people on board, the silence is amazing. The majority of passengers have taken off their jackets, and from here I can see a sea of blue and white shirts. The air hostesses are calmly going through their routine of handing out drinks and sandwiches.

Where I am sitting, I feel different. I can see nearly the whole plane without them being able to see me, and that makes me reflect. The truth is, you never have much time for thinking and you have to take advantage whenever you can.

Things are changing. You can sense it even if you don't really know how or in what way. I suppose it is normal and I relax, but I know that something is changing, and seeing this plane at this time of night tells me that it is so.

The truth is I don't know why I am surprised. All I need to do is look at any media of communication, it doesn't matter which, to see that change is possibly the most common denominator of our times and, strangely, one of the few things that we all agree about. Orientals, Latin Americans, Slavs … it doesn't matter. We can all see that this time the change is here to stay, like it is something stuck to the sole of our shoes that we have started to get used to.

I think that change always happens and always has; it is the lever of progress that has got us to where we are today. But now it seems like these changes are determined to overcome the barriers of space and time and become everyday reality.

Something on this plane tells me that things are changing; and things at my company, with all its modern touches, tell me so too. The organization chart says it with statistics that are cold and clear; in my company there are more women than men, whereas 40 years ago that would have been unthinkable; and almost half my colleagues are from countries and cultures that I haven't even seen in a travel agent's brochure. I take over 40 international flights a year, and at the meetings I go to I am the only person who speaks my mother tongue. I live and share with people from all classes and cultures; people who 6, 8, 10 hours ago were in an environment with habits and customs worlds away from mine. And this is beginning to be the everyday reality of my life.

Things have definitely changed, and continue to change, although I don't know exactly how far things are going to go.

We live in a diverse world. Perhaps that is one of those few things that do not need any explanation. We can see it and feel it at every moment in the reality that surrounds us. The question is not whether we are diverse or not, it is whether we are capable of understanding what this means and, more importantly, taking advantage of it, so that this diversity can become a major asset for this century.

For a long time the US has looked to the East and Latin America for cheap labor to help its economy. Europe is doing the same; opening up to the emerging economies of Eastern Europe, whilst continuing to care for its delicate network of relationships with Africa and the Arab world. Japan looks to the US; Spain disembarks in Latin America. Nothing that happens anywhere in the world is alien to the rest of the world. Look at it how you will, globalization is a reality, whether or not we know how to understand it and deal with it, and companies, industries, markets and even entire economies are becoming ever more sensitive to the smallest change that happens anywhere in the world.[1]

A new film has its premiere everywhere in the world within a couple of days; there is no one anywhere in the world who can honestly say that they do not know what Coke is. Most people use the same operating system for their PC, Nike decides how we mortals should run and what the ball that half the planet watches should look like. To the extent that we are able to overcome the globalization–diversity debate, we should not look at globalization as something negative; we should look at it with the sense of security that comes from glimpsing an amazing opportunity.

As the European Commission recognizes, there are many reasons for an increased interest in diversity and two of these stand out:

1. **Demographic change:** the population structures of all European countries have changed and are continuing to change. This affects the type of person we employ, the type of person we supply products to and the type of person from whom we buy goods and services:
   - An increasing number of women have joined the labor market, and are becoming entrepreneurs
   - Population migration has resulted in multicultural and multiethnic populations throughout Europe

- The average age of the workforce is increasing: there are fewer and fewer young people as a percentage of the workforce.
2. **Changing expectations:** it is becoming increasingly obvious that people are interested in the social and ethical dimension of their working lives, and the way in which they consume products and services. The idea that companies should treat their employees fairly is one of the most widely shared beliefs we have. The increased expectations that employees have of management are focussed on fairness and the need for the employee to achieve a reasonable work–life balance. The speed of change suggests that cultures, values, tastes and needs cannot be taken for granted. In addition to guaranteeing that no group suffers discrimination, the European Commission has indicated that the recognition of diversity and similarity means understanding how they can be exploited to the benefit of the individual, the company and society in general. Managing diversity and guaranteeing justice and equality is no longer "a good cause"; it is an imperative in a changing world.[2]

In the context of Spain, the social and professional diversity of the Spanish workforce is being increased by the incorporation of women, the ageing of the population, the single European market, population migrations and the use of multidisciplinary teams within organizations; teams are now more diverse in gender, age, culture and functional composition. Senior managers in large companies are becoming more interested in this growth of diversity and in the most efficient methods of managing the needs of a diverse workforce, as Professor Mayo indicated.[3]

Diversity is becoming one of the defining themes of our time. We are different because our ways of doing things are different; we are diverse in gender, where there are distinct masculine and feminine values, diverse in cultures enriched by the contribution of different ethnic and racial groups, diverse in personality, diverse in age, diverse in the way we manage time. Diversity has probably always been with us, feeding the most open forms of human genius. The importance of the age that we are living in is the richness that can be achieved by managing this fundamental asset, which differentiates and renews all humanity.

The fundamental challenge for companies, particularly those with an international focus, is managing this diversity. Today's companies operate in different markets and different countries, with different products and services and distinct lines of business, responding to growing needs from different sectors; employees, governments, clients, social agents and the media.

Companies by their nature are advocates of expansion and growth, and this, in an age like ours that has overcome the limits of space and time, means that in a relatively short space of time companies can become international structures with a presence in many countries. Today it is normal that the car we drive was bought in Spain, after being assembled in Germany using parts from Korea to a blueprint developed in the US. Whoever is going to manage such a process will inevitably be confronted with different cultures, with different ways of doing things and different ways of understanding. But, above all, they are going to be confronted with a different way of interpreting and understanding the way we relate, manage and act; this is something that should not only be understood and respected, but also can be taken advantage of.

Diversity, understood as meaning putting different people in different positions, does not necessarily guarantee success; quite the opposite. If the different points of view and opinions are not handled well, then the decision-making process can become enormously difficult. Diversity has to be managed in such a way that differences are transformed into a catalyst of business success.

The first step to managing diversity correctly is to recognize the contribution that different people can make, so as to then integrate the different points of view into a more general framework. This is where we find the first difficulty, as it is difficult to describe categories without falling into the trap of generalization and dogmatism, which can result in prejudice, stereotypes and unfair policies.

The problem is that each person sees the world differently. Their view of the world is colored by their culture, their gender and the way in which their personality and experience modify this legacy. As a result, it is safer to talk about general tendencies or archetypes that can be attributed to masculine or feminine behavior or to a specific culture, independently of whether or not such traits are common to all the members of the group.

As Jung indicated,[4] feminine and masculine archetypes give us all a representation of the masculine ideal, reflected in the ideal of the father, and of the feminine ideal represented by the ideal of the mother. Does this mean that all women correspond to the feminine archetype? Of course it does not. There are aggressive and independent women just as there are sensitive and dependent ones. Likewise there are sensitive men. Nevertheless the archetype persists in the collective mind and as a result it is normal to talk about a woman with masculine characteristics (you only have to recall the comments about Margaret Thatcher) or a man who has feminine characteristics. The archetype that we have recorded in our minds develops as roles and social functions evolve throughout history so that, although there are always trends, they do not correspond to men or women as a whole. And so, studies of men and/or women and their relationships only show us tendencies at a particular point that, no matter how well defined they might be, are not always fulfilled.

Something similar happens with culture. We can perceive major differences between English and African culture, for example, if we examine their ways of understanding time or social relationships. However, if we undertake cultural tests on a sufficiently varied group, it is very likely that we will find more than one English person with a collective mentality and more than one African with an individual mentality. Nevertheless, as categories or mental archetypes, individualism or collectivism are real and present and we often find ourselves faced with these parameters, accepting them when they are accurate and rejecting them when they are less so.

Personality is another complex parameter. Many people are surprised to find that, wherever they may be, there is a range of personalities which in some way or another repeat themselves; the way someone acts ends up reminding us of Aunt Julia (or some other close friend or relative). Films and novels, once translated, can become universal simply because the personalities described in them are in no way strange to us. These stereotypical personalities represent the egoist, the hero, the artist and so on, and it is easy for us to identify with them or to recognize them in someone we know. As a result, it seems that there are a limited number of personality types; it may be 9 or it may be 90, but a finite number sifted through a cultural sieve. It is equally difficult to find a personality type in its pure form outside the novel. No matter how accurate a personality test might be, it will always be an approximation of a particular type, never a 100 percent match.

Nevertheless, gender, culture and personality provide a series of parameters for understanding the world and so are useful tools and resources for surviving in it. Choosing one or another depends on human history and individual personality, but we all recognize that they exist. We may be individualists, but we recognize a collective personality, which we may or may not be comfortable with, but we at least understand how it functions.

And to complicate our understanding of diversity further, it is important to point out that we do not act in an isolated laboratory, but rather in human groups who influence one another immediately and dynamically at every moment. Many of us, often without realizing that we are doing it, have ended up imitating the accent of the person we are speaking to, or their gestures, an idea or a pithy expression. And as we interact with others, we may change our way of doing things and thinking, whether by emulation, rejection or simply in order to compensate. The technological media invented in recent times, from television to the Internet, mean that ideas can be transmitted globally instantaneously, so that adolescents from Amsterdam to Bogotá will all use the same fashionable phrase.

So, there are no absolutely pure personalities, cultures or genders. But there are cultural, personality and gender parameters of action that most of us use without thinking. Being able to examine these parameters in detail and understand their advantages and disadvantages provides us with useful tools. This diversity provides us with new resources with which to grow, understanding not only the way in which we work, but also understanding how other individuals function in the same system.

Different rules of behavior based on gender, culture or personality help the individual to develop in a process that Maslow calls self-realization, or in Jung's terminology, to fuse the archetypes that constitute the person in their process of individualization. The person who can harmonize their actions with their self will be more complete and less affected by external conditions; this means that they will have a greater capacity to act as independent individuals in the system, with the clarity of being able to see the common objective of the organization and to contribute as best they can to the achievement of those objectives.

The more variety exists, the more likely it is that we will find different visions of the world and more specific problems. As a result, it is important to discover different attitudes and ways of working and a way of integrating these visions and different personalities into a general framework within a company. This makes it possible to change and transform traditional management styles and so take advantage of new abilities.

If we accept individual idiosyncrasies, the next question that we have to ask ourselves is if the organizational framework has sufficient flexibility to allow the coexistence of these different behaviors, or whether an organization can use this diversity to obtain the maximum potential from its employees and so a competitive advantage. If we observe the world around us, we can see that the potential for exploiting diversity has far to go to reach its potential. Women, independently of whether they display feminine or masculine gender traits, make up around 40 percent of the global workforce, but on average only occupy 5 percent of the top management positions.

In 2001 there were 65,000 transnational companies, with 850,000 subsidiaries employing around 54 million people all over the world.[5] If we examine the senior managers in these companies, we observe that the majority come originally from the US, or from the base country of the group.

The person and the organization should have the same mission and the same objective. But this requires effort from both sides; the individuals must contribute their differences and their particular way of growing and creating, and the organization must provide a background against which the person can grow. This requires a series of human resources policies that promote work–life balance, communication across cultures and mobility.

The second part of this book is dedicated to business practice. It analyzes business policies and instruments that companies have introduced over recent years and the successes achieved as a result. But before describing international best practices, it is important to understand diversity in both its historic and current context. It is also necessary to consider some of the studies that have been made of the management of gender, personality and multicultural differences, which may improve our understanding of the potential that the management of diversity offers and some of the challenges that it presents.

Therefore the opening chapters of this book examine the environment of diversity from a historical perspective, before moving on to analyze diversity from the point of view of gender, culture and personality.

# Section 1

# **BACKGROUND**

# Diversity in Business Management: Perspectives and Trends

# 1 Dominant and Rising Values

## Change and organizations

Things are changing; there are few things that we can be more certain about. A well-known president of a Spanish bank recently stated to his board of directors, "Ladies and gentlemen, the only certain thing is change." Our society, and in particular the organizations that serve it, is subject to a continuous process of transformation and change. Anybody who works in a company can be absolutely certain of this. You only have to open a newspaper or read any of the thousands of reports that analysts produce every day to see that the majority are trying to explain these changes to us, but they seldom help us to grasp the real implications that they have.

It is obvious that change is out there and it forms part of the background to our everyday life just like anything else that we have become used to. Jonas Ridderstråle and Kjell Nordström recently wrote a best seller (*Funky Business*)[1] that uses enormous quantities of data to analyze, in an amusing way, the paradox of a reality that seems to be changing at a uniformly accelerated rate. The authors give several examples to support their theory; for example in 1990 it took six years to develop a new car model, whereas today it takes two, that most of Hewlett-Packard's profits come from products that didn't exist a year before, in Tokyo you can order a personalized Toyota on a Monday and be driving it on Friday, Seiko produce more than 5000 models, whilst Sony brought more than 5000 new products onto the market in 1996 alone.[2]

Change is out there and it is important that we know about it. A few years ago a major multinational consulting company gave a seminar to senior managers of a Spanish electricity generating company. The objective of the seminar was to make them aware of the importance of their company paying attention to change and knowing how to adapt to it. During the course, most of the participants seemed a little skeptical about what they were being told, even though several well-known American businesspeople had been invited; then the speaker produced a fact that grabbed everyone's attention:

If you wrote a list of all the great scientists from the history of humanity, you would see that 90 percent of them are still alive. The important point isn't that they are still alive, it is that they are still thinking of ways to transform the environment that we live in.

Yes, change exists, and it has affected our way of working and our environment; it extends from small physical changes (physical changes to the workspace, the tools we use) to profound changes in our vision and way of understanding our organizations, and how they perform the mission for which they were established.

In fact, we live in a **culture of change** that we have incorporated as a natural part of our behavior. We only want the news from this precise moment; yesterday's news is already out of date. We get irritated when a web page takes more than a couple of seconds to load, and we don't understand why we can't yet see the face of the person that we are speaking to on the phone (although this latter has been resolved whilst we were writing these lines). We want planes to fly faster, cars to go faster, boats that can go anywhere, communications to be more efficient and the processes simpler and more responsive to our needs. In short, we want change. And there are few things that we demand more than that change should make things more practical and efficient. In reality, we live in a world where we have become **prescribers of change**, and the majority of our consumption habits are the demand for new ideas, products and services that improve on what went before.

What has made us such addicts to change? Probably there isn't one single answer, but rather a range of factors with a more or less direct influence on us. The one certain thing is that our age has been able to overcome two fundamental concepts, space and time, like never before. Distance is no longer a barrier between people. Today, getting anywhere in the world in less than 24 hours has become a reality, and you can work with the texts stored in the Library of Congress in the US from the smallest village anywhere in the world with just a couple of clicks of a mouse. On the other hand, we live together and demand that everything happens in real time. As we have seen before, we want to know about things the moment they happen, and most of the value of the news resides in it being instantaneous. Overcoming these two barriers, which the fundamentals of human thought have been built on throughout history, means that our visions of things and the way we organize our time have changed, and means that we need to have a global vision, and that a businessperson needs to take into account not only the variables within their organization, but also those within society as a whole.

In reality this is nothing new. Throughout history companies have done nothing else but change. In some ways, the capacity for change

supports the efficiency of the company and its ability to meet the requirements of its clients and consumers, and so enables it to survive. Henry
Ford was not only the founder and president of the largest motorcar
manufacturer of his day, and today, but also was the person who, at the
beginning of the 20th century, changed the traditional industrial model,
in which each worker did things as best they could, to a systemized
production line, which was a real revolution in production processes.

Recent decades have seen a transformation in our organizations from
a compendium of extraction of raw materials, transformation and generation of added-value, marketing and finance to a harmonization of a
perfect set of management activities. In less than a century, our
companies have moved from basing their wealth on the complexity of
large-scale industrial processes, to basing their value on the correct
management of a group of elements that fit together to complete the
jigsaw that is the modern company. The appearance of new technology
signifies the move from the industrial society to the knowledge and information society, and this transformation means a radical change in the way
companies are managed.

The knowledge society demands a new focus and a new vision of
how organizations should be managed. And companies have come to
two conclusions about this new focus; that the person is the major asset
and the company cannot be alien to the environment in which it lives
and develops. The company's ability to assimilate and take advantage of
these ideas is fundamental to its ability to be efficient and profitable in
today's world.

Management literature has been a faithful witness to this reality, and
many authors have dealt with this topic in some depth. As Professor
Drucker says in his book *Managing in the Next Society*,[3] this change is
taking place without being planned, and without even having been foreseen. He argues that something is happening in the relationship between
staff and managers that does not square with what they teach at business
school, and neither does it fit with the way in which the majority of
human resource departments in business, government and nonprofit
making bodies were designed to function. He believes that from the
1950s to the 1990s executives did not need to take society into account,
and as a result they didn't, but today they need to understand the reality
of the society of the future and base their strategies and policies upon it.

## Dominant values and rising values

Our first objective is to understand in depth the evolution of organ-

izations, that is, to understand the transformation in the criteria that
predominate in a company and which orient its strategy. As has happened
at other important points throughout history, change is not something
that happens traumatically, but rather a process of evolution that at some
moments is hardly noticeable. It is for this reason that when we try to
analyze these changes, it would be more accurate to talk of tendencies or
at best of criteria that have evolved and adjusted to the reality of the
company and society. We are going to examine this change in tendencies
that is happening in our organizations and the extent to which there is
consensus about it. We will base our analysis on the work done by Professor Llano.[4]

Following Professor Llano's analysis, there is a series of dominant
values coexisting with a series of rising values in a series of corporate
parameters. So, for example, the aim of the company has a dominant
value to make profit and the associated rising value would be to service
society. The basic human tendency in the traditional parameter will be
to acquire and possess and the new rising tendency will be the desire
to create and share. We can analyze some of these changing values in
more detail.

## Aim of the company

The aim of any company is to make money. It is probably one of the few
things that we all understand about companies, even if we don't know
much about business. A company has making a profit as its first and most
important aim; it is part of the fundamental essence of the company, and
even figures as such in the company's legal incorporation documents –
various people bring together their capital and labor to achieve a profit
to the benefit of everybody who has taken a risk on the venture. If this
were not the case, we would be talking about a different type of organization, which has always existed and is labelled as "nonprofit." There is
a wide range of organizations, such as foundations, NGOs and associations, with well developed activity, which were created for a specific
objective other than making a profit.

A commercial organization has, and must have, **making a profit** as its
principal objective and the one that justifies its existence. It should
generate the economic added-value (profit) expected by the executives,
shareholders and society. Orthodox liberal economic theory says that if
the objective of the company, or more precisely the management responsible for it, is not to make the maximum profit for shareholders, the
corporate executive would be spending someone else's money for

general social interest. Insofar as his actions, in accord with his "social responsibility," reduce returns to stockholders, he is spending their money. Insofar as his actions raise the price to customers, he is spending the customers' money. Insofar as his actions lower the wages of some employees, he is spending their money.[5]

However, if we asked a member of the public if the only objective of a company was to make money, there would be a certain degree of doubt in the reply; it appears that society is beginning to feel that while the company has making money as one of its objectives, it is not the only one and other reasons are becoming more important. As Professor Carlos Sotelo, a member of the Public Relations Society of America's Association for Corporate and Institutional Communication, says in the context of corporate reputation:

> It is a long time since commercial institutions were judged solely on their economic results. In the 21st century, the company is just another citizen; and the community demands that it participates actively in the pursuit of the common good, in addition to its business activity.[6]

Obviously a company needs to fulfill its mission, but not at any cost. In today's companies it is important to demonstrate **respect for the environment, the community, employees, clients and investors**; giving to charity is no longer a demonstration of an organization with a social conscience. The media, both locally and internationally, has performed a key role in bringing to light shady practices and overseeing business activity more closely than ever before. Making a profit has its limits, and if it were not so, then drug trafficking networks would win all the businesspeople of the year awards. Additionally, if companies' only objective was to make money, their policies would have a primary objective of cutting staff costs to obtain greater profitability, whereas what we are hearing from everybody is that their greatest assets are their human resources.

The aim of today's companies is a concept that is evolving, influenced by the changes in the development of the market economy. The change from an industrial economy to a service economy and then to an information economy has multiplied the importance of the intangible aspects of economic relationships. As Professor Sotelo explains, "Products are important, but so are the values or attributes that the consumer attributes not only to them, but also to the companies that produce them."

A company's success no longer depends on the quality and competitiveness of its offer, but also on enjoying a favorable perception among its market. This favorable perception is what we call "reputation." As

Alan Greenspan, president of the United State's Federal Reserve has argued, in today's world ideas have come to displace tangible elements in the economic process and the competition for reputation has become one of the driving forces of the economy.[7]

From the point of view of the aim of every company, we can observe an evolution from the eternal dominant aim of making money, to the social responsibility that presides over today's organizations and which conditions all their actions.

Obviously a company must make money, but at the same time it must achieve another set of aims, which are becoming more important and constitute part of the company's identity. We can observe how a company, at the same time that it is making money, must **provide a service to the community**. In a free-market economy, it is believed that companies must meet the social necessities that are required; something tells us that we prefer L'Oreal to make hair conditioners or that pharmaceutical companies should put all their resources into developing a vaccine that could cure AIDS. At the beginning of the 20th century, only 10–15 percent of the world had a market economy; by the 1970s this had increased to around 40 percent and today it is around 90 percent.[8] If we truly believe that in a free-market economy, the company is the social agency par excellence, then today's companies have a grave responsibility that goes far beyond making an economic profit. The 300 biggest multinationals control 25 percent of the earth's productive resources.[9] They control and condition these assets in such a way that their activity has enormous responsibility over the rest of society. The company today is the agent that identifies and meets the needs generated by society; the role of the state is to oversee and regulate the market in which the company meets its objectives.

This service to the community also affects how it meets the norms and regulations in force in a state governed by the rule of law. The company must make money, but at the same time it must protect the environment, developing it wherever it can; it must respect the law and simultaneously create the necessary environment for it to be complied with and for the company to develop.

An objective that is complementary to the aforementioned, and which is becoming apparent in many organizations as part of this social obligation that we are discussing, is providing its members with **personal satisfaction and growth**: if a person does not develop as a person within a company, they will not do it anywhere else, if only because the majority of people who work (practically the whole world) dedicate the majority of their time to working, with only a small percentage left over for rest, leisure and other aspects of life. In today's world, the company is the natural environment for personal development, and should endeavor to ensure that the necessary conditions for this exist.

Moreover, it is becoming increasingly clear that this investment in staff is a profitable asset. Professor Guido Stein explains this, basing his argument on the thoughts of Peter Drucker:

> From a general point of view, the capacity of an institution to produce leaders is more important than their capacity to produce cheaply and efficiently. Cheap and efficient production can always be obtained given organization and human capacity. But without responsible and appropriate entrepreneurial leadership, willing and able to take the initiative, even the most efficient institution will not be able to maintain its efficiency or to increase it.[10]

The company has an obligation to assist in the personal development of each of its members, if only because its own existence depends on it. In all human activity there are psychological and ethical values that cannot be measured by economic means, although they are the key to generating economic value. It is obvious, for example, that confidence, affection and honesty cannot be bought and sold. Nevertheless, these qualities are essential in order to facilitate economic transactions. In fact, there are writers who argue that the change that is happening in the management of our companies is a change from the preponderance of formal structures to informal ones. However, this is not for reasons of aesthetics or fashion, but because of efficiency. Increasingly, what companies supply and sell is intangible; it is sensations and perceptions. The vehicle manufacturing sector has shown, for example, that the decision about buying a car is really one of perception. The client believes that at the moment most cars are more or less the same, and they make their purchasing decision based on the car they think is most appropriate for their lifestyle. And this perception is, increasingly, something that is not achieved through production processes and systems, but through the intangible things provided by the members of the organization.

A new objective that complements the earlier ones is the obligation on the company of **self-perpetuation and permanence**. Today's society is increasingly hard on bad management by company directors, from whom it demands continuity and viability. Strict business criteria would lead many companies to close plants or installations and move them to other areas where costs are lower. However, when this happens, we can observe that such decisions meet with immediate opposition from society, which demands that the company finds a solution that guarantees viability and the protection of jobs. There have been several recent examples of this in Spain, such as Ford, Santana, Gillette and, more recently, IZAR.

The conclusion is obvious. Companies, the ones that have always been with us, are here to make money, and that continues to be their principal aim. But together with this primary objective, other objectives that are vital for the development of their activity are becoming increasingly important, such as respecting the environment, generating a service to society, creating an environment in which their employees can grow and guaranteeing their own continuity.

## Basic human tendencies

A second aspect to consider whilst studying the development of our organizations is what Professor Llano calls "basic human tendencies." These are the questions that constitute the principal motivation, both for companies and the people who work for them – the basic reason why they pursue the objectives the company has set.

People, like organizations when they are considered as living entities, are active to the degree that they have a motivation to act. A brief glance at history shows that the fundamental reason for companies and people to organize themselves has been to meet their basic needs for survival. This is a reality that is inseparable from the human condition that has pushed the individual to organize in order to achieve something collectively that would have required greater effort on the part of an individual. People undertake an activity to meet a necessity. This has been, without doubt, the path of people at the core of an organization. Even in a period as recent as the end of the Second World War, the primary objective of workers was to obtain the economic resources necessary to maintain themselves and to live a stable life. Even today, when faced with necessity, people see work as a means of making a living.

To a certain extent, this has been the traditional view that has predominated among individuals and, by extension, companies. Until now, economic motivation has been the motor driving both people and companies. We judge people according to what they have or what they can obtain. The leader is, in reality, the person who has managed to acquire the most material possessions, knowledge and resources. Companies value what they have and this has led to strict internal policies of control and productivity.

Together with this way of seeing things, with the vision that people and companies have of reality to the fore, it becomes possible to refocus our attention in new ways that reveal a different picture, which has much in common with Maslow's hierarchy of needs[11] once the basic needs have been covered, both people and organizations seek to transcend these basic necessities.

Until now, it has seemed that the principal reason for action was to obtain things and keep them. Nevertheless, we can begin to observe elements that are beginning to change these tendencies. People are no longer solely interested in their remuneration when they sign a contract. They also evaluate, and give almost equal importance to, the characteristics of the company they are going to join, the person they will report to, their career path, and the working environment. In a nutshell, people value the opportunity for self-development within an organization. Almudena Rodríguez, director of Bassatt Ogilvy, puts it very clearly: "Don't look at where you are going to work; look at who you are going to work with."

Enthusiasm, the need to contribute, to share and to create have become priorities that are as fundamental as subsistence. The reason for action is no longer simply the economic impulse, but rather a range of diverse reasons that value quality rather than quantity; a person values a company to the extent that the company values them and enables them to develop.

In the knowledge and information society, the leader understands that retaining without sharing is not enriching, not even for the leader. As Professor Llano explains, when the objective is to obtain, sharing diminishes and devalues it, but when the objective is to expand, it increases when there is participation.[12]

Without doubt, companies are going to continue to have this acquisitive tendency. But more and more concrete signs that this road will not lead us very far are appearing. Business Professors Sumantra Ghoshal and Christopher Barlett have commented that, in the 1990s, with a low growth rate, overproduction is the norm for most companies, ranging from 40 percent in vehicle manufacture to 100 percent in chemicals, 50 percent in steel production to 140 percent in computers, among other examples. Technological progress and changing client needs lead us to reduce batch sizes and diversify products.[13] Obtaining, producing, accumulating ... in a globalized society where the entire world can obtain and produce in a similar way, these are no longer indicators of the strength of a company. Asian economies and, more recently, those of Eastern Europe have given sufficient proof to the US and the rest of Europe of their capacity to produce more quickly, with higher quality and lower cost.

We all agree that the efficiency of a company resides in the promotion of its creative tendencies and that the principal source of riches in our day weighs less than 1,200 grams and is called the brain. As it is becoming common to say, "true value is not the money in the hands of a few, but the information in the hands of the many."

As reported by Carlos Llano, Jack Welch, the strategist who took the company General Electric and made it grow for decades, when asked the secret of his success, replied without the least embarrassment, "We built a team that valued intellect and human performance. We gave people a voice and dignity. It wasn't difficult."[14]

Returning to the same point, companies are worth what their employees, their human resources and their ability to develop them are worth. Microsoft only has 27,000 employees, so it isn't the biggest company in the world, but it does have the highest market valuation. In 1993 it had 14,000 employees and made a profit of $3,750 million. In 1993 General Motors, one of the biggest companies in the world, made a profit of $120,000 million. Even so, at the end of 1993, Microsoft was worth more than GM; and today it is worth six and a half times as much. Microsoft doesn't have as many offices or warehouses or as much machinery as GM; neither does it employ as many people. In fact, the only asset that Microsoft has is human imagination. It is a company based on the power of the mind.[15]

Competitive advantage lies in intangible assets; in individual abilities (the capacity and motivation of human capital), internal structure (ways of working and managing the company) and external structure (relationships with agents outside the company). For example, Volkswagen Navarra has developed techniques aimed at the creation and management of these assets. Training, continuous improvement and communication are the most relevant, comments Cristina Etayo, a motor industry specialist, in the *Ideas de PricewaterhouseCoopers* magazine.[16] Training is based on the detection of needs rather than on implanting a system. The process of continuous improvement is developed on two tracks. Firstly, the KVP 2000 system relies on the use of workshops involving everybody affected by a problem, from technicians to manual workers, to resolve it; in 2000, more than 115 workshops were organized, resulting in 1,657 improvement measures being adopted and forecast savings of €5,472,000. Secondly, the other track is the possibility of offering suggestions for improvements, which must be set out in detail; in 2002, there were 5,925 suggestions resulting in estimated savings of €4,174,228. Finally, in order to improve decision making, VW Navarra introduced a company Intranet to identify and structure information, distribute it internally and reap maximum benefit from the effort.

From an operational point of view, we also observe a change in the tendencies in remuneration policies applied by the human resources departments of some of the major companies, as Carlos Delgado, director of human resources consulting of PricewaterhouseCoopers, points out.[17] "Up until today, remuneration to employees by companies has centered on economic compensation. Fixed income, short-term variable income, bonuses, long-term variable income, loyalty bonuses or fringe benefits, characterized by "coffee for everyone," were sufficient incentive for employees to feel sufficiently compensated by the company and so decide to invest their intellectual capital with us and not with our competitors.

Nevertheless, although payment in cash is very easy, it is not sufficient; it is unimaginative and even less profitable. We put an agreed quantity of a resource into our staff's current account, without observing that they hardly have time to use it adequately or, what is worse, we provide more and more social benefits that do not meet the needs of the staff at the time. The company provides expensive invalidity and life insurance cover for the employee, medical cover for their family, systems of social provision, high-spec cars and so on, when the employee's real need is to be able to pay the rent or the mortgage at the end of the month.

We end up with the paradox that the company is investing a lot of resources in compensating their employees, without them being aware of the effort that the company is making, and, what is worse, feeling that their compensation package does not meet their needs."

A recent study by PricewaterhouseCoopers reported that 64.71 percent of the companies consulted were planning to put in place systems of flexible compensation that were responsive to the needs of each employee in the short term:

> The ability to involve employees, creativity, new forms of proposing solutions, compensation that meets necessities ... these are all policies that human resource departments are trying in their search to find solutions that meet the needs of the modern company.[18]

The need for the company to create an atmosphere of personal development where its members can expand and develop to the fullest of their abilities is not only a necessary strategy that will enable the company to compete in an ever tougher environment; it is a vital necessity for the organization itself.

## Definition of strategy

Another essential aspect of the company is the definition of strategy. All organizations have a strategic plan, and it is often the only way in which all the members understand the point of what they are doing at a particular moment.

Until now, the dominant tendency in the company with respect to the definition of strategy has been the establishment of a series of objectives and ensuring that the members of the organization were aware of them and met them. The major problem with managing by objectives is that the objectives become the only way of measuring the success of the strategy and, as we well know, this is a high price that no company can afford to pay.

The principles of business strategy that are becoming more important belong to those we know as "company culture," which is nothing other than the way of understanding and acting in the company. This culture is the inspiring principle of a way of doing things: the company's. Experience shows us that, at the moment, companies with the strongest culture are the most flexible and have the greatest ability to innovate and adapt to changing situations. At the same time, they are also the most stable and creative.

In order to manage increasing complexity, the most dynamic organizations of our time have not made their organizational systems more complicated. On the contrary, they have filed their minutely detailed organization charts away with full honors, and are establishing more flexible structures, where personal autonomy and mutual support become increasingly important.

In a changing environment like the one we live in, there is hardly space for the old recipes, in which each position in the organization had a minutely detailed manual of functions. The proliferation of information and constant modifications to the ways of doing things demand inspirational models that make activity, whilst adaptable in its form, respond to the needs of common schemas with similar identifying characteristics.

In this context, Jose Antonio Muñoz-Najar, certified quality manager of the American Society of Quality, draws our attention to the interesting case of Inditex:

> Since Inditex floated on the stock market, the IBEX 35 index has lost 40 percent of its value. However, the shares in Inditex have increased in value by 50 percent over the same period. What has Inditex done to make it one of the more admired companies in the world, with revenue of 3250 million in 2001 and a presence in 44 countries? Professor Muñoz-Najar suggests that the basis for its success is down to the strategy it uses, which can be described using the term *"value innovation."*

> When the Japanese began to make inroads into the American vehicle market, it awoke a feeling of global competition. Since then, company strategy has focussed mainly on competition, leading to companies imitating rather than innovating, reacting to the actions of the competition without being able to identify emerging opportunities.

Kim and Mauborgne, according to Professor Muñoz-Najar, undertook a study of the profit growth of 100 new businesses, and identified the value proposition in most cases (86 percent to be exact) to be simply minor improvements compared to the competition. This accounted for 62 percent of income and 39 percent of the profits of the companies in the study. However, the remaining 14 percent of the new companies, that small group that was not simply offering minor improvements on competitors' products but rather real business innovations, accounted for 38 percent of the total income and 61 percent of total profits across all the companies in the study. This latter group included companies like Wal-Mart, Home Depot, Toyota, IKEA, Microsoft and CNN. The first conclusion that can be drawn from the study is that the productivity of these companies, measured in terms of income and profits, is much higher than the majority group.

In contrast to the traditional focus of business strategy, the concept of "value innovation" is not based on competition, as this is irrelevant when you are offering a new concept to the client in an existing market, which is clearly superior to what has existed up to that time. A market is created by this leap in quality and as a result the value innovating companies stand out, even at a time when trading conditions in the industry or sector are not favorable.

Traditionally, Professor Muñoz-Najar goes on to explain, innovation in companies has centered on improving or redefining solutions to specific problems with the help of technology. Value innovation seeks to redefine the problem. By doing this, the competition becomes irrelevant, because the problem that the industry had been focussing on until then has become irrelevant. In this sense, value innovators are not necessarily technological innovators. IKEA is one example, as its value proposition "design at reasonable prices" redefines the traditional problem of the furniture industry – design or cost. In this way, the company has developed a business model that resolves the apparent contradiction that existed between competing on design or cost. IKEA is not a market leader by chance.

"Inditex meets all the principles discussed because, since the outset, Amancio Ortega has concentrated on redefining the problem that the textile industry had always faced, design or cost. He set himself the challenge of providing a designer product at a reasonable price, which at the time represented an important leap in value compared to what had traditionally been offered to clients. In order to make this value proposition reality, Ortega developed a business model that resolves the apparent contradiction of basing a position on design and on cost at the same time, and this is what makes the resulting model so innovatory."[19]

From the point of view of defining a strategy, concentrating only on the consequences of the results, reacting when the competition attacks you, is not sufficient. Companies need a way of doing things rather than a detailed job description. When we employ someone, we cannot give them a manual telling them how to react in every case and every situation, if for no other reason than that in the world in which we live, change is so rapid that these recipes would be out of date in no time at all. Microsoft gives licenses to many of its providers for six-month periods, and when the provider asks why the license is for such a short period, Microsoft replies that in six months things could have changed a lot. It is essential to discover and promote new principles, new ways of seeing things and focussing on them. I should provide each member of my organization with the tools that will permit them to react to a changing world. That is why I can only provide things that do not change, principles that in some way preside over and establish the know-how of the organization, which constitute what we call "company culture." Only in this way, getting results and facing new challenges, will companies be able to face the future.

## Consequences of business activity

A fourth criterion in the analysis of companies is the consequences of their activity. Up until today, companies seemed oriented to achieving primary objectives, whilst it was beginning to become obvious that they needed to be forecasting possible secondary effects. In reality this is a natural consequence of the criteria we have already analyzed, where there was only one vision of the company's objectives and the situation that it is in.

If organizations do not calculate the consequences of their activities, they run the risk that these effects, without being looked for, will damage the organization and the environment in which it is developing. The problem is that, in the information society, these consequences become apparent very quickly thanks to the media and the sensitivity of society to social, environmental and reputation questions, the consequences of which are unpredictable.

Until today, as we analyzed in the previous point, it appeared that we expected our businesspeople to be capable of meeting their objectives, and doing so in an efficient and practical manner. Today that is not enough. The effects of an activity happen with such rapidity that the consequences become apparent almost at the same moment at which they happen. If a motor vehicle manufacturer (and there have been several cases recently) brings a new model onto the market that does not meet safety standards, it becomes known about very quickly. The consequences of having to withdraw and repair all the vehicles, compensate people affected and the damage to the brand image have economic repercussions possibly far greater than the profits that a successful launch would have generated.

Today's businessperson needs to take all this into account. Factors of production, competition and commercial prospects are all aspects that can be calculated with some objectivity. But today the interconnectedness of the market and the company with the environment in which it operates is so strong that the businessperson has to have a more diverse vision, taking into account aspects and details that at first sight appear not to be relevant to the activity. It is no surprise that today's companies and business schools are engaging people with more humanistic profiles than they did in the past; people who devote more time to thinking than to acting, to measuring the consequences of their actions rather than acting. It is a question of trying to find a balance between the objectives that are set and the effects they will produce.

But there is a further step that we must take. In order to perceive and create harmony, which is essential in order to face successfully concrete situations characterized by complexity of knowledge and information, it is necessary to understand what is possible and the internal unity of a multidimensional situation. The company must design its human relationships, production and control procedures, sales and distributions channels and, especially, its interactions with its environment in a harmonious way. Toshiba has recently gone through a situation that demonstrates some aspects of this criterion:

In 2004, Toshiba was one of the market leaders in the field of information technology and particularly in the portable computer market. Despite this position, Toshiba was aware of its lack of penetration in the younger market, where its sales were scarce, and its brand image was not known by the majority of young people aged 18–23.

To remedy this situation, Toshiba, with the aid of the company Universia (a company 70 percent owned by Spanish universities and 30 percent by the Santander Bank, and to which all Spanish universities belong) and the Santander Bank, designed a campaign aimed at making it possible for every university student who wanted one to acquire a high-spec computer, complete with wireless technology, at a price far below the market rate. The objective was to place 25,000 computers on the market.

The campaign was organized in great detail by the parties involved, but even so the original launch date of May 2004 had to be delayed to November 2004. As a result, Toshiba had to keep 25,000 computers in its warehouse for almost seven months, when a new version would not normally be stored for more than three months. Despite this, Toshiba kept the computers in store, without putting them on the market, even at the risk that after seven months, if the computers were not sold in the university campaign, it would not be able to place them in the traditional distribution chain, as they would be out of phase with the models they would have on the market at that time. Toshiba was not concerned about this risk. Its real concern was to obtain a positive brand image among university students in the 18–23 age group. As the company's Director General, Alberto Ruano, said at the presentation, "We aren't here to sell computers. We want to be the technological partner of the universities and the university students, and we are willing to risk whatever may be necessary to get that." Toshiba was well aware that, over and above the possibility of selling 25,000 computers, there was the opportunity to begin to be part of the alternatives that students would have when they took an interest in new technology; something which was not hugely important in the short term, but which in the long term would be fundamental. At the end of the campaign, Toshiba had sold 19,649 computers to Spanish university students.[20]

## Development of people within the organization

A new criterion for analysis in the company is, without doubt, the development of people within the organization, the place they occupy and the way they are promoted internally. The attitude of people within the organization is fundamental: not only for the way in which work and activity is organized, but also for the way in which this conditions their personal development, something that is without doubt directly linked to internal promotion and mobility within the company. To a certain extent, the organization is one of the defining factors of company culture, as the organization and its norms are the framework and rules of the game controlling how people develop within it.

Until now, companies have given this aspect great importance, and company structure has been characterized by a system of grades. The fundamental objective of a person within the organization is to be promoted, to climb the pyramid of the organization, dedicating all their efforts to this ascent as a reward in itself. Within the company, the person is defined by their grade, and their abilities and development are directly linked to the position they have attained. Our organizations, when looked at in this way, appear like a vertical framework of categories, with functions and responsibilities directly related to the position that is occupied; and companies have tried to ensure that every employee acts in accordance with their position as a basic premise of good company management.

This way of understanding the organization is directly linked to the other criteria that have governed the company. If the fundamental reason for these criteria was to meet a series of objectives, for processes to function appropriately and the generation of added-value based on mass production, then it is clear that organizations should have the discipline of a military unit, where everybody knows their place and where everything functions with the precision of a perfectly honed machine.

As we have said, the changes we are living through today are affecting many of these criteria. A hierarchical structure inevitably suffers from rigidity, which makes it difficult to adapt to the continuous changes that the market demands. The information that flows both upward and downward cannot enjoy the luxury of taking months to travel from one extreme of the company to the other, particularly if the message becomes distorted along the way. Companies have managed to achieve their objectives under these criteria up to now because, as we have seen, their major priority was maximizing production capacity, commercialization and transformation, where each person had to complete a minutely detailed mission, and where their only aspiration was the ability to be promoted within this structure, which only leads to competition.

As we have said, business processes within companies do not respond rapidly to sudden change, but rather they evolve, in some cases almost imperceptibly. As a result, within companies, without anybody having planned it, an informal process of communication and contact between members of the organization begins. People feel the need to talk to other members of the organization in order to resolve the problems that the organization does not resolve for them. So a series of networks and subnetworks are created within the company as a spontaneous way of working; and, spontaneously, new relationships begin to work within the company that are more horizontal than vertical. People need to communicate with the rest of their colleagues, to share and work together to improve the processes that the organization itself does not know about. Verticality is making way for horizontalness; information flows from top to bottom no longer just compete with information from bottom to top, but also with flows from one side to the other. Far from alienating the person from the organization, this results in integration and boosts loyalty; it commits the worker to the objectives and success of the company. Competition gives way to cooperation, not only as a natural form of human support, but also as a necessity for the person in order to complete the mission that the company has assigned to them.

The modern company should offer personal development space where the identity and the importance of the person is not ascribed by the company, but springs from the creative capacity of the person. People understand that they no longer just want to order others around; they also want to have specific importance within the company and to be capable of drawing on the team resources to meet the challenges they face. Verticality is no longer being pursued, today it is the center. A US executive explained the secret of her success to her boss over dinner in a distinguished New York restaurant. She took a glass and placed it upside down on the table; that is my team – we work in a circle with a strong attraction from one to another, and from all to the center.

## Attitude to spontaneous impulses

The attitude to spontaneous impulses is no more than a summary of the ones already mentioned. If all the aspects of the dominant values are true, then the principal objective is satisfaction; the tendency to enjoy immediate sensory gratification puts the capacity for projection to sleep, encourages complacency, and redefines the luxuries of the past as necessities.

Today's companies cannot allow themselves to feel satisfied; it would be the first sign that they do not fit into a society that all the time is demanding new efforts. The challenges of the future point more deeply to the person as the major resource of the organization – a person who in their capacity for self-control and development holds the only key to providing companies with solutions to the coming social and business challenges.

# Future tendencies

We have summarized existing tendencies; on the one hand, those that have been constant in the company, setting its style and way of acting and, on the other, the tendencies that are growing in importance and starting to have a more or less open presence in the majority of organizations. It remains for us to interpret the tendencies that will affect businesspeople in the future. The criteria that Professor Peter Drucker details in his book *The Effective Executive*[21] are particularly relevant and can be summarized in eight points:

1. They always ask, "What should be done?" They set priorities and concentrate on them.

2. They always ask, "Is this correct in the company?" Drucker draws a clear distinction between the company, the shareholders, the executives and the employees; anything that is not good for the company will not be good for any of its components either.

3. They develop action plans. Executives have their reason for existing defined in their name – they execute, they do. Knowledge is important for action, but action is the essential thing. The action plan needs to include a monitoring process to verify whether it is being achieved and adjust it as necessary. And this plan should be the guide for the day-to-day organization of the executive's time.

4. They take responsibility for their decisions. A decision is not a decision until someone takes responsibility for it, it has an execution date, the names of the people affected by it are known, as are the names of the people who should know about it.

5. They communicate their decisions. They make sure that their action plans and the information necessary for them to be undertaken are understood. They share their plans with their peers, superiors and subordinates, and they are ready to listen to the comments they provoke.

6. They focus more on opportunities than on problems; they take the view that solving problems prevents damage, whereas taking advantage of opportunities produces results.

7. They have productive meetings.

8. They think about "us" and not about "me." They know that, although they have the ultimate responsibility, they cannot function without delegating. They have confidence in the organization and do whatever is necessary to be able to draw on trusted colleagues.

From this analysis, it is easy to draw the conclusion that the management style of today's executive should be a perfectly harmonized set of dominant and rising tendencies, drawing on the synergy of two ways of acting and doing that have always and will always be with us.

A report by PricewaterhouseCoopers[22] reflects many of these aspects when it concludes that corporate social responsibility has a positive effect on a company's profitability, and that it has a more long-term vision of the business and includes ethical considerations, transparency and responsibility to society in its decision-making processes. According to the report, the factors that lead a company to adopt, proactively and voluntarily, corporate social responsibility strategies are intangible but they are strategic. They are not purely financial, but rather aspects that influence improvements in the company's reputation or allow the company to obtain competitive advantages. At the same time, it is a way to react to the increasing pressure from the different stakeholders in the company, who all make new demands on the company against the background of sustainable development. One of the basic conclusions of the report is that the future belongs to those companies that know how to anticipate the changes that today's society is demanding and to convert them into competitive advantages and a source of value creation, for the company and all other interested parties.

The study was prepared in 2003 with the assistance of 43 companies, many of them leaders in their fields, which together represent a significant part of Spain's turnover. The report concluded that the majority of the companies included in the survey incorporate the values of "good, sustainable corporate governance" in their management and decision-making processes, which are summarized as:

- Integrity
- Long-term vision
- Responsibility to all interested parties
- Openness to dialogue with all interested parties
- Diversity.

The company is changing. Hundreds of books and articles have been written that deal with the subject and this demonstrates how relevant it is. Change is here now, and the only thing that matters is our capacity to take advantage of it. The next chapter analyzes to what extent, both from a historic and from a business point of view, diversity is present in these changes, harmonizing and giving form to them, being a motor of growth and a basic impulse for action.

# 2 Diversity in the Historic Perspective of Business Management

In Chapter 1 we saw how business management in recent decades has been dominated by a series of dominant values. These values represent for the most part the conception we have of the company today; companies with clear separation between management and ownership, based on management procedures that are rational and scientific. In this chapter we will look at the historical roots of these dominant values and then examine to what extent diversity has played a part in the development of a new vision of business.

There are, as far as we are aware, two key aspects in the process of company development and the way organizations have been configured. These factors are shared with many other human disciplines:

1. The first is experimentation as the foundation of progress. As the poet says, *caminante, no hay camino, se hace camino al andar* ("traveller, there is no path, you make the path by walking," which can be translated into the language of management as "learning by doing"); this has been the key to business advances in the last century. The capacity of people and organizations to adapt to external reality by experimenting has led to innumerable failed experiments, but at the same time has provided us with valid models for action that led to some of the great corporate achievements of the 20th century.
2. The second aspect that has been constant in the development of business capabilities has been the idea of development through integrating old parameters with new ones, so that, without rejecting the key instruments of the old model, it has been possible to incorporate them into a paradigm of action that is more appropriate for the new context.

This ability that companies had to experiment and integrate new parameters into something that already existed is the key to survival for any organism; it has left us a rich legacy of knowledge and experience that forms the basis of corporate structure in the 21st century. Following the thesis of Rosemberg and Birdzell,[1] the key to economic success in the West is the combination of three elements: autonomy, experimentation and diversity, which together achieve a unique use of technology and organization to channel resources so as to satisfy human necessities.

Without intending to develop a work of profound historical analysis, we do want to dig into the past to find clues that can help us to understand the evolution of the company to the current concept of management. To do this, we will briefly analyze four key moments in the history of the company, leading up to the 1970s when a new paradigm made us aware of diversity and its management as an important element in business strategy. This new paradigm incorporated both the old values and the new ones within a broader framework.

1. In the first instance, we will go back to the origins of the company in the sense of an institution for business activity, bringing together resources to meet needs, which dominated business activity until the 16th century.
2. We will briefly analyze the business spirit that developed in Europe from the 16th century onward, which represented a key landmark in the rational concept of the company.
3. Then we will analyze the development of the first modern companies, up to their consolidation at the dawn of the 20th century, which will enable us to understand the process of experimentation and integration of new parameters in structures that were already consolidated.
4. Finally, we come to the appearance of management science and its relationship with the values of the time (the beginning of the 20th century), and the culture in which it predominantly developed, that of the US, which forged the dominant values of the company until well into the 20th century.
5. This brief historical summary will bring us to the 1970s, when the first explicit policies for managing corporate diversity began. We will see how, as we enter more deeply into the information and knowledge age, diversity has become a permanent element in the process of business innovation in the 21st century.

We should make clear at this point that we are focussing our attention on the creation and subsequent development of shareholder corporations. We will not be looking at other forms of company organization, such as family companies or public sector companies, which have their own complexities that are outside the scope of this study.

# Business development from its origins to the 16th century

There have been important commercial institutions since the beginnings of civilization, and these have had enormous influence on the economic life of society. Micklethwait and Wooldridge[2] mention some examples that go back to the year 3000BC, such as those in ancient Mesopotamia, where there were business agreements that went beyond simple barter, and those of the Sumerians who developed commercial contracts similar to those of risk capital in the year 2000AD. These types of commercial operations developed and expanded in the Mediterranean, through the Phoenicians and the ancient Greeks. The Romans achieved great advances in the understanding of business development, with the creation of their *societates*. Roman law was the first to introduce the idea that an organization of people could have a distinct legal personality from those of the people who constituted it, with legal figures such as the *paterfamilias* and the *collegium romano*.

In the early mediaeval period we can look at the city-states of Italy and the advances in the mechanisms for facilitating trade that they introduced. Traders in Venice, Florence and Prato, from the 9th century onward, developed formulas for diversifying risk and eliminating the possibilities of fraud, some of which were crucial to the subsequent development of business.

The *compagnia*, which began as family companies where all the partners were responsible for the value of their assets, appeared in Florence and other Italian cities in the 12th century. These cities provided the commercial impetus in the 14th century that led to the first deposit institutions, with the creation of the Banco de Medicis in 1397, and institutions for traders, such as the Compagnia of Francesco di Marco Datini in Prato in 1335.

In 1494, Luca Pacioli wrote a book about mathematics that includes a chapter on double-entry bookkeeping, which is considered to be the base of modern accountancy. The focus of the system was to make a series of entries in order to facilitate a periodic summary of the value of a company on a certain date and to analyze how it had performed over a certain period.[3] This system was a huge step forward for accountancy. It enabled the prevention and detection of fraud, the description of commercial transactions and the determining of profit and how it should be applied, in addition to making each person responsible for possible errors and fraud.[4]

Nevertheless, this commercial impulse was not accompanied by the necessary institutions or an appropriate political, religious or social framework to enable these early initiatives to bear lasting fruit. The fundamental problem was the disasters that beset Europe in the 14th century, with epidemics, plague, famine and wars that left it devastated and reduced its population dramatically; in fact, it was not until 1600 that the population of Europe again reached the numbers that it had in 1347.[5] In a period of such instability, the only institutions that were capable of surviving were the Church and those created by powerful feudal lords.

The 15th century coincided with the peak of feudal society in Europe, where society was integrated around a powerful central authority, whether a feudal lord or religious authority, with a strict hierarchy. Nevertheless, this society provided the seed for a new, pluralistic civilization that was to develop in the 16th century.

## Formation of the entrepreneurial spirit from the 16th to the 18th century

From the 16th century onward, Europe began to undergo a process of change, which saw the end of mediaeval feudal society and the beginnings of a pluralistic society. Some of the factors that caused this change were:

1. Technological advances in the countryside pushed large numbers of people into the cities, generating widespread commercial activity that was outside the control of the feudal lord.
2. The expansion of international maritime trade created the conditions for new networks of markets and raw materials, and the need to create institutions that could support such high-risk activities.
3. Advances in military technology reduced the power of feudal lords as defence became organized by professional armies built around centralized monarchies.

Little by little, the rural society based on the feudal system was transformed into an urban society ruled over by centralized monarchies that ended the political power of the feudal lords. These changes created the conditions for the development of a pluralistic society with an unprecedented degree of liberty, which facilitated the development of new institutions that acted independently within society.

The expansion of commerce and the new climate of deregulation and relaxation, together with a period of growth and economic development, resulted in a background against which individual entrepreneurs could develop the foundations of what would become the modern company; the climate for innovation was much more favorable at this time than that experienced by the traders of the Italian city-states of the 14th century.

Until the 16th century, Western society was no more advanced in its commercial innovations than the two other great civilizations of the time, China and the Islamic world. In earlier periods, both Islamic society and China had produced important innovations that facilitated their enormous commercial empires, which were in no way inferior to the European ones. As an example of the interest of the Islamic world in commercial matters, it is interesting to note that more than 1,400 of the 6,226 verses in the Koran refer to economic matters.[6]

However, the growth experienced by the European economy from the 16th century onward set it apart from the other empires of the time. The explanation for this is partly related to circumstances intrinsic to these empires, such as the progressive closing of China to the outside world from the 15th century onward or the colonization by the Turks of Arab lands. Nevertheless, the fundamental reason for this separation resides in the profound changes experienced by European society from the 16th century onward. This process, which has come to be known as the techno-scientific, represented a fundamental transformation, with a series of scientific revolutions that created a new frontier between scientific thought and philosophical thought.

Many hypotheses have been developed to explain economic development in the Western world. Perhaps the best known is the one proposed by Max Weber at the beginning of the 20th century, which explained the growth of capitalism as a result of the Protestant Reformation.[7] This German psychologist, considered one of the founders of economic history, argued that the Calvinist concept of vocation, and in particular its Puritan followers in Britain, created a capitalist spirit and, as a result, capitalism itself and led to the Industrial Revolution in Britain.

According to Weber, the influence of the Puritan conception of life not only favored the formation of capital but, and this is even more important, was favorable for the formation of rational bourgeois behavior, of which the Puritan was the most typical example; as a result, this conception of life led to the birth of the modern economic man.[8]

Since first put forward by Weber, this theory has been criticized by many authors. Rothbard,[9] for example, argued that modern capitalism did not begin with the Industrial Revolution but rather in the Middle Ages, in particular in the Italian city-states, where there were notable examples of economic rationalism, such as the development of double-entry bookkeeping. In addition, pure Calvinist states, such as Scotland, did not enjoy the same degree of capitalist development as England, whilst many of the great financiers of the time were of the Catholic faith.[10]

Leaving aside the discussion about the influence of the Reformation on the appearance of capitalism, one of the most interesting aspects of Weber's argument is the emphasis on European rationalism as the basis for economic development, through the creation of a range of political, economic and religious institutions organized to regulate a rational society.[11] Patricia Crone[12] argues that the rationalism perceived by Weber in the institutions created from the 16th century onward is fundamental to understanding European society.

Whilst in primitive societies all the functions of society are grouped together, European society separated them systematically. In modern society, each function is assigned to a specialist group. Once a function has become independent, it is no longer subject to the unified system of beliefs and can develop its own credo, that is, a system of rules and functions that should be followed by all practitioners independently of their wider role in the rest of society.

This rupture in basic feudal unity affected all areas of Western society, including the intellectual sphere, which until then had been dominated by the doctors of the Church and the universities of law and theology. In this period, scientific analysis, proposed by Francis Bacon (1561–1626) among others, appeared. Bacon proposed that empirical analysis should be the fundamental base for scientific investigation, and that this should extend to social sciences in addition to natural sciences.[13] The scientific method, based on observation, reasoning and experimentation, allowed sufficient objectivity for other scientists to be able to trust the results obtained, resulting in the creation of a scientific community organized by independent individuals with a common set of objectives.

The result of this relaxation of authority and the consequent formation of a pluralistic society was the development of all the social disciplines: sciences, politics and education and, of course, economics. This capacity for experimentation led to new technological developments, which in the business world led to an increasing diversity of products and needs (and, at the same time, ways of satisfying them) and so to the creation of new business institutions. The value that the company as an institution contributed to Western society at the beginning of modern times is that these new forms of private organization were able to take decisions that in other societies would be taken by government or religious authorities; this made it much easier for the company to innovate and so develop.[14]

The different business initiatives that emerged during from the 16th to the 18th century were consolidated in the final decades of the 19th century; but before the appropriate legal framework had been established, throughout most of Europe there was an entrepreneurial spirit, in a pluralistic society, with unprecedented freedom of action in all aspects of human activity. As society adopted these values, which emphasized rationality and individual responsibility, reducing enormously the influence of the clergy, an individual ethic of work and responsibility developed which favored wealth creation and business development.

## Consolidation of the modern company from the 18th to the 20th century

As many times before throughout history, the process of creation and development of the company was one of trial and error, and various formulas were tried that met the necessities that arose, with greater or lesser degrees of success. Different forms of business associations arose, including the guilds of Northern Europe, the chartered trading companies and franchised corporations which undertook projects such as roads, infrastructure and universities based on a government mandate, without which the project would have been too costly. By the beginning of the 18th century, the first limited liability companies owned by shareholders had appeared. These companies were formed by individuals and aimed to operate as profit-making concerns, without political rights or exclusive rights to any particular trade.

It is therefore true to say that the concept of the company and the demand to create them was fully present before the Industrial Revolution began in 1750. From the 16th century, different forms of organization had tried to channel the opportunities opened up by commercial development. Nevertheless, the Industrial Revolution was to change the forms of production and distribution dramatically and as a result would give rise to the development of new business forms that would meet the new necessities; and at the same time they would limit the enormous risks associated with the new forms of production. Finally, and following the introduction of various earlier pieces of legislation, the UK's Companies Act 1856 (subsequently reformed in 1862) marks the beginning of the modern company, with shared ownership and liability limited to the amount invested. This was followed in 1867 by the Sociétés Anonymes law in France and similar laws in other European countries and in the US. Demand for this new form of institution was so great that between the introduction of the law in 1856 and its revision in 1862, 25,000 new limited liability companies were formed in the UK.[15]

The society created by the Industrial Revolution and the need to create economies of scale led to the company playing a leading role in the capitalist economy. This saw its maximum expression at the beginning of the 20th century in the US where, by 1913, companies were responsible for 36 percent of national output (compared to 14 percent in the UK).[16]

### Development of industrial conglomerates and financial markets

The Industrial Revolution caused significant changes in the production process; among others we can note the transfer of production from the shop to the factory, more efficient use of energy, the change of production of wooden objects to those made from iron and steel and of course technological innovation.

Little by little, the idea of the role of the company expanded from one of simply operating a factory to include creating and exploiting changes in the product, production methods, raw materials, distribution and organization and taking on an ever wider range of functions. These changes led to the formation of large industrial groups, which were helped by the parallel development of financial markets capable of meeting their enormous demand for capital.

From the moment Wall Street was opened in 1798, the stock market developed rapidly, accelerating the economic revolution and the industrial reorganization that the US was experiencing. From 1888 to 1896, there was consolidation across a range of industrial sectors, for example tobacco, textiles, furniture, paper, machinery and oil. By 1904 American industrial production was in the hands of no more than 50 companies, whose pioneers, such as Rockefeller (1839–1937) and JP Morgan (1837–1913), have become part of history.

Business innovation up to the beginning of the 20th century had been led by France and the UK, but since then the US has become the driver of innovation.

By the end of the First World War, the company had developed the fundamental traits that would lead it to dominate the economic panorama for the majority of the 20th century. It had developed a clear structure, separating ownership from management and, on the other hand, it encompassed the values of the society in which it had developed, emphasizing rational criteria and the responsibility of individual work. As the 20th century progressed, the company continued to develop its ways of understanding business organization and the management of its workforce.

# The company in the 20th century: the outbreak and growth of business management

## Business organization as key to the modern company

Alfred Chandler asserts that the modern industrial corporation is the result of the integration of mass production with mass distribution[17]. Andrew Carnegie (1835–1919) was one of the pioneers of mass production when he introduced a chain of production into his factory. The production line system was later perfected by Henry Ford (1863–1947), who, following the ideas of Frederick Taylor, had the clever idea of introducing a moving belt so that the parts to be assembled moved, not the workers; as a result of this system the company was producing 1,000 cars a day in 1914.[18] Ford was therefore the first to integrate mass production with mass distribution, achieving economies of scale that further increased the efficiency of production. Within a few years of this process becoming generally accepted, shops in the US were filled with all types of product, from cars to concentrated fruit juices, produced using these techniques.

Once a major part of the production process had been integrated in one company, it became increasingly necessary to incorporate an active process of innovation to link the new possibilities being created by science with the market. Following Rosemberg and Birdzell,[19] one of the keys to the development of the West was the association of scientists and managers to achieve a common objective, which facilitated the process of change and growth. The West managed to develop a bridge over the traditional divide between science and the economic sphere, and to convert scientific explanations into economic growth. Western society was unique in combining the marketing and manufacturing functions of traditional companies with centers of scientific knowledge, all within the same management structure and with common objectives and incentives.

## Business management as a science

From the First World War onward, the structure of companies grew ever more complicated, with the ownership structure increasingly distant from the day-to-day management of operations. This resulted in an increase in the importance of the manager, who up to this point had had a minor role in the company accounting procedure and the supervision of operations. The new manager, in addition to supervising and coordinating, began to have a role in deciding the thrust of business strategy.

As Alfred Chandler famously said, modern companies were only viable when the visible hand of management showed itself to be more efficient than the invisible hand of the market.[20]

It is widely agreed that Alfred Sloan (1875–1966) was the first executive to become famous simply for being an executive. Alfred Sloan was the president of General Motors from 1923, and he became famous as a result of being the first to use a multidivisional company structure. He understood that the activities of a company were too diverse to all be managed under one single central structure. As a result he decided to create autonomous divisions: cars, lorries, parts and accessories. Each division defined itself by the market in which it acted. This decentralized structure was controlled by an executive committee, a control center comprising ten men, from which in turn there was a strong central system for supervising and controlling all the divisions. This system had the advantage of making it possible to develop new products for the market rapidly. His idea was to establish a rational organization, based on clear procedures for all that was not subject to the subjective influence of different personalities, which was normal when the owner managed operations directly. This multidivisional structure became the standard for all the major companies in the US and later in Europe and the rest of the industrialized world from 1920 to 1960.

These new corporations, with ever more complicated organizational structures, led to the emergence of management science in the early decades of the 20th century. We can take the Harvard Business School as an example. It opened its doors for the first time in 1908, with the objective of training people in the organization of administrative tasks and accountancy, but within six years it was offering courses in marketing, company finance and business strategy.

In a simplified way, we can divide the predominant management theories of the 20th century into two tendencies:

- A first period stretching from the beginning of the century until the 1970s, when a series of management models (aimed at finding the single best form of organization and the single best mode of managing people) were developed and instilled in a more or less homogeneous workforce.
- As suggested by Drucker,[21] from the 1970s onward the paradigm of a single best form of organization and a single mode of managing it disappeared, to be gradually replaced by the idea of a diversity of people and organizations, initiating a period of change that is transforming the traditional way of understanding the company.

# Business management until the 1970s

The first phase of the development of business management is character-ized by a vocation for uniformity. It was trying to establish procedures that were rational, objective and scientific, to which managers should adhere, independently of their differences. This concept triumphed, among other reasons, because of the uniformity of the workforce where these models were first applied; something which has come to be repres-ented by the figure of the company man.

## The appearance of the organization man

The figure of the executive began to be clearly defined; they were people who were obviously diverse in a multitude of ways, but who shared a sufficient number of values and ways of thinking that they began to conform to a type of behavior that became defined by the term **organ-ization man**.[22] These organization men came to dominate companies in the large American cities, and became almost a class in themselves. They shared a set of common values and often a common way of thinking about themselves that closely identified them with their position in the company. Their ethics were based on the values of solid professional stan-dards, strong loyalty to the company and personal ambition based on professional progress and competition.

During the 1950s and 60s this group became well established and their routine almost a cliché, which was often caricatured in books or films based on the everyday office life they shared; the Christmas party, competition for promotion, hierarchy, diligent secretaries, the problems caused by excessive hours dedicated to the office, the common search for social status, which in turn was based on professional position and repres-ented by salary increases, bigger offices and bigger parking spaces.[23]

This typology of organization man, who was obsessed with fitting in, was criticized for its excessive dependency on external factors, which resulted in annulling their inner drive, even in their tastes, not only for work, but also for where and how to live. Nevertheless, and leaving crit-icisms to one side, the company man formed a class that was fundamen-tal for Western economic development. At the same time, the excessive concern for fitting in and forming part of the company had important compensations that few others had access to in this period, including a job for life and other rewards not directly related to their professional lives, such as the provision by many companies of a pension scheme.

These men had to adapt to the new management models that appeared, models that gave the company such efficiency that soon they had to be imitated outside the US. Some of this efficiency was derived from the fact that organization men, setting aside the natural differences between individuals, shared a sufficient number of traits to enable them to adapt to a common culture, which reflected an important part of their values and way of thinking and which meant that it was not overly difficult for them to suppress individual tendencies. For this reason, up until the final decades of the 20th century, the company was normally characterized by a uniform culture that all its members had to subscribe to, giving a picture of homogeneity and uniformity which undoubtedly resulted in a highly efficient system.

The organizational model they were looking for was rational and scientific, based on a series of procedures that all could subscribe to, whatever their personal vision. Subjective personal values were relegated to private life, whilst professional life was governed by fundamentally rational criteria. The impression of uniformity given off by company men was in part due to a common set of values, but also to the separation of private life from professional life, with each having its own objectives, values and behaviors.

This uniform, rational behavior was one of the elements that produced most surprise when the model was exported to other cultural contexts. For example, Jean Jacques Servan Schreiber argued in 1967[24] that America's competitive advantage over Europe did not reside in its technology or its financial power, but rather in the extension to Europe of an organization that the Europeans found frankly mystifying. This French intellectual's opinion was that the real competitive advantage that the Americans had was their mastery over the instruments of organization. European companies, first in the UK and later in the rest of Europe, decided that if they wanted to compete, they would need to learn this American way of organizing. Micklethwait states that by 1970 more than half the 100 most important British industrial companies had asked the American consulting company McKinsey for advice on reorganizing.[25]

## Theories and models of business management

It would be beyond the scope of this book to undertake a detailed study of the different models and theories of business management that appeared throughout the course of the 20th century. Nevertheless, so as to be able to understand how diversity affects management in our later analysis, it seems appropriate at this stage to take a brief look at a series of theories that summarize the main tendencies and how they have developed.

The earliest theories focussed on developing ways of perfecting the organizational structure of the company, using the scientific model as a basis for action.[26] *The Principles of Scientific Management* by Frederick Taylor (1856–1915), published in 1911, is considered to be the first book on business management. Taylor tried to organize work scientifically; his major discovery was the identification of the principles that govern the productivity of manual labor. By analyzing the productive process, he established a simple chain consisting of the following links:

1. Observe the task and analyze the movements involved
2. Record each movement, noting the effort and time required
3. Eliminate all unnecessary steps
4. Reorganize the necessary steps so that they are simpler
5. Reunite all the new movements in a logical chain and design appropriate tools for them.

Taylor did not see any need to decentralize the hierarchical structure, which was contrary to the opinion of Albert Sloan who, as we have seen, revolutionized GM by adopting a multidivisional, decentralized structure. In 1942, Peter Drucker, who was to be one of the most influential management theoreticians of the 20th century, analyzed the structure of GM at Sloan's invitation, and came to the conclusion that GM's success was in large part due to its multidivisional structure. The results of his study were published in a book that went on to be an enormous success.[27]

This first phase of management theory is normally referred to as "rationalist."[28] The majority of the theoreticians from this period were trying to identify a rational structure for the company, marginalizing the variables of human behavior in the organization. Nevertheless, there were some isolated voices in favor of the management of people as a resource, not simply a cost. Among these was Mary Parker Follet (1868–1933), one of the female pioneers in the field of management, and one of the first theoreticians to argue for the need to discuss the treatment of people within the company. Nevertheless, as Peter Drucker indicated, the paradigm of the period was not open to such ideas and as a result they were not taken seriously by the mainstream until long after her death.[29]

The consideration of the worker as a resource and not a cost came into focus in the 1960s with the work of McGregor and Abraham Maslow, among others. The fundamental theme of their investigations and theoretical work was the analysis of the human factor, their feelings and aptitudes, the importance of management, job satisfaction and personal motivation. In his book *The Human Side of Enterprise*, published in 1960,

Douglas McGregor[30] argued that managers had to choose between two different ways of managing people, which he termed theory X and theory Y. Theory X is based on punitive management, derived from a relationship between managers and workers where there is a mutual lack of trust. Theory Y, on the other hand, proposes that the worker is an active being who is capable of assuming full responsibility.

Both the rationalist theories of organization and the humanist theories are fundamentally based on the reigning paradigm at the time of uniformity: they were looking for the *single best method of organizing or the single best way of motivating the workforce*. The problem was not so much the ideas that were suggested, but rather the underlying belief in uniformity. As Drucker has indicated,[31] the ideas of the pioneers of management about creating an organizational structure or managing human resources are still valid; the mistake was simply to believe that there was only one possible way of organizing them or only one valid system for managing people.

During the 20th century, the company evolved to include an ever wider range of structures, incorporating new ideas that arose over time. Creating a scientific division of work and establishing an organizational structure remain valid and necessary ideas to this day, and are fundamental to the successful operation of a company. Nevertheless, in addition to an organizational structure, companies need to treat their staff in a different way to their material resources, and as a result humanistic theories complement the earlier theories, adding new elements to them. In this way, throughout the 20th century, new theories appeared that complemented some of the advances that had already been made, always with a belief in the need to find the best way of organizing, and that the conclusions would be universally valid. This belief in uniformity began to break down in the 1970s.

## The new company and business management from the 1970s

### Background

As the century progressed, the speed and range of changes faced by the company increased exponentially. As technology advanced, production cycles became increasingly short, new models appeared and disappeared with great speed, and the speed and unpredictable nature of changes made the context the company would be operating in impossible to forecast. There is no valid model for the company to apply when the context is one of permanent change. Rather than looking for a model to adopt, the company tried to learn how to manage among diversity.

Change affects everybody, from the senior director to the company man, who started to feel the pressure from young competitors with real entrepreneurial spirit, flexibility and no permanent ties. And women had ceased to be diligent secretaries and become another competitor.

In the final decades of the 20th century, the concept of a multi-divisional, hierarchical company guaranteeing a job for life to its employees was beginning to shake. Before the disbelieving gaze of everybody, governments, businesspeople and workers alike, some of the biggest and most robust corporations, such as Pan Am and Barings, disappeared. The majority of large companies drastically reduced their workforces in the 1980s. Then there were major scandals like Enron and WorldCom that shook the foundations of the company.

There were many causes of this instability:

- An increase in competition from countries like Japan, who managed to adapt American management methods and drastically reduce costs, increasing their efficiency of production enormously and so reducing prices.
- There was an increase in competition from small companies with flexible structures and high technology, such as those of Silicon Valley, which began to develop an identity in the 1970s and floated on the stock market in the 1990s. These companies, leaving aside the subsequent bursting of the dot.com bubble, showed that it was possible to function with structures that were very different to the traditional models.
- The structure of investment changed, from a large number of anonymous small investors to investment structured by large investment and pension funds, who were able to exercise control over their investments and, more seriously, remove it if a company did not meet its expectations.

At the same time, from the 1970s onward, governments began to demand that companies played a bigger role in solving social problems, requiring equitable treatment of their employees and greater control over the effects of production on society and the environment.

## Paradigm shift

The traditional structure of the company and its values began to be insufficient to meet the demands of a new context that required flexibility and the ability to innovate and change perpetually. Faced with such rapid change, and against an ever more complicated background, management theories came to conclude that it was not possible to continue believing that there was a single best way of managing an organization, nor a single best way of managing people. Each situation was different, and the employees were increasingly different and, as a result, the company began to change its focus to become a responsive and flexible organization capable of adapting to continuous change.

This paradigm shift toward greater openness and diversity was not restricted to the company, but extended to cover all areas of human knowledge. Thought was no longer based on a rigid scientific method, but looked for ways of integrating complex and dynamic systems. Many scientists at the end of the 20th century began to evaluate and realign the different branches of science, believing that discoveries in the field of physics, for example, could be applied to psychology or to the company. As a result, management theorists began to adapt ideas from the field of biology (Francisco Varela and H. Maturana), engineering and mathematics (Joseph Weizenbaum), quantum physics (David Bohm and Wolfgang Pauli), psychology (Carl Jung and Abraham Maslow) and anthropology (Clifford Geertz, Luis Dumont and James Clifford). And, in turn, they were influenced by new sciences such as cybernetics and new theories of human knowledge.

The changes that have begun are going to affect our way of understanding at the most profound level, making us rethink the way we act in addition to the way we think, and require new concepts to incorporate these new conceptions of reality. Emmering,[32] for example, has argued that the concepts we have developed for understanding reality have supported a definite reality that is fixed, stable, clear and reducible. Nevertheless, when reality is changing, not very stable, unclear and irreducible, as is the case, for example, with the processes of innovation required by today's organizations, the concepts of traditional science no longer support the necessary process of understanding. The limitation of the traditional scientific method is especially evident when we are faced with a dynamic process, with many contributors and different perceptions of what each understands by reality, which can lead to fragmented vision, and not the harmonious, integrated vision that is required. It has therefore become necessary to develop new concepts that support the process of the group, to convert it into an intelligent, knowledge-based organization. These are concepts that can be taken from other relevant sciences, such as the sciences of cybernetics and evolution.

Everywhere people are beginning to break some of the parameters of the traditional, rigid scientific method based on the objective observation of reality, which has its origins with the ancient Greeks and was reincorporated into Western European thought in the 17th century. At the end of the 20th and beginning of the 21st century, formulas are being looked for that are more in accord with a dynamic, changing reality, above all in social sciences, where it is difficult to separate reality from the interactions of its participants and the new realities that are coming into being.

Important theorists from the world of management, such as Chris Argyris, Peter Senge, Peter Drucker and Edward de Bono, are some of those who are applying concepts from other sciences, from neurology to cognitive sciences, to the world of organizations, taking advantage of the new possibilities for learning that are emerging as a result of information management systems.

## Theories of business management for the new company

These new modes of thought and the emulation of other fields of knowledge are giving rise to a wide range of new theories on organizations and the management of people, which are outside the scope of this study. Nevertheless, and in so far as it is going to affect the management of diversity, we would like to highlight three key ideas which are going to progressively liberate the potential of diversity in companies:

- **The conscious participation of the individual in the organization.** Workers increasingly see themselves not as receptors of external ideas but more as individuals who are becoming more active and capable of innovating and being the impulse for change and innovation within the organization.
- **Organizations as dynamic and interactive systems.** If logical positivism saw the world as fragmented, today the world is basically integrated. Systems theories from mathematics will be particularly useful in enabling an understanding of the organization as a dynamic and interactive system projected in time.
- **Organization based on permanent collective learning.** The development of an organization that, supported by knowledge management technologies, can channel the learning of its members into a common objective.

We will now look at these three ideas in more detail.

## The conscious participation of the individual in the organization

As the 1990s progressed, companies became increasingly aware that if they were to obtain a competitive advantage, they could no longer ignore their **human capital**. This term, although first used by Theodore W. Shultz in 1961,[33] took on new importance in the final decades of the 20th century.

Davenport,[34] one of the precursors of the idea of human capital, argued that the company needed, first, to employ the appropriate people and establish a solid contract with them through the creation of an environment that stimulated their contribution to the job and encouraged their capacity for innovation. As a result, management should not so much manage people, as develop a high-return environment for them to operate in. He was an advocate not only of what the individual can contribute to the company, but also of what the company can contribute to the individual.

The focus should be on maximizing the potential of knowledge individuals who supply their skills, competences and experience to the company, which in return meets their requirements.

The idea of the closed concept of the organization man who responded to external stimuli is disappearing, to be replaced by the **knowledge worker**, who is responsible for their function and how they belong to the system, based on managing themselves and continuous learning. Managing oneself is a revolution in human affairs, which aims to maximize the development potential of each of the members of the organization; individual development that enables them to know themselves and their potential and to be able to apply this potential to the needs of the organization.[35]

An organization of responsible individuals who manage themselves will need a change in the attitude of individual members of the organization and a change of focus in the organization.

## Systems and networks: organizations as dynamic and interactive systems

In the 1990s, Peter Senge's book *The Fifth Discipline*[36] revolutionized the way many people thought. In this book he discussed creating an intelligent organization based on individual and group learning. He thought of the organization as a dynamic and integrated system, in contrast to the earlier period when the company had been thought of as a static organization, based on the scientific organization of the organization and its workers.

The system is understood as something holistic, in which all the parts are related and in a continuous feedback process. As a result, the total is often more than the sum of the parts, as the parts, acting interactively, can make the system grow.[37]

Senge based his view of the organization as a dynamic system on the capacity for self-realization of the individuals who constituted it, which he called their *personal domain*, which transcends competences and skills, approaching life as a creative task, not a reactive one. In addition to the need for individuals' personal domain in order to create an intelligent organization, the author goes on to state that a profound analysis of the *mental models* that dominate our way of thinking and acting, of which we are not necessarily conscious and which may not be shared by others, is required. The organization also needs a *shared vision* and to live against a background of *constant and common learning*.[38]

An organization of developed individuals, with shared mental models and shared vision and a common system of learning can achieve a common purpose for the members of the organization to develop a living and dynamic learning system, which he called the **intelligent organ-ization**: an organization that learns continuously and expands it ability to create its own future. The fundamental issue is to change to a longer term perspective where, beyond the annual profit, the company manages to create a living and innovating system that can guarantee its survival.

Senge, in his work with companies like Shell, Ford, Digital and P&G, developed leadership programs based on dynamic and different experiments, which have helped to consolidate this type of thinking in the corporate world.

### Information and knowledge management: organization based on permanent collective learning

The development of *systemic thinking* was influenced by the increasing development of the theories of knowledge management supported by advances in information technology in the final decades of the 20th century.

According to Baets,[39] technology helps us to live and work in a different way; it promotes flexibility in the workplace, without being limited by time or space, which in turn leads to higher productivity and less stress at work. The revolution brought about by the information era will be crucial for the management of diversity, enabling different people to work in different ways whilst still being coordinated and connected. In addition, technology is moving us rapidly from an industrial to a knowledge-based society, where knowledge and its appropriate management networks are a key factor of production.

The objective of the company now is not only growth, but above all sustainable development. As a result, in addition to knowledge, companies require the competences and skills to activate collective knowledge and so convert themselves into **continuous learning organizations**. They need to form self-managing networks that facilitate the continuous learning of their members, which at the same time generate new ideas and ways of thinking from their members.

It is about finding mechanisms to manage a complex organization, to capture individual and collective experience and establish permanent, dynamic communication. In this sense, there are instruments that come from knowledge management that can support collective and individual learning. Some systems that have been appropriated for information and knowledge management include *case-based reasoning, group decision support systems, cognitive mapping* and *artificial neural networks*. Many of these are based on theories of artificial intelligence and neurology, how the brain works individually, and how the collective is the result of sharing individual units and not their sum.[40]

## Diversity management and the new company

### Diversity in the new paradigm

The search for a model of organization based on developed individuals contributing as much as possible to the system has liberated the potential of diversity. Earlier models took for granted the elimination of individual differences in search of rational efficiency. The new paradigm, however, without rejecting the earlier model but rather trying to integrate it into a new framework, maximizes individual differences to achieve greater creativity and competitiveness for the company, resolving the apparent contradiction of unity and diversity.

The contribution that the individual can make is increased enormously if the company does not impose a single culture and allows diversity. In addition, the commitment of the individual to the company should go much further than a salary payment for the hours worked and become a mutual compromise in which the company, for its part, fully supports the development of each individual.

Individuals need to function in an environment that meets their needs, which includes, among other things, achieving an appropriate work–life balance. As a result, one of the questions most clearly posed from the 1990s onward was how to achieve self-fulfilment through work when the demands of working life make it impossible to lead a full family life. The need to reconcile work with family life, one of the pillars of the management of diversity, began to become clear. These conflicts between work and family are considerably reduced when the company has values in accord with the sentiments of the workforce, values that have the same significance in the workplace as the home, accepting the diversity of needs of all those who make up the company. It is in the context of flexibility in the working environment that individuals can contribute to the maximum of their potential and therefore provide the innovation that the organization requires.

## Management of corporate diversity

Diversity management exploded on to the scene explicitly in the 1970s. Nevertheless, diversity was nothing new at the time. As far back as 1911, Mostyn Bird, in the book *Women at Work*,[41] illustrated how cities were being transformed by women working in administration, affirming that even then, the *city* was not a place exclusively for men. Nevertheless, women did not enter the workplace in the same way in every country, and the vast majority of women basically undertook administrative work, with very few reaching management, and particularly senior management, positions. The same is true of ethnic minorities and immigrants, who joined companies throughout the 20th century, particularly multinationals, but very few of whom reached senior management positions.

The dominant model of business management at the time was based on male, Anglo-Saxon values, which resulted in individuals who did not share these values accepting them in order to fit in, which thus resulted in a loss of efficiency.

The moment of change in diversity policies came explicitly to companies in the 1970s in the US, when new civil rights laws were enacted that made the penalties for gender or racial discrimination at work much tougher. In order to comply with the laws against discrimination, companies adopted a range of positive discrimination measures, the principal aim of which was to correct the underrepresentation of certain groups.

The traditional focus did not look at this as a way of managing diversity, but rather a way of correcting injustices from the past. It stemmed from the assumption that for historic reasons, equal opportunities had been denied to women and ethnic minorities. This discrimination was due, above all, to the existence of a series of collective prejudices against these groups; as a result, the elimination of these prejudices and other associated practices would result in equality of opportunities.

The policies were fundamentally based on the principle of the illegality of discrimination, and the policies adopted by corporations led to special selection processes, training to make employees sensitive to the issues and producing lists of candidates with high potential for promotion.[42]

The traditional model of understanding the management of diversity offered some advantages, among others a greater representation of minorities and improved promotion possibilities for them and women, an increase in self-esteem, fewer discriminatory incidents and an improved company image. However, the traditional model also suffered some disadvantages, such as:

- White male backlash, generating resentment and resistance
- The reaction of ethnic minorities and women at being stigmatized in this way and, in some cases, resentment at not being able to demonstrate their real "qualification" for the job without these special measures.

And the traditional model, in itself, did not help the efficient management of questions related to diversity. In general, positive discrimination policies often backfired against companies as they increased the diversity of behaviors, which, when not managed effectively, can have a negative effect on the company and slow down its work in the fields of integration and equality of opportunity.

These policies were maintained in the 1980s, but as the decade progressed, and in particular as it moved into the 1990s, companies in the US and Europe began to apply a more integrated approach, known as **diversity and integration policies**, which aimed not only to correct certain social injustices but also to profit from the potential benefits of diversity. These new policies stopped focussing on groups who were insufficiently represented to focus instead on the culture of the organization, with the intention of creating a general atmosphere of integration, in which all members of the organization could develop their full potential.

In order to understand the process that these companies have been through in the last 20 years with regard to diversity, it is helpful to study the work of Thomas and Ely[43] and the three paradigms they proposed on corporate diversity:

1. **Nondiscrimination and fairness** is based on the recognition that discrimination is wrong. The paradigm idealizes assimilation and color and gender-blind conformism.
2. **Access and legitimacy** on the other hand, celebrates differences. According to this paradigm, organizations want to reach a wider range of clients. The problem with this paradigm is that when you

look for a demographic makeup of staff that reflects that of the target client, employees belonging to other identity groups will probably feel marginalized or exploited.

3. **Learning and efficiency** occurs when organizations link diversity to work perspectives and organizations learn from the potential of diversity. This paradigm, in contrast to the previous two, revolves around the general theme of integration. The new model of management of diversity transcends the first two. As with the fairness paradigm, it promotes equal opportunities for all employees. As with the access paradigm, it acknowledges cultural differences between people and the value these differences have. But this new model of managing diversity enables the organization to internalize the differences between their employees in order to learn and grow as a result of them.

The new focus requires a firm commitment from senior managers and a cultural change in the organization:

> Leaders in the third paradigm are proactive about learning from diversity; they encourage people to make explicit use of cultural experience at work; they fight all forms of domination and subordination, including those generated by one functional group acting superior to another; and they ensure that the inevitable tensions that come from a genuine effort to make way for diversity are acknowledged and resolved with sensitivity.[44]

## The company of the 21st century: the century of diversity?

At the beginning of the 21st century, we are living through a process that, according to Drucker, is producing changes in the forms of management resulting from the new realities and their demands that are so drastic they require a total change of the practices that functioned well during the last century; more than this, it requires a change of mentality on the part of both organizations and individuals.[45]

It will surely be necessary for several decades to pass before it will be possible to evaluate this process of change. In the meantime we are living through a period of transition without anyone being able to tell us where this process of change is going to lead us. Without a clear model on the horizon, companies are obliged to adapt to a context of permanent change and find a way of functioning that is responsive and allows them to change course quickly; above all, they need an entrepreneurial spirit and the ability to innovate.

The practices and values that have worked well during the last century do not need to be thrown away; it is only necessary to enlarge their focus in order to integrate them into a wider concept of the organization. In the same way that evolution absorbed simpler organisms into more complex ones, organizations need to encompass the useful and necessary practices and values in a wider focus that understands the company not as a series of separate fragments but rather as a dynamic and active system in which the members consciously contribute to the harmonious and integrated functioning of the whole.

The objective today is not to manage people, but to manage objectives and results, and provide an appropriate atmosphere for the individual, through their own development, to be able to give more of themselves to the company. In this context the idea of exploiting the potential of diversity has developed. It will permit the company to open up to new ideas, values and markets but at the same time it demands a search for an appropriate way of managing; an open system in which, instead of having a business culture in which the employees have to "fit in," it is necessary for the company to adapt to the diversity of its members. In conclusion, instead of looking for models of management, the company will be obliged to find an organizational model that leads to a dynamic and flexible system.

# Section 2

## CONTENT

Gender, Culture and
Personality: the Values
Provided by Diversity

# 3 Gender and Management

Until relatively recently, gender diversity was not taken into consideration, and companies have not known how to take advantage of it. Women did not receive the same education as men and there was one simple reason for this: it was unquestioningly assumed that women were inferior to men and as a result did not need a man's education to prepare them to be able to transform and change the world.

In the work of Pythagoras and Aristotle and many other ancient philosophers, women were considered "imperfect men." This way of thinking may seem incomprehensible and brutal to us today, but it was accepted throughout history without anybody proposing an alternative. The attitude to women was, at best, paternalistic and protective, considering them as muses that inspired male thought or diligent housewives, whilst men were responsible for all the important decisions of the day in the social and personal fields.

In 1870 only 10 percent of European women knew how to read and only a small percentage of this number possessed a level of cultural knowledge that could be considered anything more than mere adornment. In 1890 the Congreso Pedagógico Latinoamericano affirmed that the "natural frivolity"[1] of women constituted an insurmountable barrier to their universal education. Today these prejudices have been largely overcome; although many types of thought still exist that try to justify these prejudices in one form or another.

After being faced with this situation for centuries, women have finally awoken. In the last century, with the beginning of the feminist movement, women attempted to claim their rights, demonstrating their abilities in public and demanding to be judged by the same criteria as men. The equality seeking feminist of the first half of the 20th century, fuelled in large part by the attitudes of Simone de Beauvoir, gave rise to the radical feminism of the 1970s, advocating the differences between men and women and proposing a model in which the feminine identified with the masculine in order to achieve equality.

In the 1980s a different feminism appeared that welcomed and highlighted the differences between the genders. Among the leading figures in this movement was Bárbara Sichtermann, who proposed that men could only be the model for women up to a certain limit, firstly, because the masculine world had given sufficient proof that it did not work and, secondly, because women did not aspire to convert themselves into quasi-men. In this struggle, women, in the necessary search for equality, have in many cases found themselves obliged to renounce their femininity in order to be able to compete in a man's world, particularly at work.

Women began to be admitted to male universities in the US in 1837, with the foundation of the first female college, which was in Massachusetts. In Europe the process began in the UK in 1848 (Queen's) and extended to France (1880) and then Germany (1894).[2]

Over the last few decades, women have taken decisive steps forward in their development, with the achievement of three important objectives: access to education, universal suffrage and incorporation into the world of work.

This brief historical summary might make us think that the presence of women in public life, their access to professions that previously were male only, to university courses, to the ballot box and even to ministerial office means that the process has been completed and that today women have the same rights as men.

Women are arriving, it is true, but they are arriving in a society that is still masculine, with concepts, programs and objectives which are made by and for men. Without doubt there are many women today who are capable of adapting to this world without losing their femininity; but there are also those who are not capable of doing so and appear committed to assuming a masculine role or being relegated to an inferior level. Although we believe that women have won a space for themselves in professional and social life, in the majority of cases their rights are still restricted for reasons of social class or geographical location.

Men have set the rhythm in social and professional life throughout history and this continues to be true in our companies and institutions today. To this day, the value and importance of things is still largely assessed by the methodical male criteria of rationality. The interesting thing, the thing that is motivating us today, is that, more than at any previous moment in history, it appears that the feminine style is also being recognized and valued. From a historical point of view, women have been relegated from the world of work and limited to performing some social functions. It is only in the last few decades that women have been incorporated in significant numbers into the world of work and the company, contributing their diversity.

Women may have joined both the worlds of society and work, but in this first phase it has been at the high price of taking on and adapting to the male way of thinking and doing things. Women have hardly had time to contribute their own new ways of seeing and doing, the richness of their diversity, which will be one of the great achievements of the 21st century.

John Naisbitt and Patricia Aburdene argue that women are transforming the world we live in and this will have an effect on education, the professions, marriage, companies, investments, publicity campaigns and politics, both for men and for women. Women are rising to the highest levels in the worlds of politics, the media, sports and religious organizations in a way that threatens to alter the status quo for men, by bringing with them a new feminine point of view and values and so giving a new impetus to today's social, political and economic trends.[3]

Few writers today turn a blind eye to this new reality. As the sociologist Amando de Miguel recognizes in his study on Spanish society, change has happened quietly but continuously and this change is going to have further consequences. This change has been spontaneous; it was not foreseen by government, set out in a party political manifesto nor included in the objectives of any organization, even those representing women. It is an example of what sociologists call "the unforeseen consequences of social action."[4]

Women are present at all levels of social life, and in particular at all levels of the world of work. Up until now they have taken part, regarding it as "a game that had to be played away from home," in a stadium designed and built by men. But in the same way that in Chapter 1 we talked about the existence of dominant and rising tendencies in business management, we can also observe that the majority of organizations are beginning to value a range of feminine styles and values as being the most appropriate and adequate for the environment in which we are living today. The Argentinean labor market consultant Alcira Romano argues that we should recognize that the feminine style of communicating, resolving conflicts and taking decisions, and the values and ethics of business and strategies for achieving objectives are different to the masculine style. They are different; but they are complementary and the combination of the two fits perfectly into the trend for integration in the modern company.[5] Tom Peters, the author of *In Search of Excellence,* points out that we can predict the value of a new type of company, but we don't ask who will be the most appropriate people to lead them. His point is that if we take seriously the central role that talent has in our new economy, then the obvious connection between "talent," "leadership" and "women" makes women the obvious candidates.[6]

In this chapter we will attempt to analyze some of the present-day realities of women and companies, and go deeper into the idea of a feminine management style and what this can contribute to the company.

## Current situation

Women are widely dispersed throughout the workforce; women make up more than 40 percent of the global workforce.[7] Between a quarter and a third of all companies are in the hands of women and they represent between 40 and 60 percent of students of tertiary education. Female participation in the labor market, in particular in sectors other than agriculture, has increased in practically the whole world. Between 1980 and 1990 the range of occupations in which women were employed increased in most countries, especially in those of the OECD and in small developing countries where occupational segregation was very high. Nevertheless, it appears that whilst horizontal segregation (by sector) is decreasing, vertical segregation (between positions) often seems to be increasing.[8]

Despite this tendency, we can observe that discrimination on grounds of gender continues to exist: as a result policies aimed at the liberalization of world trade and corresponding privatizations continue to affect women above all. Women have the greater difficulty in accessing finance, technology, and specialized training and support networks. Women are the group that suffers most from poverty, lack of culture and illnesses, even in developed countries like the US, where one in four women of colour and American-Indians live in poverty.

We will now examine some of the characteristics of the female labor market, looking in particular at activity rate, remuneration and access to senior management positions.

### Activity rates

According to a report produced in 2003 by the International Labor Office (ILO),[9] participation by women in the labor force between 1990 and 2000 varied enormously from region to region. Whilst in developed countries, Latin America and the Caribbean, the rate of female participation in the labor market continued to increase, the growth in Asia was more moderate; and the economic crises suffered in some countries appear to have had a greater effect on women than on men. In countries that are in transition and those in subSaharan Africa, the participation rates for both men and women have been decreasing. The overall picture is that the difference between activity rates for men and women is decreasing, principally due to the masculine rate not changing whilst the feminine rate increases. If we look at activity rates in the EU, we can see that the activity rate for men is higher than that for women; 65.5 percent compared to 48.2 percent, a difference of over 17 percentage points. Spain has the highest difference in activity rates between men and women in the EU, with a difference of 24 percent.[10]

Despite this lower rate of activity, overall the rate of female unemployment has almost always been higher than the male rate. This difference has been narrowing in recent years, although there have been some notable exceptions, such as in the Baltic states, parts of Eastern Asia and some developed countries such as Australia, Canada, Japan, New Zealand and the UK (although this may be due to the preferences of employers for certain characteristics, for example in export processes, or that women are more liable to accept jobs and contracts that have little security or are badly paid).

**Table 3.1** Women in Spain: occupation rates by gender (2003)

| | Spain | % | Male | % | Female | % |
|---|---|---|---|---|---|---|
| Total population | 42,717,064 | 100 | 21,034,326 | 49.24 | 21,682,738 | 50.7 |
| Population over 16 | 34,285,700 | 80.26 | 16,647,800 | 79.15 | 17,637,900 | 81.35 |
| Active population | 18,989,100 | 55.38 | 11,245,200 | 67.55 | 7,743,800 | 43.90 |
| Occupied | 16,862,000 | 88.80 | 10,323,100 | 91.80 | 6,538,900 | 84.44 |
| Unemployed | 2,127,100 | 11.20 | 922,100 | 8.20 | 1,204,900 | 15.56 |

*Source:* Active Population Survey INE 2003

**Table 3.2** Women in Spain: occupation rates by educational level and sex (2003)

| | Both sexes | Women | Men | Difference |
|---|---|---|---|---|
| TOTAL | 49.18 | 37.07 | 62.01 | 24.94 |
| Illiterate | 6.26 | 3.87 | 11.49 | 7.61 |
| Unqualified | 14.33 | 7.98 | 23.20 | 15.22 |
| Primary | 32.23 | 18.76 | 47.62 | 28.85 |
| Secondary or medium (except technical and professional medium) | 56.29 | 41.90 | 69.66 | 27.75 |
| Professional technicians (medium and higher grades) | 72.01 | 63.40 | 80.91 | 17.51 |
| Universities (1st cycle) | 69.37 | 67.05 | 72.55 | 5.50 |
| Universities (2nd cycle) | 78.44 | 75.57 | 81.09 | 5.52 |

*Source:* based on Active Population Survey, INE

The situation in Spain is similar to the global pattern, being toward the bottom of the list of developed countries and the EU. As can be seen from Tables 3.1 and 3.2, female activity rates are lower than male activity rates at all educational levels in Spain, although the difference reduces for those with university-level education (but, as we have just seen, the active population is more restricted). Female unemployment in Spain is double the male level, and it is the third highest in the EU.[11]

## Access to management

The greater presence of women in paid employment has made their contribution to the economy more visible, but the type of job to which they have access is still far from that of their male counterparts. In general terms, men are in central, higher paid positions, whilst women occupy peripheral, insecure and less highly valued positions; women have higher representation among part-time workers. In Japan and the US, almost 70 percent of part-time workers at the end of the 1990s were female. These are jobs that involve working from home; they are temporary, dependent on demand or are "women's work"; in general they are less attractive, and tend to have lower remuneration, less prestige and fewer possibilities for development.

In the 1980s and 1990s there was a reduction in "horizontal segregation," but "vertical segregation" continued, with women continuing to have difficulty in breaking through the glass ceiling and obtaining the positions with the greatest responsibility.

Women have not managed to rise to positions of leadership. Among directors, senior executives and the highest levels of the professions, men are still in the majority, whilst women are predominantly to be found in junior management positions. In 2003, 13.6 percent of the directors on the boards of Fortune 500 companies in the US were women,[12] whilst in Spain the figure for IBEX 35 companies was 4.6 percent (see Table 3.3).[13]

The results of *The 2004 Female FTSE Report*,[14] on the composition of boards of directors, shows that only 29 companies had 2 or more women on their boards; of these, 8 companies had 3 women directors, 2 had 4 women directors, whilst 31 large companies did not have a single woman on their boards. This study also showed that on a measurement of ROE over the previous three years, the companies with women on their boards had a return of 13.8 percent, compared to 9.9 percent for those formed solely by men. The study for 2002[15] showed that 16 (80 percent) of the 20 largest companies in terms of stock market valuation had women on their boards of directors, whilst only 8 (40 percent) of the 20 smallest companies had women on their boards. This could be used to defend the cause of gender diversity, based on the argument that the relationship between high stock market valuation and the presence of women on the board of directors is closer than ever.

**Table 3.3** Women directors in Spain

| Total working population | Total | Women | % women |
|---|---|---|---|
| Directors of companies and public administration | 16,862.0 | 6538.9 | 38.78 |
| Directors of public administration and companies with 10 or more salaried employees | 359.4 | 65.3 | 18.17 |
|    Executive and legislative power and directors of organizations | 14.1 | 4.2 | 29.79 |
|    Directors of companies with 10 or more employees | 345.3 | 61.1 | 17.69 |
| Managers of companies with fewer than 10 employees | 456.7 | 120.7 | 26.43 |
|    Commercial | 152.6 | 50.7 | 33.25 |
|    Hospitality | 86.7 | 23.3 | 26.87 |
|    Other | 217.5 | 46.8 | 21.52 |
| Managers of companies without salaried staff | 437.0 | 199.3 | 45.61 |
|    Commercial | 260.8 | 142.0 | 54.45 |
|    Hospitality | 107.3 | 38.1 | 35.51 |
|    Other | 68.8 | 19.2 | 27.91 |

*Note:* Figures in thousands
*Source:* Data from the Active Population Survey, INE, 4th quarter 2003

These studies lead us to ask why, if women have managed to access the labor market, is it so unusual for them to reach the highest managerial positions?

The difficulty of access for women to the highest managerial positions is not limited exclusively to companies, as we can see in Figure 3.1, but rather it is a constant in all professional areas. For example, following the elections of November 2004 in the US, 456 of the 535 members of Congress were men, more than 85 percent, and only 79 were women. There are five states (Delaware, Iowa, Mississippi, New Hampshire and Vermont) that have never sent a woman to Congress. This difficulty for women to reach the highest directorial positions represents what has been referred to as "the glass ceiling."[16]

According to Meyerson and Fletcher, it is not just this glass ceiling that prevents women from progressing, but rather the whole structure of the organizations for which they work: the cement, the beams, the walls and the very air they breathe. They argue that the solution lies not in dismantling the organization but in searching out the hidden barriers that stop equality and efficiency. They urge leaders to act like good architects and reconstruct the buildings beam by beam, room by room, and rebuild the structure with practices that are more robust and fairer, not only for women but for the whole workforce.[17]

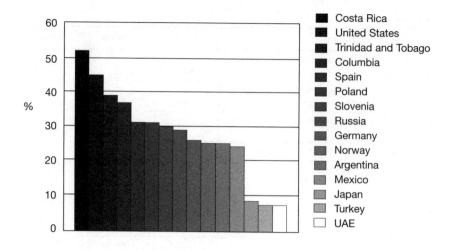

Figure 3.1 **Women directors, legislators and senior administrators**
*Source:* UNDP Human Development Report 2003/ILO 2004

An interesting study by Catalyst[18] hints at some of the barriers that obstruct the career paths of European women. The study comprised interviews with 500 women and 132 men in senior positions in large companies and professional firms in 20 European countries.

The study reached some interesting conclusions. In the first place, women consider stereotypes to be the principal barrier they meet in their professional lives, whilst men do not consider stereotypes to be an important factor at all. Other issues that had an impact according to the women interviewed were their lack of visibility in senior positions, lack of experience and commitments to their personal lives.

The conclusions also identified some other barriers. Some of these are related to issues such as motherhood in the early stages of a professional career, between 30 and 40 years of age. There were also social barriers related to achieving a work–life balance. Other barriers are more closely related to the psychological perception that men and women have of the suitability of men and women for positions as directors. However, there were a number of sectors that, in general, were considered more open to women, these included retailing, food shops, financial and savings institutions, the media and the public sector in general.

Training in management

The majority of studies consider training in senior management to be a key element in breaking the glass ceiling restricting the progress of women managers. Nevertheless, the number of women taking postgraduate training in management has not increased; in fact it has decreased over recent years.

In 2000, 56 percent of graduates within the EU were women; however, only 46 percent of postgraduates were female, and this falls to between 25 and 30 percent of MBA students worldwide. Despite this, according to studies by the *Financial Times*, there is a worrying decline in the number of women taking MBAs. In the EU, the percentage of MBA students who were women decreased from 56.5 percent in 2001 to 27 percent in 2003. In the same period, in the US the reduction was from 51.9 percent to 25 percent.[19]

## Salary levels

Although pay differentials between men and women have been reducing in many places, there is still a huge gap, particularly in the private sector. This gap has been reducing in Latin America, central and Eastern Europe and, from the 1970s, in the countries of the OECD, although very slowly.

Contrary to what is generally believed, the causes of this pay differential are not lower educational achievements or career breaks; the causes are rooted in other factors, such as the occupational segregation that arises from predetermined structures and systems of classifying work or from weak collective negotiation.[20]

According to the November 2004 study *The Status of Women in the States* produced by the Institute for Women's Policy Research,[21] women on average receive 76 percent of the salary of men in the US, and at the current rate of progress it will take then a further 50 years to reach equality. The situation is worse if factors such as race are included in the equation; an African-American woman receives 63 percent of the salary of a man, and a Latin American only slightly more than half. There has been practically no progress in the situation of Latin American women, where, if anything, the difference has increased. This is the situation in the US, one of the most developed countries in the world, and one of those that has been concerned about improving the situation of women for the longest.

In the EU the situation is very similar.[22] In Spain, a January 2005 study[23] showed that, on average, women earn 34 percent less than men. The gap is 50 percent in the private sector, compared to 10.7 percent in the public sector.

## Achieving a work–life balance

Throughout Europe, it is mostly women who take responsibility for domestic chores, something which presents a special problem for women in management positions, whether they have children or not. Long working days make it difficult to combine professional careers with family responsibilities.

The difficulty of reconciling personal life with a professional career is one of the principal questions that companies have to confront with their diversity strategies. The majority of companies in Europe and the US are increasingly committing themselves to flexible working conditions, which make it easier to balance professional and private life. These new policies that are being adopted are aimed primarily at women, but corporate experience shows that these policies are also increasingly being extended to men as well, so that all members of the organization can find a more appropriate work–life balance.

## Women and professional life: options and/or choices

The overall situation of women in their professional life appears, from the preceding pages, to be far from reaching equality. Nevertheless, we cannot point to a single cause, or say that there has been a conspiracy by men or society to impede the full professional development of women. On the contrary, there are many factors that have resulted in the difficulties that women face in their professional lives. Some of these stem from a lack of options whilst others arise from the personal choices that individual women have made at different times in their lives.

The principal problem, according to all the studies, is the difficulty of combining family life with a full professional life; this produces difficult choices that in many cases stop women reaching senior management posts, or result in them accepting lower remuneration in exchange for more flexible working conditions, or missing out on training opportunities due to lack of time.

Everywhere and nearly all the time, women continue to take the basic responsibility for family life. At the same time, they have joined the workforce, taking on all the responsibilities that that implies; on many occasions this leads to a difficult balance and a great deal of stress. Meanwhile, men have not taken on the same responsibility for family life, and at times even seem to be being overcome by a loss of territory that is leaving them without a clear social role.

The reality is that we are immersed in a process of transition from a society with clearly defined and separated roles, to a society where roles will be decided by each person, or by each family, according to their particular circumstances, not by society, government or a company. In our opinion, this process of transition is the root cause of the current lack of equilibrium. Leaving to one side strictly biological matters, each woman will decide the degree of responsibility within the family that she wants or is able to delegate. Each couple will have to decide together the degree of responsibility that each partner is going to take.

The degree of balance between family and professional life is moving from being something dictated by society to something freely chosen by each person. The individual mentality of men and women is changing toward a personal choice of their way of life; at the same time, society and the company are adapting to facilitate this flexibility. At this moment in time, synchronizing the rhythm of change is the biggest difficulty.

## Gender studies and anthroplogy

Toward the end of the 19th century and especially at the beginning of the 20th century, psychiatry and philosophy, through the work of writers such as Feurbach, Freud and Jung, discovered the importance of the sexual element in the understanding of human behavior.

As Anne Moir and David Jessel argue in their book *Brain Sex: The Real Differences Between Men and Women,* men and women are different – they are the same only in so far as they all belong to the same species – and insisting that they are equal in aptitudes, skills and behavior would result in creating a society founded on a biological and scientific lie. They argue that a large part of the failure of women to occupy their rightful place lies in their determination to be like men, which they regard as being mistaken.[24]

As we are different, our ways of doing things at work are different. They are not better and they are not worse. There are different qualities, and these different qualities are those that have not been taken advantage of in the world of work, which as a result is only working at 50 percent of its possibilities.

Nevertheless, we should make clear before we go on to look at any analysis that there is a difference between sex (man/woman) and gender (masculine/feminine). Culture consists of masculine and feminine qualities and values, rooted in the roles that each society ascribes to men and women. Depending on the situation, a man can act in a feminine way and a woman can adopt behavior that is considered masculine. Looking at the anthropological differences between men and women may help us to understand certain forms of behavior. However, taking this too far would be a form of reductivism that would not help anybody; they are purely for guidance, which is how they should be understood.

The differences between men and women have been demonstrated in numerous studies that look at the different characteristics of each gender from different points of view: genetic, physiological, psychological and educational. Here we would like to give a quick overview of these studies, which will give us a greater understanding of gender diversity and the richness that the complementarity of the two genders contains.

From the beginning, these differences are obvious: women are the combination of two X chromosomes, whilst men are the combination of an X and a Y chromosome. As a result it is the man who dictates gender, being the only one who carries a different chromosome.

It can be observed that women are less prone to hereditary illnesses; 70 percent of babies born with congenital defects are male. A study undertaken by 16 experts concluded that the differences between male and female are much greater than initially appear, especially with regard to health, both as a result of the number and the seriousness of the wide range of illnesses to which they are susceptible. "The male or female sex really does matter, it has an importance that we did not expect and could not even have imagined," commented Mary Lou Pardue of the Massachusetts Institute of Technology (MIT) in the prologue to the report.[25]

From a more local point of view, Francisco Flórez, head of endocrinology at the Hospital Clínico in Madrid, showed that there are various differences that favor women: genetic, metabolic and immunological.[26]

At birth, girls weigh an average of 2,750 grams, compared to 3,250 grams for boys, who in addition are 7 percent larger. Boys' hearts are bigger (310 grams compared to an average of 260 grams in girls) and beat more slowly (72 beats per minute compared to 80 beats per minute for girls). Girls burn fewer calories (2,000 compared to 2,700 in boys), breathe more rapidly and have 20 percent fewer red blood corpuscles. Girls' voices are sharper; they are livelier and have less muscle fibre (30 percent less than boys).

The physiognomy of both sexes is clearly different, in their features and the different ways in which they develop. Males have greater muscle mass, are stronger and have more sweat and sebaceous glands, whereas females show greater coordination in all its forms.

It is perhaps in the neurological aspect where the most important differences can be observed. *Time* magazine published photos showing that when women think about a definite thing, neural networks in both hemispheres of their brains are active, whereas in men only one specific part is used. This has led to the justification of women being able to perform various operations at the same time, together with their greater facility for verbal expression, compared to the greater spatial awareness of men. Research undertaken by the University of Sydney confirmed that the areas of the brain related to language are between 20 and 30 percent larger in women[27].

Women hear better, have better vision, even in the dark, and have more acute senses of taste and smell. They are much more sensitive in all areas of their bodies. On average they suffer more minor illnesses but fewer cardiovascular problems.

Men perform better in mathematical tests, compared to women who do better in verbal tests and have greater ability with languages; both genders represent different learning styles. It is also widely appreciated that females mature intellectually more rapidly than males and this is leading to a revision of the models for mixed primary and secondary education.

From the various different studies that have been undertaken, it is possible to conclude that, anthropologically, we have to talk of men and women as two radically different sexes, which when they are manifested in people are different and complementary. Considering them to be equal would lead to uniformity and a single way of thinking that would impoverish the richness that humanity represents.

## The influence of gender on management

It is now time to look at what women do, and are able to do, for companies; we will leave to one side the discussion of what the company can do for women. It is time to identify the aspects that gender can bring to the management of our organizations, which, as we have argued, is becoming increasingly important in today's world. In order to do this, we will try to identify some of the characteristics that define what we call the "masculine style" and the "feminine style" at work.

As we begin to reflect on this, it is important to reiterate the fact that defining masculine and feminine styles does not mean they can be applied to all women or all men. To be more precise, it means that an ideal type exists that can be considered feminine and another that can be considered masculine, irrespective of whether women and men behave in this way.

Carl Jung[28] postulated the existence of masculine and feminine principles as basic components of personality. According to Jung, the ego, or conscious identity of a person as a man or a woman (as socialized and articulated in a temporal, cultural context), is balanced by an unconscious, unarticulated complement. For men this is the interior feminine component or *anima* and for women it is the interior masculine component or *animus*. The anima is associated with eros (the principle of love) and the positive and negative associations with the general maternal figure (transmitter of life, carer or manipulator). The *animus* is associated with logos (the principle of discrimination and cognition) and the positive and negative with the general paternal figure (protector, provider or tyrant).

This Jungian vision leads to an abstract concept that underlines the differences in personality traits, where masculine signifies discrimination, orientation to objectives, desire to explain, improve and provide, whilst the feminine signifies care, holistic vision and acceptance. Although there are other psychological approaches to gender, the Jungian approach offers an initial perspective of the masculine and feminine visions of the world (in developed Western economies).[29]

As a result, numerous studies have defined idealized forms of masculine and feminine conduct in management; these forms are not common to all women or all men, as everybody has a unique individual perspective. However, overall, these ideal types are real and influence some of the fundamental perceptions in the workplace, such as how to motivate others, the role of the mentor and management and leadership styles.

It is interesting to observe that the majority of writers and studies that have been done agree on the characteristics that identify what has come to be called the "feminine management style." In this context, the results reported by a group of female executives from 14 Latin American countries, organized by the Network of Latin American Women in Organization Management in Mexico City, are relevant; they recognized responsibility, working in teams, orientation to achieve, interpersonal relationships, time management, safety, tenacity, perseverance, intellectual capacity, language skills, justice, organization, commitment, creativity, enthusiasm, experience, motivation, tolerance, loyalty, flexibility and positive image as being feminine traits.[30]

If we asked any executive in a large company, without doubt they would recognize these as being the principal personal characteristics required in order to develop and progress within the organization, without necessarily identifying them as belonging to a "feminine" style. And to a certain extent, men continue not to recognize some of this contribution that is developing in a natural way in their companies.

Feminine management characteristics, whether accepted by men or not, are becoming natural features in today's organizations and a key factor in forming behavior and models in the modern company.

Lidia Séller, a consultant and author of various works on the subject of female leadership, argues that the principal strengths of the feminine style are greater communication skills, greater patience and listening ability, a greater capacity for interpersonal relationships, the ability to handle multiple situations at the same time, the ability to decentralize and greater ease of seeing things in their true perspective.[31] No matter how you look at it, more and more of the professional literature and studies are beginning to identify these characteristics.

Perhaps John Naisbitt and Patricia Aburdene have produced the best synthesis[32] of the appreciation of the difference between the traits that constitute the feminine style and those more traditionally identified with the masculine style. These authors define traditional management with the main objective being control, in contrast, the feminine management style is based on an objective of change. As such, traditional management will be based in some of the following characteristics: position, having all the answers, giving orders, discipline, punishment, restricted vision, rigidity, mechanical and impersonal, among other traits. Feminine management by contrast will be based on: enabling, connecting, asking the appropriate questions, serving themselves as examples, valuing creativity, wide vision, flexibility, integrator and personal style, among other traits.

The majority of recent studies on business management agree about a series of generic aspects that are more or less directly applicable to women or, more accurately, to a feminine management style. They identify these aspects as if they were proof of a series of elements that are repeated in the majority of behavior that can be observed in management. We will now examine these and the reasons used to justify them in greater detail. We would like to try to understand how gender diversity provides new elements and focuses, which will allow both men and women to adopt new styles and behaviors. Our objective is to try to shed a little more light on this reality, which enables new ways of acting in everyday management. We are conscious that this is a challenge that is happening at the moment and that only by understanding its origins and its cause will we be able to extract all its positive consequences. To this end, and to flesh out what we have already said, we will now highlight some of the behavior that characterizes the feminine style of management.

## A transforming style

The masculine style has been defined as *transactional leadership*, which means that managers reward or punish employees based on their performance. The masculine style is characterized by a more competitive atmosphere, more difficult communications, individualistic attitudes, a certain taste for bureaucracy and respect for hierarchy. Men do not like asking for help; they try to conquer the situation on their own and convert situations into personal challenges.

The feminine style, on the contrary, is considered *transformational*, that is, it is an interactive style that values diversity and promotes partic- ipation and teamwork. If the masculine style looks to formal and rational structures as the magic formula to unite the efforts of the organization, the feminine style promotes concentric structures, creates collaborative teams around the individual, who in this way becomes the center of their own structure. If the masculine conception sees structure and methods as the magic formula for resolving any situation, and information flows fairly freely upward and downward, feminine style leadership surges from inside to outside, from the person to the rest of the organization, creat- ing new management formulas that mesh with the new realities of the company today.

### Diverse thought

The first contribution that gender diversity brings to the company is precisely the fact that diversity exists and that this is a good thing. The masculine gender has always shown a natural capacity for abstract intel- lectual activity; this type of intellectual activity carries with it the risk, which is rarely overcome, of missing the point of life and leaving just pure, general concepts, which are skeletal and empty. The masculine model of thinking is, in many ways, the mathematical model. Even in activities far removed from the appropriate rigor of professional activity, the masculine model tends to impose order, which is the consequence of this rationality. The masculine model agrees with the Cartesian models, when ideas are clear and distinct, and where geometry, method and reason are the norms for behavior. Probably the most frequent complaint made by men about women throughout history has been that they are not reasonable. The point is that for men, the only reasonable way of thinking and acting is the masculine way. And this is the root cause of many of the frustrations that lead men to think that the feminine is not as rational as the masculine, without realizing that it is not a question of who is most or least rational, but rather of two distinct ways of under- standing what is known as "reason." If men surpass women in the level of abstract conceptions, they are merely apprentices with respect to women when it comes to the realization of the vital values of life and the existential and concrete knowledge of people. In other words, the femi- nine surpasses the masculine in its attitude to life. The masculine has a compartmentalized attitude to life, with a rationality which makes him move from one concept to the next successively. The feminine, on the other hand, has a global vision of things, with a certain unity about the important questions of life that values them according to their true worth. The masculine takes things apart, divides them up and analyzes them, whilst the feminine has an extraordinary faculty for intuition, of understanding things in the whole without grandiloquent discursive reasoning. The feminine sees and understands things, resolving them with certainty and efficiency, where the masculine loses itself in lengthy algebraic analysis of the questions that really matter in life.

### A new way of knowing

There are two distinct types of knowledge; abstract knowledge and expe-riential knowledge. The masculine style naturally tends to value abstract knowledge more highly than experiential knowledge; it feels the need to rationalize things in order to be able to understand them. When it comes to taking a decision, the masculine style will generate a huge number of alternatives. The feminine style values experiential knowledge more highly than abstract knowledge; the feminine sees and evaluates. When it comes to decision making, women evaluate the multiple alternatives more effectively. The masculine style is more focussed on objectives, whilst the feminine style focuses more on the policies. The masculine style looks upward (to the abstract), whilst the feminine keeps its feet firmly planted on the ground (experiential). As a result, we are comple-mentary: without masculine values, there would be immobility; on the other hand, without the feminine, contact with reality would be lost.

### Allocating time

The feminine tendency is to allocate time effectively; this is almost a natural tendency. Women work intensively, trying to avoid meetings, which are so common in the masculine style, especially the interminable ones that begin at 7 o'clock in the evening. The feminine style assesses its strengths and distributes them in such a way that everything can be achieved and it is easier to delegate.

### Approachability

Men lose their concentration more easily, whilst women are normally approachable. Women are not bothered when they are interrupted whilst working. The masculine style, on the other hand, in its relationships with people, focuses more on the task in hand than in building relationships based on trust and reciprocal help; a man will happily approach a colleague with the aim of achieving an objective, whilst a woman will feel uncomfortable asking for a favor from someone with whom she has not built a personal relationship of trust.

## Work–life balance

The feminine style attributes the same importance to work as the other aspects of life. This leads to a greater degree of personal equilibrium and helps maintain calm at time of stress by treating things according to how important they really are. Some companies, faced with the huge increase in work over recent years, have adopted working practices that show that women have more of a work–life balance, whilst men are addicted to their work.

## Interpersonal relationships

The feminine style puts the accent on interpersonal relationships within organizations. The most important thing is that the circuits of communication function correctly to maintain the team. The masculine style is jealous of its power and the instruments it can use to wield it: control of information, delegation, decision making. It is difficult for the masculine style to ask for information, as if this was in some way undermining the vertical structure of the company (hierarchy), whilst the feminine style relies on horizontalness and integration (which is exactly what modern companies are trying to achieve). The feminine style is based more on cooperation than on competition. In a job interview, whilst a man will show greater confidence in himself and will "sell" himself more to the employer, a woman will downplay her role and emphasize the work of her "team."

The feminine style makes what has been called the "double life" possible, and does not make a drama out of it, although on occasions the effort of combining family life and work leads to great difficulties. The way it operates means that the feminine style has a greater capacity for resolving problems, avoiding going over an irresolvable problem a thousand times. The feminine style recognizes the importance of family life as fundamental for personal development, both for women and men. Until today, based on a purely masculine vision, personal and professional development have been kept completely separate. Today's companies have recognized that their greatest asset, perhaps the one thing that differentiates them from their competitors, is their people, and it is only by understanding this and fully developing their abilities and resources that companies can hope to meet the challenges they are facing. The greatest sources of wealth in the 21st century are creativity, the ability to form different teams for different tasks and the innovation that arises from new ideas. The person is the greatest asset the company has and it must invest in each one; but the person is not purely the sum of everything added together, but rather a unit which transforms and matures all the aspects that affect it. Personal life and professional life are not two disassociated elements; they are a perfect combination that allows a human being to reach real self-fulfilment. The feminine style is aware of this and combines both aspects; the masculine style has still to learn this lesson.

The feminine style brings a new dimension to strength, which should be understood as resistance rather than aggression. The masculine style is conditioned by its rationalistic obsession with understanding all the processes and systems, in many cases attaching greater importance to the processes themselves rather than the results. The masculine style is oriented toward changing the environment, whilst the feminine style prefers to transform it.

### Importance of informal structures compared to formal ones

The masculine style believes that human progress is based on technical knowledge, the economy and other variables related to visible structure, whilst the feminine style brings into consideration the structures that are not visible to rational examination, but which are more real in everyday life. The feminine style does not formalize more than is necessary.

### Effusiveness (sharing) as a leadership trait

The feminine style perceives delegation as an integral part of the management function, not as a loss of authority. In a meeting, women listen and let those who have most difficulty in being heard speak. The feminine style internalizes all the elements that are produced in a relationship. Today's companies increasingly base the development of their wealth on the capacity to generate perceptions that meet the needs of the client. It is no longer a case of producing products that are better or worse than the competition, but rather of creating a perception in customers that a company's product is exactly what they are looking for to fulfil their needs. Today's products are composed of material elements and a symphony of sensations that the company seeks to add to them, and in this specialization the feminine style has the advantage of grasping and interpreting all these needs.

## Ability to manage diversity

In a situation where there is a proliferation of information, there is a need to create new ways of knowing and acting based on behavior that is more intuitive. The feminine style handles heterogeneous information more effectively, precisely because it has a greater capacity for understanding than for elaborating complex systems of analysis. In the feminine style, vision is used as a step to analysis; it is intuition rather than deduction. Faced with this proliferation of information, the masculine style tends to become blocked, to become desperate when confronted with the impossibility of analyzing everything. The feminine style prefers to observe with an intuitive knowledge of where ideas should be extracted from, dismissing the information overload.

## Feelings and emotions

Decision making based on feelings is highly dangerous, but taking decisions without taking feelings into account is impossible and would be heartless. Logic is normally a magnificent tool, but it is not complete. Reality does not follow the laws of normal logic. The feminine style does not hesitate in breaking the rules if this is necessary in order to achieve an objective. Until now, feelings have seemed to be negative aspects in decision making, not because feelings in themselves are something negative, but because the masculine style had understood that they were something that had no place in management. It is not that this was the best way of seeing things; it was only that it was the masculine way of understanding them. In the feminine style, the feelings of others are important, as are their states of mind, and they should be taken into account.

The interest in ecology in our times, the need to conserve the environment and promote diversity is something that is genuinely feminine, compared to the coldness of technology that has governed the masculine style. The important issue is to enable internal growth whilst preserving the external; both can live together in harmony.

## Masculine values

Masculine values are good at generating alternatives, whilst feminine values are good at setting criteria and limits to decisions. In this way, the masculine style provides qualities such as the capacity for projection over the long term, a tendency to rationalization, exactness and technology. In negotiations, the feminine style only makes a decision when it considers that it has all the necessary information to do so.

An investigation undertaken by the psychology department of the

University of Valencia (under the direction of Ester Barberá) investigated some of these aspects.[33] The study focussed on two companies in the Valencia region, one of which had a wide range of diversity in its senior management (Arquitectura e Iniciativas por la Ciudad), whilst the other was not diverse (Garrigues & Andersen). The study showed that the majority of people interviewed perceived real differences between male and female senior managers in the way they ran their departments and related to their teams. The most significant aspects that confirmed the existence of a distinct management style that brought positive qualities and benefits to the team, and as a result the organizations, were, among others, that female senior managers:

- had greater sensitivity to relationships and a greater capacity for communication
- took greater account of emotional and personal aspects in the development of the job, considering the person as a whole when it came to decision making, evaluation and so on
- took greater account of the personal needs of their staff, and had greater respect for their private and family life
- had a working and management style that was more methodical and organized, was more practical and had a greater capacity for resolving issues.

It can be concluded from the results of this study, that female senior managers had a management style that was more horizontal and people-centered.


## A conclusion: we are complementary

We are complementary. This is the crucial message of our times, which for centuries has not been understood, or has been understood incorrectly. Women have always been considered inferior to men, whom they serve, and who form the fundamental reference point for their personal and social actions. At best, social roles were distributed so that women took on subordinate or collaborative functions to the roles that were designed for and should have been carried out by men.

Today this interpretation has been overtaken and humanity is beginning to understand the debt it has accumulated throughout history to women. Today, if someone were to talk of the rights of women as something separate from the rights of men, it would be something shocking, although injustice and discrimination persist and continue to happen in many places throughout the world. We now talk about the rights of the person, whether man or woman, of personal dignity, as a single reality that cannot be interpreted in any other way.

Women are not here to complete the role of men. They are here to play their own role, and their reality as women is what makes the reality of men definitively real. We cannot talk about masculine if there is no feminine, as there would be no reference point. The masculine exists because of the feminine, and the feminine exists because of the masculine. There are few realities that are so deeply rooted. And humanity can at last consider the fundamental and basic recognition of the woman as an essential protagonist in a humanity that creates both men and women as one of the great successes of our age. It has certainly been a long process, but it appears to be about to be fulfilled in our era with the universal recognition of this reality.

This process has been even more difficult for the company. As we have already stated, in the traditional division of roles that society had made, men belonged to the sphere of public life, whilst women belonged to private life. But then women broke into this constructed reality. They did this out of necessity (society needs their help), but also because they wished to fulfil a role to which they were fully entitled. Women have left private life to participate in public life with the same importance as men. Society has come to this conclusion as a mark of civilization, but it has also been a question of necessity. The company needs the person, but the person is not something isolated, cold and compartmentalized. The person is a whole, which is influenced by all aspects, from the details of the organigrams of the company superstructures to the harmony of the balance between personal and professional life. Masculine and feminine values, beliefs and ways of doing things, age and race are inseparable aspects of the person that enrich and distinguish them, which convert them into powerful motors of progress.

The world of the company created by men was incomplete. Women, as a result of their contribution, bring into question all the realities that until today had seemed unquestionable.

In Chapter 1 we saw how the company is making an effort to transform itself. We discussed dominant values, those that have come to define company identity, and then looked at rising values. We came to the conclusion that these rising values that are beginning to be present in companies coincide exactly with the aspects supplied by diversity. The conclusion is simple; the characteristics that define modern management can be identified more easily and more naturally with what we are coming to recognize as the "feminine management style."

Does this mean that our organizations should "feminize" themselves?

No, it doesn't. We are only saying that our organizations were incomplete as they were only taking advantage of half the riches that human gender has to offer, they were only functioning at 50 percent of their capacity, and now, at last, we are entering a period when we can take advantage of the fullness offered by humanity.

Our companies have worked up to now, and they have done so efficiently. They are still functioning efficiently, but at the same time the company is conscious that it must find new opportunities and new focuses if it wishes to survive and thrive. The dominant values, perhaps those that are most associated with the masculine style of managing and organizing, are still relevant and form a solid structure that enables our companies to function. But it is becoming increasingly necessary to undertake a revision of these assumptions in the light of the new challenges and opportunities presented by diversity. Women have a head start in this, as they have no need to learn the feminine values of the new company, but, at the same time, they have already had to adapt to the pre-existing masculine concept. Men, on the other hand, are faced with a new task; they need to recognize the new values presented by diversity, and recognize that their vision is not the only valid one.

The feminine management style brings to the company a strong commitment to people; it is participative and expansive, it looks to share and make all members of the team feel comfortable and capable of proposing initiatives and changing. Company structures are necessary, but it is also necessary to change them. In order to do this, there needs to be a will to change and create the conditions necessary for people to be able to propose and activate the mechanisms of change.

Women have been to an exceptional school. As Naisbitt and Aburdene point out, many of the attributes for which feminine management styles have been praised are deeply rooted in the functions that society has attributed to women. Today's companies require managers who have the capacity to motivate, an interest in people and a disposition to encourage the creation of teams. The traditional organization continues to exist with its masculine methods and processes, but the management of these processes demands new styles that combine the personal with the professional, something which the feminine style has been doing for some time.[34]

There is no longer a space in our organizations for the arrogant boss who thinks they have all the answers, or there is a space, but only on a limited number of occasions. You have to read between the lines and understand what people really want. And, above all, you have to manage a multitude of situations, data and perceptions that make up the structure of a business reality that is ever more complicated. And, what is more, it needs to be done quickly. The objectives continue to be the priority for any company, but meeting them today is a complex process in which hundreds of variables are intertwined in a way that we cannot always control. In addition, feminine and masculine styles are becoming complementary in order to achieve perfect harmony and an appropriate and effective way of managing.

The analysis of the disposition of organizations merits separate attention in its own chapter. The advances made by moving from pyramidal structures to horizontal ones are widely accepted and we will not go into the positive contribution that this change has made here. Our companies continue to have a certain degree of hierarchy and chain of command, but these have been enriched and complemented by the management of teams and projects based on horizontal structures; a new parallel between the transformation of the company and diversity. The masculine style has created efficient structures that today are being enriched by the incorporation of the feminine style. This style prefers to be in the center of the organization instead of at its apex, so that all those collaborating in a project can revolve around this center without necessarily belonging to a determined position. The center will not cease to exist and should attract other things to it, but without assigning immoveable positions.

Gender diversity is complementary; just as the transformations that are developing the company are complementary. Masculine and feminine are mutually enriching each other at the heart of our organizations and opening new perspectives for a new management model. It is now up to each one of us to take advantage of the possibilities that this opportunity is offering us.

# 4 Culture and Business Management

*And now we are alone. We have swapped biological diversity for cultural diversity. In this sense, if human beings in the future wish to continue evolving, it will be essential to integrate diversity so as not to waste energy and in this way to accelerate the process of hominization and humanization.*

Eudald Carbonell, co-director of the Sierra de Atapuerca project[1]

## What is culture?

One of the oldest definitions of culture is the one formulated by the British anthropologist Edward Tylor in 1871, which has been widely used as a reference point, for example by the *Encyclopaedia Britannica* (2000), which defined culture as "a complex whole which includes knowledge, belief, art, morals, law, customs and any other capabilities and habits acquired by man as a member of society".[2]

The large number of definitions that we can find for the term "culture" reflects its great complexity. Schein,[3] one of the most influential experts in the field of cultural studies in the 1980s, defined culture as a basic model of suppositions that have been invented, discovered or developed by a group, with which it has learnt how to deal with problems of external adaptation and internal integration, and has functioned sufficiently well for the model to be considered valid and so taught to new members of the group as the correct way of perceiving, thinking and feeling in relation to such problems.

This definition touches on the operative character of a culture, that is, something that can be taught and, therefore, learnt. As a result, for some experts, such as Katan,[4] the importance of culture is not so much what it is as what it implies, what it has behind it: a complex system of congruent beliefs interrelated with values, strategies and cognitive contexts that guide the shared bases of knowledge.

Understood like this, culture is a dynamic and practical process rather than a static concept. In addition to reflecting a series of beliefs, culture provides guidelines for facing the future, orientations for living and resolving everyday problems, and a single interpretation of the collective concepts of time and space.

## Culture and business management

For many years, business management was perceived as a "culture-free science." The earliest management theories believed that the keys to success for a company were the universal application of a series of rational and scientific models, which were perfectly applicable to any business context, without the need for any particular special adaptation.

As Hoecklin[5] shows, the majority of management models were first developed in the US and were based on some commonly held assumptions about the nature of science, technology or human behavior, which were in their turn based, as we saw in Chapter 2, on a scientific and rational conception of the management process. Nevertheless, these models began to lose their efficiency when they were applied in culturally different contexts.

The problems experienced by multinational companies during their massive expansion in the 1960s and 1970s led management theorists to conclude that culture was important in the business world and convinced them that, for example, the things that motivate a worker in the US would not necessarily be the same as those that would motivate a worker in Venezuela.

A greater degree of interaction between cultures is inevitable in today's world, and the cost of ignoring this issue would be too high. As a result, from the 1970s onward, and at an ever accelerating rate, management theorists began to study cultural differences between countries and their influence in a business environment.

Research into cross-cultural management began to show, little by little, that culture should not be considered as an obstacle, but instead as something with the potential to help compete in a marketplace that is more and more globalized.

In today's competitive environment, individuals within an organization need to develop cultural competences that will enable them to communicate, negotiate, commit themselves and understand the values and views of others. As Lisa Hoecklin[6] indicates, ignoring cultural differences or not handling them correctly can result in, among other things, a lack of ability to motivate and retain staff, failure to adequately grasp the potential for strategic alliances in different regions and not being able to construct an adequate foundation to achieve a competitive advantage.

The demonstration of the importance of the cultural element has led management theorists to focus on theories developed by anthropologists, which have led them to a deeper understanding of the way that these cultures function and to develop models with practical applications for business management, as we will see below.

## Models for explaining how a culture functions

It is interesting to note that the models that have been most widely used to explain the way a culture functions have been developed by social anthropologists who, in the majority of cases, have performed important roles as consultants for the major international companies.[7]

We will look at three models which have been widely used in recent decades for teaching culture in business management: Trompenaars' layers of culture model,[8] Hofstede's onion model[9] and, perhaps the most widely used, the iceberg theory of culture, which became popular in the 1950s as the result of the work of Hall[10] and others. These models provide practical elements that enable us to understand culture and its influence on organizations.

In the **iceberg theory** Hall proposed a series of **external** (visible and objective) and **internal** (invisible and unconscious) elements. In turn, the internal elements are composed of two levels; one is **formal**, made up of elements such as rituals and customs that can be taught and learnt, and the other is **informal,** consisting of elements that are acquired without being consciously aware of them, where the concepts of time and space and individualism and collectivism stand out.

In the **onion skin theory**, Hofstede described culture as a series of layers, some of which are more visible than others, divided into two main sections; the least visible part, the heart of a culture, consists of its values, whilst the most visible part consists of its practices, which in turn can be divided into three parts: symbols, heroes and rituals.

In the **layers of culture theory**, Trompenaars distinguished three levels, ranging from the most to the least explicit. The most explicit level is made up of **artefacts and products** (which include institutions and laws, among others). The second level is formed by **norms and values** (norms of social behavior), and the third, and least explicit level, are the **basic assumptions about life**, which are almost inaccessible from outside; they are acquired unconsciously and reflect the forms of behavior that had been crucial to the survival of the group at a specific moment in time.

The interesting thing that the three models have in common is that they define culture in levels, some of which are external and some of which are internal, some visible from outside and others that cannot be recognized from outside. Also, all three models have in common the theory that the most profound base of a culture is made up of a series of unconscious elements, which form what at one definite time was the group response to a concrete problem that implied the survival or otherwise of the group. These responses conditioned typologies of behavior in relation to time or other people, which are reflected in the distinct dimensions of culture that can be observed today, as we will now see in detail.

## Cultural dimensions

Fons Trompenaars[11] conceived culture as being the way in which communities resolved a range of universal problems that could be divided into three types:

- Those that arise from relations with other people
- Those that arise from the passing of time
- Those related to the environment.

There are other ways of analyzing cultural conduct, such as communication, negotiation or the existence of hierarchies, nevertheless, the dimensions that we will now describe are those that are most deeply rooted in culture, the cement that forms the base on which cultural elements are constructed. In the first place, we will analyze this basic cement, and then go on to apply it to business management and examine how far the cultural dimension affects the conduct of people at work.[12]

### Problems arising from relationships with other people

#### The concept of self: individualism vs collectivism

One of the basic cultural differences in society is the extent of individualism compared to collectivism. It is important to highlight that there is no such thing as an entirely collectivist or an entirely individualistic culture and that in all cultures people present individual differences.

In an **individualistic culture**, the individual puts their needs before those of the group. For an individualistic person, the best form of guaranteeing the welfare of the group is to make its members self-sufficient. The general values appreciated by the group are those related to self-sufficiency and self-confidence. In general, individuals tend to have a distant behavior at the emotional and psychological level. They may decide to join a specific group at a certain time, but belonging to this group is not fundamental to their sense of identity or their social success as a person.

In a **collectivist culture**, a person's identity depends on the role that the individual has in the group, whether the group is represented by the family, the team, work and so on. The success and survival of the group guarantees the welfare of its members. The individual normally puts the needs and feelings of the group before their own, believing this to be the best way to ensure their own survival. Interdependence and harmony among members of the group are the most appreciated values. The members of a group are psychologically and emotionally close, but distant to those who do not belong to the group.

### The concept of obligations: universalism compared to particularism

When obligations to family and friends interfere with social obligations, individuals belonging to different cultures normally position themselves at one or the other end of the spectrum ranging from particularism to universalism. It is important to highlight that no culture is entirely universalist or particularist and that in all cultures there are individual differences. Nevertheless, the majority of cultures and the majority of people position themselves along the two sides of this dichotomy.

**Universalist cultures** apply absolute concepts in certain situations, independently of circumstances or particular situations. As far as is possible, the person should always try to apply the same rules to similar circumstances. The concept of justice consists of treating everybody in the same way, without exception for families or friends. And to the extent that it is possible, the person has to set aside their personal feelings and analyze a situation objectively.

**Particularist cultures** have no absolute concepts and the way that individuals behave depends on the circumstances. Each person will behave with their family and friends in the best way possible, believing that everybody else will receive the same protection from their own group members.

### Problems arising with the passage of time

### The concept of time: monochronic or polychronic

Time is probably one of the perceptions with the deepest cultural roots in the organization of life and work. Time is tightly bound to the rhythm of nature. Different cultures have different concepts of time, resulting from their environmental conditions, their history, their traditions and their general customs.

Hall and Hall (1990)[13] identified two main types of time systems, monochronic and polychronic. For people with a monochronic concept of time, time is something that is almost tangible; they talk of it as something that you can "find," "save," "fritter away" or "lose." On the other hand, people with a polychronic concept of time do not consider it to be tangible and pay more attention to human transactions than calendars. Hall and Hall analyzed how each of these systems can define the behavior of the people who subscribe to them.

**Monochronic people** will thus have some of the following traits:

- Only do one thing at a time
- Concentrate on their work
- Take time commitments seriously (deadlines, appointments and so on)
- Do not depend greatly on context and need information
- Are committed to their work
- Follow plans to the letter
- Avoid bothering others; respect rules of privacy and are considerate
- Show great respect for private property; seldom borrow or lend
- Are accustomed to short-term relationships.

**Polychronic people** by contrast will have some of the following traits:

- Do many things at the same time
- Are easily distracted and suffer from interruptions
- Consider time commitments as objectives to be achieved if possible
- Depend greatly on context and already have the information they need
- Are committed to people and human relationships
- Change plans easily and frequently
- More concerned about those who are closely related (family, friends, colleagues) than privacy
- Show a tendency to form lifelong relationships.

In general, northern cultures such as those in the Nordic countries, the UK and Germany are closer to monochronic systems, whilst southern cultures such as Mediterranean, Arab and Latin American countries are closer to polychronic systems.

Polychronic people do not consider things like socializing, talking on the telephone, doing several things at the same time and not setting priorities to be bad things; quite the contrary, they regard them as being necessary conditions for doing business well. For example, in the Arab world, receiving many visits in the office is an essential aspect of business life, where personal and professional life have much closer links than they do, for example, in Nordic countries.

## Control of the environment in cultural diversity

### The concept of control: activism compared to fatalism

Cultures differ in their perception of the relationship of the individual to the outside world. Above all, they differ in their perception of the influence that a person can have on the exterior world and whether they can manipulate external forces and their own destiny. The two extremes of this dimension are represented by fatalist and activist attitudes.

In an **activist culture**, control is in the hands of individuals. There are very few givens in life and the majority of them can be manipulated and therefore modified. There are no limitations to what a person can achieve if they really commit themselves and make the necessary effort. Life is what each person makes it.

In a **fatalist culture**, control is not in the hands of the individual. Some aspects of life are predetermined and inherent in the nature of things. There are definite limits beyond which nobody can go and circumstances which cannot be changed and which therefore should be accepted.

## Cultural dimensions applied to the organization

Cultural dimensions influence our perception of time and space, and our way of relating to others. This, in turn, affects our way of exercising authority, working in groups and other fundamental aspects of an organization.

Hofstede[14] was the first to study the application of Anglo-Saxon management methods to different cultural contexts, analyzing the relationship between organizational culture and the culture of the country. One of the most well-known studies related to a study of IBM and its branches in 64 countries. This enabled him to identify five national cultural dimensions. According to Hofstede, these five dimensions, which were learnt within the family or at school, are inherent in the perception of the human adult and determine behavior in the workplace.

The five dimensions identified by Hofstede are as follows:[15]

## 1. Power distance

This dimension refers to the degree that the members with least power in the organization or institution accept and expect an unequal distribution of power. It suggests that the inequality that exists in a society is accepted both by its leaders and its members.

## 2. Individualism vs collectivism

At the extreme of individualism, we find societies where the bonds between people are loose. In these societies all individuals are expected to look after themselves and their immediate family. At the extreme of collectivism, we find societies where their members form strong, cohesive groups from the moment they are born; these are often extended families, including aunts and uncles and grandparents, which continue protecting each other in exchange for unconditional loyalty.

## 3. Masculinity vs femininity

Studies show that some cultures are dominated by masculine values, such as domination and control. On the other hand, there are other cultures that can be identified as feminine, where typical feminine values such as sensitivity and concern for others are predominant.

## 4. Uncertainty avoidance

Uncertainty avoidance refers to the tolerance that a society shows to uncertainty and ambiguity, and therefore to the search for the truth about humanity. It indicates the degree to which a culture programs its members to feel comfortable or not in situations that are not highly structured. These unstructured situations are novel, unknown, surprising and different to what normally happens. Cultures that are averse to uncertainty try to reduce to the minimum the possibility that these types of situation will arise by applying laws and strict rules, adopting precautions and safety measures and, at a philosophical and religious level, believing in an absolute truth – there can only be one truth, and it is the one that we believe in. People who live in countries that are averse to uncertainty are also more emotional and feel more motivated by internal nervous energy. At the extreme opposite, cultures that have no aversion to uncertainty are more tolerant of differences of opinion; they try to reduce rules and regulations to the minimum and, at the philosophical and religious level, they are relativists and allow the coexistence of different currents of thought. People who belong to these cultures are more phlegmatic and contemplative, and their environment does not expect them to express emotions.

**5. Short-term orientation against long-term orientation**
The fifth dimension was identified in a later study based on a question-naire designed by Chinese scholars in which 23 countries took part. According to this dimension, the values associated with a long-term orientation are saving and perseverance, whilst the values associated with a short-term orientation are respect for tradition, meeting social obligations and the protection of personal "image."

The power distance and aversion to uncertainty dimensions are undoubtedly the two that have most influence over management styles. Both help to answer two fundamental questions:

- Who should have the power to decide?
- What rules and procedures should be followed to reach the desired outcome?

The cultural dimensions identified by Hofstede have served as a base for the development of numerous studies in different areas of management, such as motivation, leadership, relationships between superiors and subordinates and the sources of existing power in an organization, in addition to the structure and the culture of the organization.

## Cultural diversity and nature

The categories we have looked at are not rigid, and change according to the circumstances and internal and external pressures. As a result, in the same country or even in the same organization, different characteristics may be present at the same time as a result of the multiplicity of elements that coexist in our companies today. According to Sackmann,[16] the perspective of cultural complexity suggests that the culture of organizations is more complex, pluralistic, diverse, contradictory and intrinsically paradoxical than had been previously recognized. It is now highly unusual for all the members of an organization to belong to the same culture, or subculture, as a person can identify themselves by gender, ethnic origin, their role as a parent or spouse, their sports club, their profession, department or division, their trade union, their geographic region, their industrial sector, their country or region, whether it be Europe, America or Asia. All these possible cultural identities can simultaneously influence the cultural context of an organization.

From what we have seen so far, classifying the members of an organization by their culture, sexual affiliation or age can be counterproductive and can cause some confusion; the fact is that in all organizations many ways of seeing the world and the everyday problems of life coexist. This means that different competences also coexist, and these differences and the way they are taken advantage of are what give the company the ability to survive in a competitive and ever changing business world.

Diversity is the vehicle through which nature adapts, competes and evolves. The existence of diverse elements in a group can be its salvation when environmental conditions change and traditional ways of seeing things no longer guarantee survival. At such times, without warning, a marginal element that was hardly noticed before can spring into the limelight, allowing the group to compete and survive.

The fact of being a woman does not automatically mean that someone is sensitive, in the same way that being Italian does not necessarily mean that someone is polychronic. However, the characteristics of sensitivity and being polychronic are real, and it is important that managers know the advantages and disadvantages of an employee who is sensitive or polychronic, and knows how to utilize them to the benefit of the organization, independently of the label we put on these feminine or cultural traits.

## The reconciliation of opposites

In order for the complexity of diversity to be handled efficiently in an organization, it is necessary to allow the existence of differences and tensions, and to channel them toward an acceptable framework for action in which the different elements can compete. The challenge is to confront the complexity inherent in today's business organizations, integrating the different forces and the different cultures to obtain better results.

One way of promoting the diversity that modern companies need is to accept that two totally different ways of focussing on the same problem, whilst being opposites, can at the same time be equally valid. In this way you can ask the question again and present the problematic dimensions of group life in a paradoxical way.

For the members of a group, there are numerous experiences that come to the fore and contradict each other, generating tensions that appear to threaten both the group as a whole and each of its members. Nevertheless, when these experiences are focussed on in a holistic and paradoxical way, things that seemed impossible to resolve by conventional linear logic become manageable and, on occasions, become a source of inspiration. This paradoxical mentality allows us to perceive the potential that the differences inherent in a multicultural group offer.

Smith and Berg[17] have identified seven different paradoxes in the multicultural group:

1. **The paradox of involvement:** this looks at the dilemma between confrontation and conciliation; the paradox of involvement is linked to the possibility of exclusion. Action is based on reflection, and reflection is based on action.
2. **The paradox of identity:** this looks at the dilemma between the individual and the collective. The paradox of identity is found in those repetitive cycles in which individuals and groups try to establish a common and significant identity, where each forms an integral part of the other.
3. **The paradox of authority:** the dilemma between the autocratic and the participative. The paradoxical perspective of authority in groups affirms that the authorization of others to act in their own name is equal to authorization for oneself, and that the authorization of oneself to act in the name of others is the equivalent of authorization of the group.
4. **The paradox of democracy:** the dilemma between the spontaneous and the orchestrated. The common commitments to liberty and equality have to be faced from different, and at times opposite, starting points, knowing that both commitments are necessary for the survival of the group and the creativity of its members.
5. **The paradox of boundaries:** the dilemma between task and process. In a certain way, a group becomes the sum of individual anxieties arising from the frustration of not being able to undertake some tasks alone. These anxieties have to be reined in sufficiently for the tasks to be completed, but they should not be so structured that they impede the natural development of group processes.
6. **The paradox of abundance:** the dilemma between quality and quantity. The paradox of abundance is that, in order to generate quality, members of a group have to contribute a lot and accept that much of their contribution will not be used, but in order to maintain the motivation of the group, the group needs to increase the quantity of individual contributions, whilst imposing fewer demands on its members.
7. **The paradox of face:** the dilemma between criticizing and diplomacy. The paradox of face is that the diplomatic route is only possible when it is accompanied by criticism, and criticism can only be directed with diplomacy.

These paradoxes described by Smith and Berg help us to acquire a broader vision of the competences and skills necessary to compete in the current business world. Faced with ferocious competition in a context defined by change, no manager can ignore the capital of competences present in the workforce. Each person has a natural tendency toward a way of understanding work, whether individual or group, process or task. However, the opposites are complementary and a manager needs to know how to make best use of the person whose competence is most appropriate at each and every moment

## How do you acquire cultural competences?

The importance of the cultural dimension has enabled the elaboration of different theories about learning cultural competences. Many of these theories come from the field of linguistics and in particular from the science of translation, which investigates the best way to translate a cultural content from one universe to another.

In recent decades, the theories of the neurolinguistic programming school (NLP)[18] have become popular. NLP proposes the reorganization of concepts at a linguistic level as a way of organizing some internal structures. Robert Dilts,[19] one of the leading proponents of NLP, developed the theory of logical levels within the hierarchy of cultural experience. He saw culture as being formed by a hierarchical scale of experiences. The highest levels, whilst the most abstract and the furthest removed from everyday experiences, are the ones that are going to have most influence in our experience.

These levels, organized by their greater or lesser degree of abstraction, are:

- the *environmental level* (climate, temperature)
- the *behaviors level* (gestures, health, spoken language)
- the *capabilities* level (how you learn, how you negotiate, how you communicate and so on)
- the *beliefs and values level* (what is taboo, what is absolute and relative)
- the *identity and role level* (the frontiers that belong to the culture)
- the *spirituality and purpose level* (cultural models of nature, the meaning of life, representations of the absolute and so on).

These levels represent a cultural map symbolizing the connections between events in the physical world and their internal representation. In this way, culture is converted into a filter that is responsible for our behavior. They are filters we are not normally conscious of, and from which a whole host of misunderstandings can arise.

Taking these hierarchies as a starting point, Dilts proposed a series of necessary competences for cultural competence, which include:

1. **Personal aptitudes:** the ability to analyze internal thoughts on personal reality and the ability to learn.
2. **Interpersonal aptitudes:** which recognize the forms used in communication and social relationships.
3. **Contextual skills:** the aptitude to understand time and space and be able to talk about them.
4. **Creative and imaginative competences:** the capacity to understand the imaginative and creative aspects of a culture.
5. **Leadership capacity:** learning how to suggest, persuade and convince using particular language.

Just as with learning a second language, acquiring a second culture requires competence prior to action; in a culture you first learn some discrete actions and then include them in a system for expressing meaning.

Our way of understanding the world is limited by our mental map, and so we have a limited comprehension of the world as experienced by another. In the process of acquiring cultural competence, distinct models have been defined that signal a series of basic stages to pass through on the route from our cultural world to that of another and then finally to integrate both of them into a wider framework of action.

Bennet[20] developed a **model of cultural sensitivity** based on six steps of fundamental changes in our way of understanding:

1. **Denial:** first it is denied that any other way of conceiving the world distinct from one's own is possible.
2. **Defence:** noticing that an alternative different to one's own causes fear and this activates a defence mechanism which rejects this difference.
3. **Minimization:** from this moment it is accepted that the difference exists, but it is not very important, and the common base is sufficiently wide so as not to have to fear this different behavior.
4. **Acceptance:** it is accepted that other ways of functioning are possible.
5. **Adaptation:** a period of adapting in which new competences are learnt which function in other contexts.
6. **Integration:** finally there is a process of integration of one's own culture with the alien culture into a wider frame of reference, where the distinct identities include many options, any of which can be used in any context at will once they have been acquired.

At the end of the process, and thanks to the acquisition of ways of behaving that are different from our own, not only do we not lose our identity, but we amplify it by being able to draw on a wider range of resources that we are able to use as best fit the circumstances. As a result of cultural learning, we develop from being individuals who react unconsciously and in a similar way in all circumstances, to being conscious beings who can react in different ways in response to the specific needs of each situation, drawing on the increased resources available to us.

## Conclusions

The reconciliation of supposed opposites in wider frameworks of action enables the coexistence of a wider range of points of view on the same problem. Nevertheless, it is important to signal that differences also present a series of challenges and can disorient the organization's objectives. In order to avoid possible risks, organizations should provide clear and visionary leadership that is capable of placing the differences in a wider framework and managing possible tensions. Managers should establish clear rules and procedures that will be respected by all within a flexible framework of maneuver.

Today's companies, characterized as they are by their global scale and the changing environment in which they function, need above all to be capable of innovating and growing, and to do this they need to adapt to the potential of the diversity provided by their employees, who in turn need to grow and innovate, in a context in which they feel recognized and valued. In a labor market context, in which differences of gender, culture and personality are ever more marked, and in a changing economic environment it is not easy to decide which style of behavior is the most appropriate for the company: a multifaceted person capable of generating work rapidly in many directions, or a monochronical planner who is focussed on details and capable of producing rigorous work. Ideally, each person should be capable of both approaches, and training helps each to acquire the skills of the other. Nevertheless, whilst we are being trained to be more complete beings, we must learn to respect and enable the complementarity of differences.

# 5 Personality and Diversity Management

Personality is one of the major areas of study in psychology today. We do not have scope in this book to explore the complexities relating to this topic, nor to discuss neurological and biological questions. We will restrict ourselves to looking at the concept of personality, understood as character, the apparent, conditioned identity of each individual.[1] Our intention is to investigate some of the results of the numerous studies that have researched character typologies and how they affect behavior. Individual and collective behavior within organizations has been an important area of study in recent years and has produced interesting results relating to the development and acquisition of competences and new skills by managers.

## Archetypes and personality typologies

From time immemorial, the work of the great artists has been universal as a result of their ability to reflect values that are common to all. The works of Shakespeare and Molière are universal in part because of the mastery with which they analyzed a range of typologies of human behavior. The profundity of some of their masterpieces reflects not simply isolated behavior, but the inherent complexity in each character typology, with all their quirks, desires and ways of interacting with others. The analysis of these archetypes of behavior leads each of us recognize ourselves, or someone close to us, whether we wish to or not, in the different characters portrayed, for example the coward or the hero.

The psychologist Carl Jung argued that in the Western world the suppression of everything that was not strictly rational has forced a series of archetypes deeply rooted in our primitive collective consciousness into our subconscious. Due to the impossibility of rationalizing man's relationship with nature, the unknown, the supernatural and tribal functions were pushed from our consciousness to become part of our subconscious world, where they reappear in the form of dreams, legends, symbols and myths.[2] These archetypes represent some of our fears and desires; transcendental problems that would initially have been resolved collectively, but which Western man has to confront alone. Outside the rational mind, symbols, myths and dreams represent natural attempts to reconcile and reunite opposites in the mind. By attempting to reconcile reason with emotion and thought with intuition and giving them the attention they deserve, we can begin to understand the totality of the human mind.

Archetypes and their psychological functions have been the subject of much interesting research on human behavior by many authors, including, among others, Joseph Campbell and Manuela Dunn Mascetti.[3] Many of these studies have subsequently been applied practically in training programs for managers all over the world. Through the use of simulations and group dynamics, many companies have made use of representations of basic archetypes to position a brand in the market and aim it at a specific client type, based, for example, on the characteristics of the archetype of the hero or the wise man.[4]

## Personal development systems

The study of the human characteristics related to different typologies has resulted in powerful training instruments for human resources in organizations. Numerous psychologists, investigating both individual and group human behavior, have identified a series of basic behaviors that constitute the major part of the basic personality. These personality studies have led to experimental training systems, which are used in personal development programs to improve the behavioral competence of senior managers and executives.

There are a number of methodologies based on the systems developed by psychologists such as Jung and researchers from other fields. All these methodologies have many characteristics in common and are equally valid when put into practice. One of the most widely used systems in recent years has been the **enneagram**, which has proved particularly useful in training programs in companies such as GM, AT&T, P&G, Cisco, Alitalia, Telefónica, Indra and McDonald's.[5] This personal development methodology has been integrated into business training programs for the development of competences and to help to discover the rules of behavior of the participants and their colleagues so as to improve team performance and its alignment with the values of the organization.

The roots of the enneagram lie in the distant past with the Sufi community, and it only became known in the West through the work of the

Russian Gurdjieff, following his experiences with esoteric Christian communities in central Asia. His work was developed by psychotherapists from the transpersonal school, such as the Chilean Claudio Naranjo,[6] who in turn was inspired by the work of the Bolivian, Oscar Ichazo. Claudio Naranjo has done much of his work in California, and many of his ideas have been incorporated into training programs, through group dynamics and workshops, which have been successful not only in personal development training but also in improving the group performance of a large number of organizations.

From its origins as a geometric symbol representing universal laws and as a route map for evolutionary change, the enneagram has come to represent a useful map for analyzing personality and human behavior. The enneagram, as with all other systems and models that define human characteristics or values, is based on a series of fundamental concepts that help to explain the importance of understanding diversity and how it can play a complementary role. Amongst these we can highlight the following five:

## Unity

The starting position is that all the different human typologies are equally necessary. From the potential total of cognitive resources at the disposition of the human race, some have used certain resources more than others, whether for reasons of survival, imitation or rejection. The choice of basic resources for survival results in the development of behavioral traits, which are the most visible manifestations of personality. All the traits are developed from the same resources, so they are universal and familiar, setting aside cultural differences. They represent different solutions to survival problems created by man, and as a result, in their totality, they represent the full range of human capacity. In this sense, the enneagram is represented by a circle symbolizing unity.[7]

## Light and shade

All the typologies of personality are equally valid; nevertheless, they all have their positive and negative aspects. The character of an observant personality might produce a genius capable of discovering the way that nature functions; nevertheless, this same character could also produce an avaricious person who, through fear of losing control, grasps everything that comes within their reach. In this sense, Oscar Ichazo and Claudio Naranjo associated the different personality types to the seven deadly sins of Christian tradition, which they symbolized in each of the typologies and which can represent the different pathologies of the character diagnosed in modern psychology.[8] An individual might be better or worse depending on whether they found themselves in the more positive or more negative aspects of their personality; in extreme cases this could even lead to psychological illness. Aside from extreme cases, almost nobody can escape from the shadows of their personality no matter how hard they try to hide. When we look at attraction or rejection between personalities, it is necessary to distinguish if that which is being rejected is a destructive process of the person, or if it is a way of seeing the world that is fundamentally different from ours, although equally valid.

## The development process

As all personalities are the result of the potential development of the same resources, to the extent that we integrate different typologies in our way of acting, by tackling their negative aspects and developing their positive ones, we can become more complete people. Integrating new behavioral traits, in addition to those we habitually employ, allows us to acquire new competences and human skills, enabling us draw on one resource or another according to the requirements of the situation. For this reason, working with different personalities helps us to recognize and understand them; and in addition, it enriches our work and our contribution to the common purpose.

## Basic resources

The majority of these systems are founded on a base of primary cognitive resources common to all human beings and to the way they are combined in the individual, using more of one and less of another. For example, Jung identified four basic functional types, which he related to the fundamental ways in which conscience obtained its orientation to experience. These are **sensation** (the perception of the senses), **thinking** (applying the intellectual faculty in order to orientate oneself), **feeling** (value judgement of what we do and do not like) and **intuition** (which tells you whence it comes and where it is going). The primary choice of one of the four functions to orientate oneself in life is the basis that people use to adapt to other individuals and to circumstances. Jung was never dogmatic about this, recognizing that everybody possesses all four of these functions, and that in addition to these four functions there were many other factors that affected human behavior, such as memory and imagination. Nevertheless, Jung affirmed that these four basic functions were sufficiently basic to provide a useful classification criterion and to help us to uncover our own prejudices.[9]

In a similar way to Jung, the enneagram identifies three basic centers of human resources; the **visceral center** (the capacity to act), the **emotional center** (the capacity to empathize) and the **mental center** (the capacity to organize data in logical sequence). It assumes that, when faced with an unforeseen event, all of us act, feel and reason in a constant way throughout our lives, tending to choose one of the three resources as the impulse motor that forms the basis of the way in which our character is organized.

By way of illustration, we can imagine a situation in which a basic mental person, who tends to organize their life in a hypothetical manner (analyzing the facts based on logical and objective procedures), asks another person for their opinion of a recent dramatic event; we will take the Southeast Asian tsunami of Boxing Day 2004 as an example.

Whoever is asked the questions, the replies will always tend to one of the three following orientations:

1. One group of people will always go directly to their emotional center (with its basic orientation to relationships and capacity for empathy), and will respond, for example, "Oh no! It makes me cry every time I see children drowning on TV" or "Since it happened I haven't been able to get over the feeling of sadness." Basically, all replies will indicate the closeness that the respondent feels to the suffering of others. It should be noted that whilst it is probable that the person asking the questions will also feel the same emotion, the questioner asked for the person's opinion, not their emotional reaction.

2. The impulse of the second group would be to go straight to their visceral center (with its practical attitude to life and action) and reply, something like, "What they need to do is write off their foreign debt," or "More aid needs to be sent now." Whatever the reply, it will indicate action, whether it relates to what should or should not be done, or what has or has not been done already. The person who asked the question will of course agree or disagree with the actions proposed, but, once again, that was not the question they asked; they asked for an opinion, not what action should be taken.

3. Finally, the response of the third group will be directed by their mental center; they will reflect on what they think, and their reply will be something like, "I believe that what happened was the result of an inadequate forecasting system" or "I think the catastrophe was due to the lack of resources in these countries, which has stopped them installing adequate systems." Whatever the response made, it will represent an objective analysis of the situation, putting all the data into a logical chain that explains the causes of what happened; in fact this is the response that the original questioner was looking for, and the questioner has the same orientation.

Obviously, we all have the capacity to employ all these modes of action, emotion or thought, but the primary reaction that each of us has is **to feel, think or act**. The basic primary resource that we use and the degree to which this is based on the others results in the construction of different character typologies which represent the range of human characters; these are the characters that have been described by writers and poets throughout history, and who we sympathize with and understand or reject, thinking that they were acting just like our boss, for example.

## The development of typologies

Building on the three basic primary resources, different typologies of character can be developed based on the different possible combinations of the primary resources. For example, if the primary resource is the emotional, the secondary could be action and the third thought or vice versa. As a result, there are nine different possible combinations on the enneagram.

Other methodologies are based on similar systems. For example, the Myers-Briggs system, which is based on Jung's functional typologies, has developed a system of sixteen typologies.[10]

The nine typologies of the enneagram can be represented by giving both the definition of the most positive personality trait and the least positive for each typology, following the works of Naranjo (1995) and Riso (2000), among others.

For example typology 1 can be defined as a perfectionist in its positive trait or as anger if we choose its negative quality. Typology 2 as the helper in the positive or pride in the negative. T3 as the achiever positively or deceit in its negative quality. T4 can be described as an artist or as envious. T5 can be represented as the observer or as avarice. T6 can be described as the collaborator or as a coward. T7 can be depicted as an optimist or as a glutton. T8 can be defined as the challenger or as arrogant, and finally T9 can be defined as the peacemaker or as its negative trait, laziness.

In the following description, we give a somewhat stereotyped and caricatured description of each of these typologies and try to show how each of the positive traits associated to a typology can give rise to a defect. It should be understood as a simplified illustration of the different ways in which reality can be understood and reacted to, and not as an attempt to define humanity.

This system is much richer and more complex and is more effective when it is implemented through workshops and group dynamics where psychologists and experts help the participants to know and recognize the different ways of reacting to different situations. Here we are only aiming to show the broad outline, which will help to develop our argument about the importance of understanding diversity between personalities and the importance of reconciling them within a wider and more integrated vision of reality.[11]

---

### Description of the nine characters according to the enneagram

#### 1. The perfectionist

The perfectionist is a person who is committed to action, and who is objective, just and noble. The basic resource of a perfectionist is to do things well, being a perfectionist down to the finest detail; "a place for everything and everything in its place" would be the idealist's motto. Perfectionists are tremendously useful for a society or group as they develop the plan in their perfectly ordered mind and it can be implemented without changing a comma. They are afraid of making mistakes, and as a result their negative side can lead them to be incredibly rigorous and correct, judging everything and everybody, including themselves; they do not forgive even the smallest error, and anger is their worst defect.

#### 2. The helper

The helper is generous, empathetic and sensitive. Helpers know what those around them need and do not hesitate to sacrifice their own requirements in order to satisfy those of others. Their principal fear is of being rejected, and as a result their negative aspect can be that by using their ability to provide the necessities for others, they build a network of dependency around them, which means that the helper does not need to ask for help from those around them, as they all depend on the helper and as a result they are always around. One stereotyped example of a helper would be the mother hen who has all her chicks around her without allowing any of them to leave the nest. As a result, their worst aspect can be pride.

#### 3. The performer

The performer is an empathetic person. They know what others want, and as a result they know how to be liked and be sociable. They find it easy to surround themselves with people who react with enthusiasm to the plans they propose. It is easy for them to organize meetings, parties, whatever it is that their group requires or wants. They are extremely efficient; they know how to evaluate people, giving everybody the sensation that they have achieved what they wanted. Their biggest fear is social failure, and in order to avoid it they can resort to manipulation and suppressing their most intimate desires in pursuit of social recognition, leading in the worst cases to losing their connection with their ego, as they only function in terms of parameters of external recognition.

## 4. The artist

The artist is a highly sensitive person, with a deep capacity for empathy. They empathize not only with the person, but with the deepest human sentiments; and it is in this way that the artist can manage to reflect so deeply the feelings of the majority of humanity. On the negative side, and due to this great profundity, their fear of not experiencing great passions occasionally rises to the surface, leading them to reject the ordinary life of the majority in search of the experiences they feel they deserve. They suffer enormously from the resulting solitude, which, even though they searched for it, deep down they resent, as they feel they deserve social recognition that never comes. They therefore envy those who do receive recognition and in their worst aspect eventually envy all those who, unlike them, are capable of living simple, satisfactory lives.

## 5. The observer

The observer is an intellectual person, with a large capacity for observation and relating to phenomena that occur in their surroundings. They are tremendously ingenious and subtle, surprising all when they speak, which they do not do often. Their capacity for observing everything leads them to fear losing control and that circumstances might overwhelm their capacity to reason; as a result they can be terribly selfish, using others to satisfy their needs without letting anybody enter into their protective sphere, not even those closest to them. A caricatured example would be the inventor locked in his ivory tower. In order to protect themselves and not have to depend on anybody, they accumulate everything that is within their reach, so that their negative aspect can be tremendous avarice.

## 6. The collaborator

The collaborator is a thinker and is characterized by a strong sense of responsibility. Collaborators are tremendously loyal and gregarious. They respect tradition, their elders and the values of their group. They have a clear understanding of how society works and are happy to belong to it. Collaborators make the perfect colleagues at work as they perfectly happy to work overtime in the interests of the group. Their fundamental fear is of being expelled from the group, and as a result they are almost obsessive about following all the rules. Their fear of being expelled from the group can lead as far as cowardice and can even lead them to accuse another to avoid being accused themselves and their membership of the group thrown into question.

### 7. The optimist

The optimist is capable of using their powerful intellect to make everything relative; the optimist is the perfect companion on a night out. The optimist always looks for the positive element and tries to get the most out of life and out of whatever situation presents itself to them. But their need to make everything relative hides a deep-rooted fear of seeing the ugly side of things and of suffering, and as a result their negative side leads them to run away from any potentially conflictive situation, whether it be at work, in the family or with their partner, looking for a new life and new challenges in other places. They exploit situations to the maximum, getting the most from them until they no longer satisfy them completely and they have to move on and look for new situations.

### 8. The challenger

The challenger is a person of action. They are strong, intense and realistic and have deep and clear convictions. They can be caricatured as action heroes like Zorro, the solitary hero with endless courage who does not give a second thought to risking his own life in what he believes to be a just cause. They will try to resolve an unjust situation, and will burn all their bridges without the least thought if they think that this is the right way forward. They are capable of involving everybody in their cause at first, but they are also incapable of reasoning with others who question their authority. They fear weakness, which they do not tolerate, not even in themselves, and their worst defect is the excess with which they act, exhausting the few who still follow them and survive their excesses. As a result, the deadly sin often associated with them is lust.

### 9. The mediator

The final character of the group is a person of action, who paradoxically could pass almost unnoticed as a result of how little they like to move. The mediator is calm, friendly and practical; they are decent, patient and tolerant. They have a passion for calm and harmony, and for everything around them to be tranquil as they enjoy a slice of cake with their morning coffee. They are slow in everything, including talking and walking and will finally exasperate all those around them, who, although they deeply admire the harmony they transmit, never manage to get them to do any of the things they have promised to do. Their biggest fear is conflict and they would be incapable of taking sides in a dispute or acting if this affects anyone around them; as a result they prefer not to give an opinion or to act when faced with doubt. This need for everything around them to be perfect leads them in their negative aspect to forget about themselves so that all those around them are happy and do not protest; mediators do not mind whether they eat or not, whether they go to the cinema or listen to the radio or not, forgetting in the end what it is that they really do want and as a result missing out on important opportunities to develop themselves and do something in life. They will say yes to everything that is asked of them so as not to come into conflict with anyone, although the hours will pass and they will never get around to doing whatever it is they have promised, much to the desperation of the person who asked them to do it in the first place; as a result their defect is laziness.

This system should not be viewed as something static, but rather as something dynamic. The understanding of the positive and negative aspects of one's own character helps not only to accept oneself, but also with the challenge of understanding others, both those close to us and apparently compatible and those further away and seemingly incompatible.

Figure 5.1 shows, in a dynamic way, how each of these personality types acquires some traits from the other personalities and rejects other negative ones, to evolve into a more complete individual, acquiring at the end of the maturity process all the resources that we as human beings have at our disposal.

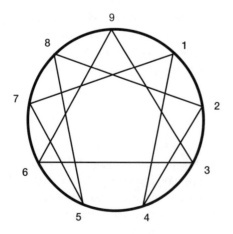

Figure 5.1 **The enneagram**

This brief representation of the different types of human character is only useful for making us think about how complementary these types might be socially. We should repeat that we are describing archetypes, not real people. Real people, in addition to having a tendency toward one of the personality types, are affected by a series of influences as a result of their gender and culture, in addition to the experiences they have lived through, which make them unique. All the different ways of understanding the world have their positive and negative aspects. Taken together, they prove highly useful in enabling us to adapt to the world and other people, although it is also possible that at times they may paralyse us and stop us from seeing other forms, which at certain times might be useful in helping us to function.

The popular saying "Not everyone is good at everything, but everyone is good at something" is useful here. Each character type brings a series of advantages and disadvantages with it to a common project. By way of illustration, in the first stages of innovation, character types such as 4, 5 and 9 would be particularly useful, with each one functioning from feeling, mind or action; they are especially creative as a result of their tendency to observation and profundity, independent of social influence. Once the project has been designed, these personality types would be less useful as a result of their difficulty in organizing others. However, characters such as types 3, 7 and 8, also functioning from feeling, mind or action, are able to organize others, convince them and direct them in a plan of action to put whatever the project might be into operation. These character types would not have the patience to consolidate the project and continue with it, and as a result types 2, 6 and 1 are ideal as they develop the established norms, respect them and ensure that the system works.

Ideally, each of us would have the capacity to be capable of everything, to design a new idea, bring it into being and create a system to enable it to continue, and it is possible for a person to develop the necessary competences to be able to carry out all these functions. Nevertheless, whilst we are acquiring these competences, observing the way in which others function is extremely useful, not only in order to understand them, but also to enable us to grow.

## Universal values and cultural influences

To bring this chapter to a close, we would like to take a look briefly and from an academic point of view at universal values and the rules for behavior associated with them. In recent years, important investigators such as Crosby, Bitner and Gill[12] and Schwartz and Sagiv[13] have under-taken cross-cultural studies of universal value systems and the influence of culture on these. Schwartz and Sagiv have developed a theory of the structure and content of value systems that appears particularly relevant to us in illustrating the idea of the values that underpin the different rules of behavior.

From the starting point of a definition of values as the principal objectives that act as a guide in people's lives, values are defined as cognitive representations of three types of human requirements: individual necessities as biological organisms, the requirements needed for coordinated social interaction and the necessities of survival and welfare of the group.

Having conducted many studies in more than forty countries, Schwartz and Sagiv identified ten typologies of motivational values derived from the three types of universal requirements. These values act dynamically, as the actions derived from the pursuit of these objectives would have psychological and social consequences that would either coincide with or conflict with other values. As a result, a system of compatible and conflicting values is formed and this can be represented in a circular form; the values at the opposite side of the circle are those that have the greatest degree of conflict, whilst those that are close together have the greatest affinity with each other.

At the same time, these ten values are organized into two higher order dimensions. The first dimension is made up of the opposites: **openness to change/conservation**. This dimension contrasts values that emphasize the independence of thought and action that is favorable to change (stimulation, self-direction) with those which emphasize preservation, stability and traditional ways of doing things (security, conformity and tradition). The second dimension consists of the opposites: **self-enhancement/self-transcendence**. This dimension contrasts the values that emphasize the acceptance of others as equals and concern for their welfare (universalism and benevolence) with those that emphasize personal success and domination over others (power and achievement). Finally the value of **hedonism** relates equally to openness to change and self-enhancement.

This theory has been used in recent years as a basis for numerous investigations, including, among many others, observing the impact of cultural elements in specific behavioral situations such as voting or giving and receiving feedback.[14]

The interesting point that we would like to highlight here is the way that the values identified by Schwartz and Sagiv, based on the basic necessities of the individual, coincide with typologies defined by the enneagram system earlier.

Schwartz and Sagiv develop a taxonomy of universal value types with associated values employing some of the following traits:

- **Power**: Social status and prestige, control, domination of people and of resources
- **Achievement:** Personal success demonstrating competence in accordance with social standards
- **Hedonism**: Pleasure, social gratification for oneself
- **Stimulation:** Excitement, novelty and the challenges in life
- **Self-direction:** Independence of thought and action, exploring and creating
- **Universalism:** Understanding, appreciation, tolerance and protection of the common good and nature
- **Benevolence:** Preservation and promotion of the welfare of people within your ambit
- **Tradition:** Respect, acceptance of ideas, traditions and commitment to tradition, humble, moderate
- **Conformity:** Repression of actions or impulses that might contravene or violate social norms or expectations or injure others
- **Security:** Safety, harmony, social stability in relationships and in oneself

Leaving aside the differences between Schwartz and Sagiv's academic models and the enneagram model, both in their conceptualization and their aims, the system of values that Schwartz and Sagiv present us with complements the enneagram, as it enables us to delve deeper into the idea that there are basic motivations in searching to fulfil specific human and universal necessities, which define, albeit unconsciously, clear rules for behavior.

## The complementarity of diversity

There have been a large number of studies and models developed in recent years, both academic and related to corporate practice, that agree on the basic idea of the existence of certain basic universal behavioral traits. The fact that these have been universally recognized, setting aside the preference for any particular system or any kind of ranking of them, shows that they are all common to humanity as a race and can therefore be assimilated by any individual.

Each person may value one way of acting more highly than another, but they have the capacity to recognize them all. On the majority of occasions, one is hardly conscious of the way one is acting or the values that underpin that particular way of behaving. The greatest challenge in personal development lies in becoming conscious of the pattern that our behavior follows, discovering why we act in a certain way, of the positives and the negatives of this particular way of behaving, so that we can go on to reconcile this, firstly, with ourselves and then with other ways of acting that are equally valid.

We would like to end this chapter by returning to the complementarity of diversity. The search for a better way of acting in preference to another or one character type in preference to another may, in the last resort, be valid in specific situations. However, in the changing world in which we live, the environment is constantly changing and a particular form of behavior that may be appropriate at one moment may be totally inappropriate the next moment (and, of course, may be appropriate again the moment after that). From an objective point of view, none of them is better or worse than the other; they are good or bad according to how they are used in their concrete application to a specific situation.

Diversity provides us with an excellent instrument for acquiring new resources and competences, in order to complete ourselves with those around us and to grow as people. Growing as a person is not simply learning a few best practices as a guide book for all occasions, but rather choosing all the best practices possible, understanding how they work and integrating them into our personalities. Growing as a person is about moving from a situation of reacting instinctively in the same way in the majority of situations to being able to react consciously having meditated on the different ways in which we can react to different situations using the behaviors we have acquired. Growing as a person means ceasing to act as an individual guided by unconscious impulses of gender, culture and personality, and acting as a human being who is aware of all the instruments at our disposal and knowing how to use them in any situation that arises.

# Conclusion to Part One
# The Correlation Between the Values Provided by Diversity and the Values of the New Company

We have now arrived at the halfway point in this book. We began by analyzing the transformation that our society and our organizations are currently experiencing, and we came to the conclusion that there are now new values that are gradually increasing their influence and opening new horizons for what we consider traditional values. We then went on to analyze the history of companies in Chapter 2; it is a story that shows a clear and important development that continues up to the present day and has not finished. Finally, we looked at one of the clearest realities of our time: diversity. This diversity is opening up new horizons for us, and has never before been so apparent or so influential.

It was interesting to observe that the transformation referred to at the beginning of the book has taken place at the same time as what we refer to as diversity has exploded onto the scene. It is worth asking whether diversity is the cause of this transformation; or is it this transformation that has freed diversity and given it its importance? In the end, the answer to these questions is hardly relevant; reality is forcefully imposing itself, showing us that the only certain thing is that both these factors are happening at the same time, now.

There are few things that we are more certain of than that the transition process we are involved in at the moment is fundamentally characterized by change and diversity; and it is precisely a better knowledge of diversity and how to manage it effectively that provides the key to surviving in an ever changing world.

Above all else, diversity provides us with variety; it throws a new and different light onto things and in this way brings innovation and new answers, which at the same time come together to produce a greater flexibility in companies to respond to the changes affecting them. The flexibility required by today's companies to meet the challenges they face shows itself, among other traits, in the capacity of workers to undertake varied roles, performing tasks in different ways and taking positions in different companies. As a result, only by having the capacity to be flexible, to change rapidly from one way of doing things to another, will the executives of the 21st century be able to compete.

As we saw in Part One, the traditional paradigm of searching for a single best way to manage a company, or a single best way to manage people, is no longer relevant in our diverse, globalized world. The wide range of parameters, whether of gender, culture or personality, provides us with the tools we need to incorporate these new parameters into the traditional models.

In the traditional paradigm, one of the most important factors was uniformity of company structures, to which all employees had to adhere strictly. But, in today's world, a good manager is one who can manage and control informal structures, those which by their nature appear in diverse organizations. There is not time to try to formalize them; but neither is there any interest in trying to do so. Why should we? Perhaps in another era this would have been an appropriate way of behaving, but not now; we are looking for people who are capable of continuously generating ideas, challenges and opportunities, and who know how to resolve them. Formal structures paralyze these processes and get in the way. Now, when companies design recruitment policies, they are not only looking for people with knowledge, methods and processes, they already exist on the hard disk of every computer with the appropriate software. Today when they are recruiting, companies are looking for precisely what is not on a computer and that which you cannot teach. You cannot teach a person to smile, to be tactful or respectful to the tastes of a client, to intuit the exact needs of someone who has a necessity that needs to be met; they are looking for those people who have the informal ability to react in a changing environment. Everything else can be taught or downloaded from a computer with a broadband internet connection.

We have seen how one of the basic criteria in the transformation of organizations is in their principal objective, where we can note an evolution from the definitive criterion of profitability toward what has come to be known as **corporate social responsibility**. This is an especially enriching concept which unites the logical necessity of the company to add economic value to include service to society, the training of employees, respect for the environment and for rules, regulations and customs. These concepts now appear natural and plausible, but it is not so long ago that they would have been far from at the forefront of the mind of any businessperson.

Corporate social responsibility is no longer just some empty piece of company rhetoric. The information society in which we live means that companies have to be more transparent and conscious that any action or practice, no matter how small it might be, can become known about instantaneously all over the world (in this context, we can recall the tremendous consequences that the Enron case had for the largest auditing company in the world). Diversity brings with it globalization, and globalization brings with it diversity, providing challenges that companies have not had to take into account until today because they simply were not affected by them. Today everything has an impact on the profit and loss account, and there is no company anywhere in the world that can afford to permit itself the luxury of not taking diversity into account.

Diversity in organizations is a very real reflection of the diversity present in society, and as a result is a natural representation of all the interest groups that exist in a company: shareholders, suppliers and clients, or, to put it another way, the stakeholders. In this way, the company becomes conscious of the need to make a financial profit that justifies its activity, but at the same time no company can now have this as its sole objective as this would present a threat to its very survival.

In Chapter 1 we analyzed how the company has evolved from being simply based on financial results to the discovery and realization of principles. In a world where everything is changing, the important thing is not the answers but the questions, and as Picasso said, "computers are useless; they only know how to give answers." There are always answers, what are sometimes lacking are questions.[1]

Today's companies are living in the so-called information era; we used to think that hundreds of television channels and thousands of radio frequencies had collapsed the information universe, but now, we have to face millions of web pages on the most diverse subjects, where Google takes hardly a fraction of a second to find thousands of pages related to even the most obscure search criteria. Nevertheless, the problem is not the information itself, the problem is analyzing all the information that is available. Companies run the risk of information overload, an illness that is much worse than being starved of information. Until now companies have functioned with the sole objective of achieving financial results; but this is no longer possible, there is no longer a magic formula applicable to the development of a task, it needs to be done and the quicker it can be done the better. Everything changes quickly and this change is based on information. The issue is that until now analysis was based on obtaining information, whereas now it is impossible to process all the available information. Today's companies do not have the capacity to process all this information and choose the best possible solution. And so now we do not talk of the analysis of results and the procedures that accompany them, but rather of the discovery and the applicability of principles.

In fact, it is starting to be normal to consider that the most competitive people or institutions in our age are precisely those that are most capable of efficiently processing the flow of information. In this new way of understanding the company and the world of relationships, the ability to combine masculine and feminine models holds the key to success. The intuition of the feminine paradigm helps to extract the essential and most interesting information in the shortest time, leaving aside the rest, whilst the masculine paradigm of rational knowledge helps to explore the essential aspects in detail. In the future it will be equally important to have in-depth knowledge of a specific area as it will be to know how to find the resources required to resolve a specific problem rapidly. On this measure of activity, the capacity to integrate the two models will result in a complete executive, one capable of analyzing information in an analytical way, ignoring everything that is not germane to the issue.

In Chapter 1 we also analyzed the changes that are taking place in companies with respect to the consequences of business activity, from achieving primary objectives to forecasting secondary effects. Our insistence on the changes that are happening in our society led us to the conclusion that companies can no longer focus solely on short-term results. Indeed, their success is based on their ability to forecast effects in the medium and longer term.

Today it would be suicide for a company to be so short-sighted as to only look at its own short-term results, without taking into account possible secondary or "perverse" effects. There are always negative effects, even when a positive goal is being pursued, but these consequences should not be so prejudicial that the damage caused is out of proportion to the value of the primary objective being pursued. The environment is a good example of the need to take care of secondary effects, but there are also other types of counterproductive social effects that cause damage to the common good or unfairly prejudice the interests of workers, clients, suppliers, shareholders or competitors. Companies are coming to believe that the production of products or services does not represent the real added-value supplied by their activity. The principal objective of a company is to sell its goods or services, but today selling is a curious mixture of the generation of confidence, perceptions and sensations that a team needs to know how to transmit to the client. The diversity of the organization brings an overall vision of the different interests and as a result improves the value of the company as a brand.

Perhaps the most important transformation in our companies is in the field of individual talent and the ability of individual members of the team to create and innovate to help meet the common objective. As a result the person becomes the focal point of the organization, replacing the central role that until now was occupied by raw materials, hard work and capital. This is a point of view that in recent times has been attracting more and more proponents, and today it is a reality. This can be seen by a global best seller like *Funky Business*,[2] the success of which is based on the exaltation of the idea that today talent is what moves capital, and the principal means of production is small, grey and weighs around 1,300 grams – the human brain. The pillars of good management are now not only economic profitability, meeting objectives or perfect company structures. The company is learning that it is in innovation, informal structures, the capacity to foresee the results and promoting working in teams that it will find the major challenges of the future. In another best seller, *Emotional Intelligence*, Daniel Goleman[3] goes one step further by considering that, if the driving force in companies in the 20th century was IQ, there is more and more evidence that in the 21st century the driving force will be emotional intelligence, with its twin forms of practical and creative intelligence.

Our rigid structures based on objective criteria have ceased to be the most important factor, to be replaced by increasing the potential for inclusion. The tendency is for vertical structures to disappear; the "summit" is no longer the point at the apex of the pyramid, but rather it has been dispersed among the members of a creative team. These configurations lead to other ways of understanding power and exercising leadership. This is where the perspective of diversity opens doors to other types of leadership, not only the traditional hierarchical forms, but also transformational leadership, which is focussed more on the motivation of the team and on achieving a common objective.

The people who are promoting inclusion and involvement are not interested in rising to the heights of the company, but rather to be influential in the organization. They do not want to be able to order people around but to be able to influence them. They are committed to the company itself, because they are attracted by what it does; they want to know more, to try new things, to discover the most effective procedures for obtaining good results. They do not usually push for promotion, and as a result they are frequently passed over when promotions do take place. They are the key figures in the company, and they are the ones who should be rewarded, even if it is only for the admirable example they set, by being placed in positions of greater influence, but without isolating them in bureaucratic tasks.

Nevertheless, it is still necessary for someone to know how to give instructions, and at certain times it is still essential to use structures and hierarchies. The key is not in changing the model for a different one, but in integrating them into a wider framework and knowing how to use them according to the circumstances. In order to do this, the people who are capable of integrating both models and thus understanding the complementarity of inclusion with the hierarchy structure will be the true leaders of the company in the future.

The studies of gender, culture and personality we have analyzed have served to create development programs for competences and skills at the heart of organizations. These personal development programs promote the capacity for creativity and innovation within the company, but it is essential that the company knows how to manage its people in order to benefit from this.

The person is without doubt the fundamental building block of value in any organization, but the person is not an isolated subject, alien to the situation or separate from its visions, values and beliefs. On the contrary, these are the fundamental reasons why the person is interested in their own personal development. The company can provide the appropriate background for a person to achieve their maximum potential and so be capable of innovation in the interests of the company.

In the period of transformation we are living through, we cannot be certain about anything, nor can we trust in a single recipe for resolving all possible situations. The ability to innovate, create and adapt to permanent change has become the most important value in the new company; and this is a value that diversity can supply, provided the company knows how to manage it. For this reason the final part of this book analyzes international best practices and looks at the useful tools for managing diversity that have been employed.

# Part Two

## *Managing Diversity*

Section 3

# POLICIES AND BEST PRACTICES

A New Framework for Analyzing Corporate Diversity Management

# 6 Diversity Management in Today's Companies

*If we can get a disproportionate share of the most talented people in the world, we have a chance of holding a competitive edge. That is the simple strategic logic behind our commitment to diversity and the inclusion of individuals – men and women regardless of background, religion, ethnic origin, nationality or sexual orientation. We want to employ the best people, everywhere, on the single criterion of merit. The importance of that goal as part of our overall business strategy has grown as competition has intensified.*

Lord Browne of Madingley, group chief executive, BP plc
*Extract from the keynote speech to the "Women in Leadership: a European Imperative" conference, Berlin, Germany, 19 June 2001*

As we saw in Chapter 1, the business environment has changed dramatically in recent decades. The development of information technologies, the liberalization of international commerce and the increasing mobility of people are some of the factors that have stimulated international competition. In a market where added-value has become the key to survival, the managers of the largest companies are becoming more aware that, in order to be able to adapt to demand, they need to diversify their management structures and introduce greater variety in the composition of their working groups, so they will be able to provide creative and innovative leadership.

The key to diversity does not lie so much in its existence, but rather in knowing how to manage it. The way of working depends to a large degree on behavior generated by the culture, gender and personality of each individual and it is precisely this diversity that can be the principal source of innovation in the company; but at the same time it can also be the cause of conflicts and tension. Companies such as JPMorgan Chase, BP, Shell, American Express and Ford have embarked on major reform processes in recent years that, from senior management down, propose an important change of strategy aiming, in the medium term, to utilize to the maximum the potential of their workforce. The reason for this is not just social justice, but rather the belief that an increase in diversity, when it is well managed, represents an important source of potential for the company, which can enable it to respond more efficiently to demand, with a wider range of opinions and the greater flexibility necessary to compete in a market that is constantly changing.

In this chapter we will attempt to analyze the processes that have begun in recent years in large international companies, using a framework of analysis focussed on the management of the different levels of diversity and the specific objectives of each level. The key point of this analysis is to try to identify best practices in the international market, its application in defined contexts and the degree of success that such practices have brought to the companies involved.

## The analytical framework of diversity

As has been said in earlier chapters, understanding diversity management is a complex process, as it affects many areas of the company and requires a range of different strategic focuses. Although these processes take place simultaneously, they have different rhythms and use different policies and tools; as a result, analyzing the results obtained is no straightforward matter.

The promotion of diversity in the company is taking place in response to two sets of stimuli. The first is external, social and legal pressure that pushes the company to meet the needs of society, which in reality consists of its clients, shareholders, suppliers, workforce and managers. This social demand is to our minds the first step to a more fundamental internal reform of the company, aimed at managing and efficiently integrating diversity to achieve efficiency increases and improve the process of innovation.

As a result, we intend to work simultaneously on two horizons. Firstly, we will look at the relationship between the different parts or members of the company and the totality of what the company represents, that is, the relationship between the diverse *parts/members* of the company, and the relationships that could exist between them to fulfill the company's mission understood as a *whole body*. And at a different level to this sociological or group scenario, there is the question of the objectives of the members themselves, that is, their desire to achieve personal realization, which without doubt has a direct influence on the realization of the mission of the whole or group of which they form a part.

The new company is an organization in which it is widely agreed that the objectives of the company should be pursued in parallel with, and convergent with, the objectives of the people who constitute the company. There are many levels at which this convergence of needs between the company and its *parts/members* can take place.

The company's aim in the medium term is to integrate the various components of the company into a single system, in which the members contribute their abilities and, as a result of their interaction, the company is able to grow and innovate. However, there are of course objectives and results that can be achieved in the shorter term, and these can be analyzed at three different levels, each of which has their own corresponding specific objectives and results; nevertheless, action at all three levels is aimed at a common objective – in the longer term the company will be an active and intelligent organization, capable of taking on the challenge of changing and diverse markets.

In Figure 6.1 we can see a summary of the three levels of diversity and the areas in which they act.

**Level 1: Society**
**Objective:** to harmonize the company to society's demands
**Benefits:** improved reputation, an effective response to demand

**Level 2: The organization**
**Objective:** to provide a flexible environment
**Benefits:** retaining talent, access to markets, organizational integration, cost savings

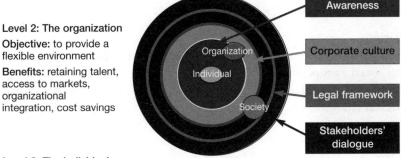

**Level 3: The individual**
**Objective:** supports the development of the individual members of the organization
**Benefits:** innovation, leadership, a variety of opinions, growth and adaptability to change

Figure 6.1 **Levels of depth in diversity strategy**

By examining this schema, we can look at the three levels of analysis according to the depth of the policies and their effect on the individual. Companies act simultaneously at the three levels; however, as we shall see, even within the same mission, each level of analysis incorporates its own series of objectives, policies and tools.

At the first level, that of **society**, the company interacts fundamentally with society in a continuous dialogue with its stakeholders, introducing diversity policies that aim to meet a social demand and as a result provide immediate benefits, such as an improvement in reputation for the company or its brand name.

In addition to acting at the level of society, the company has a level of action **within its own organization**, the aim of which is to provide its employees with a flexible environment in which they can achieve their full potential, and as a result the company is able to retain its brightest talents.

Finally, the company acts at the level of the **individual**. The company can provide systems, particularly those related to training and personal development, which support the individual in their personal growth. Nevertheless, the ability to develop in response to needs, abilities and desires remains the personal choice of each employee.

In 2003, the EU's Directorate General for Employment, Social Affairs and Equal Opportunities published a study entitled *The Costs and Benefits of Diversity*.[1] This study was based on a sample of 200 companies from four different countries within the EU. The fundamental conclusion was that diversity generates a series of positive values for the company that can be broken down into the three levels to which we have made reference:

### 1. Society
- An improvement in the company's image and reputation with external social agents
- Improved assimilation of the impact of globalization and technological change.

### 2. Organization
- Attraction, recruitment and retention of personnel in a wide pool of talent
- Reduction of labor costs and absenteeism
- A better understanding of the needs of long-standing clients
- Assistance in the development of new products, services and market strategies
- Improvements in knowledge of how to operate within different cultures.

### 3. Individual
- A contribution to the flexibility and responsibility of personnel

- Promotion of the commitment, the work ethic and the "discretional effort" of salaried staff
- Boosting creativity and innovation.

A company that is capable of innovating and learning is one in which its people innovate and incorporate knowledge. The individual capacity to grow and innovate will determine the organization's capacity to grow and innovate. This relationship between the parts and the whole is the objective of an appropriate diversity strategy. The development of human capital therefore forms the foundations of organizational strategy.

When we look at Figure 6.1, the central circle represents the heart of the organization, and so its growth will set the pulse for the growth of the rest of the company. Nevertheless, as we can appreciate from the diagram, all the levels are equally important; if the company does not expand at the organizational level, then the company will find it difficult to expand at the central level. Likewise, no matter how ready the individual and the company are to grow, they will not be able to achieve much if the company is not in tune with the demands of society. On the other hand, it is difficult for the company to expand at the social level, if the company does not permit expansion at the internal level at the same time.

As a result, policies aimed at all three levels simultaneously are required in order to achieve short-term results. Nevertheless, the combination of the different policies, each acting at a different level and with different rhythms, will achieve the final objective in the medium term, a living and intelligent organization. On the other hand, the capacity of the company to learn from the different policies and the results achieved as they become apparent, and to take action to use them in a process of feedback, will favor the development of a learning organization that is harmonious and capable of adapting to the various changes in its environment.

There is one final point that we should make before moving on to a more detailed analysis; the three levels represent relatively open concepts, and we can see that the differences between them become blurred at the edges. The division between society and organization is difficult to distinguish at the limit, and in the same way, the impersonal blends into the limits of the personal. The policies and instruments are not in sealed boxes and unable to move; rather they align themselves on a scale of depth, with the practices from one level becoming confused with those from the adjacent one.

We will now look in detail at each of the three levels, illustrating them with some examples of best international practice.

## Society level

| 1 – Society |
| --- |

**Level 1: Society**
**Objective:** to harmonize the company with the demands of society
**Strategy:** equal opportunities policies, dialogue with the stakeholders
**Instruments:** ethical codes, sustainability reports, anti-discrimination policies, CSR indicators (GRI, FTSE4Good)
**Results:** improvements in reputation, increase in brand value, effective response to demand
**Training strategy:** information and communication programs

Legal framework

International and National legal requirements

Figure 6.2 **Levels of depth in diversity strategy: society level**

### Objectives

The debate about the social objectives of companies is nothing new. As Micklethwait and Wooldridge[2] argue, there have been two conflicting trains of thought since the middle of the 19th century; one stated that the company had a responsibility to society, whilst the other stated that the company only had a responsibility to its shareholders. In recent years this debate has been reactivated and centers around the vision of Michael Porter, who sees social action by the company as a tool for obtaining competitive advantage,[3] in contrast to the traditional posture defended by Milton Friedman, who believes that the company's function should continue to be solely generating profits for its shareholders.[4]

On the other hand, the growing pressure from social groups, the reporting of abuses committed by some multinationals in the least developed countries, in addition to the Enron and WorldCom scandals, have obliged governments to take a much stricter position and propose measures aimed at limiting the potential social damage that can be caused by dubious business management.

This social pressure has enabled the emergence in recent years of initiatives at both regional and worldwide level, which principally promote:

• Respect for a series of basic principles, based on universal human rights
• Greater transparency by companies that will enable effective supervision and control by society.

These policies have come to be grouped together under the heading **corporate social responsibility (CSR)**, which has been defined as

> The voluntary integration by corporations of ethical, social and environmental concerns in their commercial operations as well as in their stakeholder relations.[5]

CSR is becoming one of the barometers for comparing companies, based on the idea that good social and environmental practices and corporate governance can be reliable indicators of a company's management and its value creation in the long term.

In a world where the informal is taking over from the formal, where the decision to buy, the basic action in any market relationship, is based more on perceptions than on reality, the perceptions felt by consumers are now an aspect that has a direct effect on the company's balance sheet. A market like ours where the majority of products have similar characteristics and conditions means that purchase decisions are supported more by the image and the concept we have of the company than the actual characteristics of the product itself. We have reached a point where the actions taken by the company are conditioned by the same factors that positively condition our society, and this parallel will, without doubt, be greatly enriching for all.

### Strategies

The demand for greater social responsibility has been crystallized in a series of general principles set out in initiatives on a global scale, amongst which we should highlight the Global Compact.[6]

The Global Compact[7] is a UN initiative which was announced at the World Economic Forum in 1999, with the aim of facilitating the alignment of corporate policies and practices with agreed, internationally applicable ethical values and objectives.

The Global Compact develops ten basic principles in areas of human rights, labor and environmental protection, which companies can sign up to voluntarily. Of those that relate to diversity, it proposes the promotion of equal opportunities at all levels of the company. Article 6 of the Compact asks companies to support the elimination of discrimination with respect to employment and occupation, and defines it as:

> any distinction, exclusion or preference which has the effect of nullifying equality of opportunity of treatment in employment or occupation and is made on the basis of race, colour, sex, religion, political opinion, national extraction or social origin. Discrimination may also occur on the basis of physical or mental disability.[8]

*Instruments*

The voluntary acceptance of inspiring principles such as those in the Global Compact is an important step forward in increased social responsibility by companies. Nevertheless, social pressure demands a greater commitment, together with increased transparency.

To this end the **triple bottom line strategy** has been developed and includes economic growth, social equity and environmental protection in what have become known as **sustainability reports**. In these reports, in addition to reporting each year on their financial situation, companies undertake to publish details of the actions they have been involved in during the year, both in social improvements and the protection of the environment.

A large number of companies throughout the world prepare these reports using the guidelines laid down by the Global Reporting Initiative (GRI),[9] which sets out a methodology for preparing reports on sustainability policies, drawn up by an independent body which includes economists, sociologists, trade unionists and NGOs. The GRI complements the Global Compact, providing a tool for preparing detailed reports with respect to the principles of the Global Compact.

With regard to diversity, the GRI proposes a series of equal opportunity indicators in the social section and in particular in the parts that refer to labor practices and decent work. To be precise:

- LA 10. Description of the equal opportunities policies or programs, as well as monitoring systems to ensure compliance and results of monitoring.
- LA 11. Composition of senior management and corporate governance bodies including female/male ratios and other indicators of diversity as appropriate.[10]

More than 625 companies from a wide range of business sectors and countries now prepare their sustainability reports in accordance with the GRI guidelines, including, among others, BP, Shell, BBVA, Telefónica, Inditex, General Motors, Eroski, Intel and Diageo.[11]

Sustainability indices

In addition to preparing sustainability reports, many companies have decided to meet a series of specific CSR criteria which enable them to be admitted to some of the most prestigious stock market sustainability listings, such as for example the FTSE4Good[12] on the London stock market and the Dow Jones Sustainable Indexes[13] on the New York stock exchange. Being included in these listings requires a high level of commitment to meeting a series of social responsibility criteria, including diversity indicators, which indicate, among other things, if the company has adopted equality policies, if they have a minimum number of women on their boards, and if they show evidence of support systems for equal opportunities both in recruitment and promotion. The analysis of whether these policies are being met or not by companies is undertaken by independent companies, one of the most well known of which is Eiris, which has its headquarters in London.[14]

## Best practices

We will now look at some examples of how various companies have used the instruments that we have been describing.

---

**Telefónica**

Together with Iberdrola, Telefónica topped the CSR index for the companies listed on the IBEX 35 prepared by *Actualidad Económica*. Telefónica prepared its CSR report using facts, data, graphics and figures to show how it was putting into practice the values and commitments that the Telefónica group had made.

The report was prepared in accordance with GRI's 2002 guide, so as to form a balanced and reasonable presentation of the economic, environmental and social development of the organization. Telefónica divided the data for the different countries in which it operates, provided data on the redistribution of the income it generated to the various interest groups involved and estimated the contribution of the Telefónica brand to its revenue streams. The interest groups, or stakeholders, that were included in its report are clients, shareholders and investors, employees, society, the environment and suppliers; a seventh interest group, the media, was also included.

Chapter 5 of the report, entitled "Employees: clarity and professional development," detailed the policies that affected employees. This chapter was in turn divided into five sections, describing policies relating to employees, development plans, social action initiatives and its nondiscrimination policies. The section on nondiscrimination policies placed special emphasis on the efforts the company had made to promote gender equality, the integration of disabled people, the achievement of a satisfactory work–life balance, teleworking and the reduction of the working day.

*Source:* Telefónica's corporate social responsibility report 2003, "The New Leaders" *Actualidad Económica*, July 8 2004.

---

**Opel-General Motors**

In its CSR report 2003–04, Opel-General Motors highlighted the efforts that it had made to promote equality of opportunity for its employees, irrespective of colour, race, gender, age, ethnic origin, nationality, civil status, disability, sexual orientation and political beliefs. The report stated the company's intention to create an environment in which the interaction between people of different ethnic origins, cultural identities and religions became an integral part of the company's corporate culture.

*Source:* Opel Corporate Responsibility Report 2003–04.

Another important tool used by companies is the sponsorship of a range of events aimed at improving their communication with society.

**Mini Football World Cup**

Since 2003, a mini World Cup of football teams of immigrants has been held every year in Madrid. The competition was held for the second time from 11–12 July 2004. Teams from 16 countries took part in a party that combined sport with increasing awareness of issues; the team representing Nigeria won the competition. This project has been supported from the beginning by La Caixa and the Madrid Football Federation, and the second time it was held it was also supported by Madrid Regional Council's Department of Immigration, Development Cooperation and Volunteering and their Education Department, by Madrid city council, Correos, Telefónica and Madrid 2012, among others.

Similar initiatives have taken place in other parts of Spain. For example, a mini World Cup was held in Valencia from 11 July to 8 August 2004 and organized by the Arí-Perú Valencia immigrants' association and Valencia university's Physical Education and Sports Department and was reported on by www.nostresport.com. The objective of the competition was to promote the integration of immigrants living in the Valencia region in 2004, which was the European year of education through sport. Eight teams from different countries took part and the winner was Columbia.

*Source:* el mundialito de las naciones", www.nostresport.com.

## Results

Policies aimed at improving the dialogue between the company and its stakeholders about diversity have resulted in greater diversity in all areas of the company, which has helped to improve society's image of the company.

At the first level, the objective is to meet the demands of society, the result of which is to improve (or worsen) the reputation of the company. As a result, the equal opportunity policies set out in the social responsibility reports serve, among other things, to improve the value of the brand, which in turn improves the stock market value of the company and also the products it offers.

Nevertheless, more important than making a profit, at the first level, the company is aiming to avoid risks that could lead to damage to its reputation, for example:

- Bad publicity in the media
- Difficulty in attracting new talent
- Difficult relationships with employees
- Legal risks
- Critical resolutions made by shareholders
- Decreases in production
- An increase in the costs of security.

The company's reputation is increasingly being affected by surveys and articles published in the media; these lead companies to try to be featured among the companies highlighted as being the best companies in the social area, and so to be featured in the listings published and in public tenders.[15]

### Legal framework

The legal framework is the minimum demanded from companies by law. For this reason it should not be seen as an objective to achieve, but simply as minimum standards that must be met. In their social strategies, companies try to go further than the legal minimum, which in any case will differ according to the cultural context that the company is operating in.

The principles of CSR, such as those identified in the Global Compact, are voluntary. It should be pointed out that there is an increasingly strong debate about the degree of compulsion that should be involved in CSR policies. Many governments, principally in Europe, but also in other regions, are considering incorporating some of the basic elements of CSR into their domestic legislation.

Setting aside the debate about the degree of compulsion in CSR principles, the area that is amply covered by legislation in most countries is equal opportunities. Looked at in this sense, diversity, understood as the attempt to achieve equal treatment for all groups, particularly those discriminated against, is established in law and there are legal remedies for workers to pursue when they feel they have been discriminated against; and at the same time, businesspeople obtain advantages by employing members of minority groups.

Equal opportunities in the EU entered into a new phase in 1997 with the signing of the Amsterdam Treaty, which gave the EU competence to legislate in social areas that until then had been outside their remit. The promotion of equality has taken place through directives and incentives, such as the EQUAL program, which was financed by the European Social Fund and has the objective of developing cooperation between the member states in order to promote a more inclusive work-life through fighting discrimination and exclusion based on sex, racial origin, religion or belief, disability, age or sexual orientation.[16]

---

**The Amsterdam Treaty**

The EU's Amsterdam Treaty is based on principles which all the Member States have in common, such as liberty, democracy, respect for human rights and other fundamental freedoms and the rule of law.

In the ambit of the application of the founding Treaty of the European Community, Article 12 (previously Article 6) made discrimination on the grounds of **nationality** illegal.

The Treaty of Amsterdam included Article 13, which set out that the Council could adopt actions aimed at **combating discrimination on the grounds of sex, racial or ethnic origin, religion or belief, disability, age or sexual orientation.**

The Treaty of Amsterdam introduced into the body of the Treaty establishing the European Community the new articles 136 to 145. Article 136 states that social policy is an area of joint competence between the Community and the Member States. Article 137 stated that the Council could intervene or reinforce its action for the approval of directives adopted by qualified majority, in co-decision with the European Parliament and following consultation with the Economic and Social Committee and the Regional Committee, in the following areas:

• Health and safety at work

- Working conditions
- The integration of excluded people into the labor market
- Information and consultation for workers
- Equality between men and women in terms of equal opportunities in the labor market and equal treatment.

Article 141 (previously Article 119) stated the **principle of equal treatment for men and women and equality of opportunity,** whilst the earlier Article 119 had been limited to questions related to equal pay.

This disposition enables the Council to adopt, following consultation with the Economic and Social Committee, and following the procedures for joint decision making, positive measures aimed at guaranteeing the application of the principles of equality between the sexes.

The Member States may adopt and maintain special measures for the sex that is under-represented, with the objective of facilitating professional activity or impeding or compensating disadvantages in their professional career. These measures may not take the form of rigid quotas, which were expressly rejected by the Court of Justice in the Kalanke decision of 1995.

*Source:* Álvarez y Asociados, alvarez.marian@icam.es.

---

### European Directives on Equal Opportunities

Directive 76/207 of 9 February 1976 on the implementation of the principle of equal treatment for men and women as regards access to employment, vocational training and promotion and working conditions.

Directive 92/85/EEC of 19 October 1992 on the introduction of measures to encourage improvements in the safety and health at work of pregnant workers and workers who have recently given birth or are breastfeeding.

Directive 2000/78/EC of 27 November 2000 establishing a general framework for equal treatment in employment and occupation.

Directive 2000/43/EC of 29 June 2000, implementing the principle of equal treatment between persons irrespective of racial or ethnic origin.

The Council Decision of 27 November 2000 which established a community action program to combat discrimination (2001–2006).

Directive 96/34/EC of 3 June 1996, as modified by Directive 97/75/EEC of 15 December 1997, on the framework agreement on parental leave.

*Source:* Álvarez y Asociados, alvarez.marian@icam.es.

**The Racial Equality Directive 2000/43/EC**

This Directive implements the principle of equal treatment between people irrespective of racial or ethnic origin.

The Directive protects people against discrimination at work and in training, education, social security, health care and access to goods and services including housing.

The Directive contains definitions of direct and indirect discrimination, harassment and prohibits the instruction to discriminate and victimization.

The Directive allows for positive action measures to be taken in order to ensure full equality in practice.

The Directive gives the victims of discrimination the right to make a complaint through a judicial or administrative procedure, with associated penalties for those who discriminate.

The Directive shares the burden of proof between the complainant and the respondent in civil and administrative cases.

The Directive provides for the establishment in each Member State of an organization to promote equal treatment and to provide independent assistance to victims of racial discrimination.

*Source:* http://stop-discrimination.info.

## Conclusion: diversity at the social level

We have seen that the first level of diversity is the society level, and that policies taken at this level are equally relevant as those developed at deeper levels. Harmonizing the company to social demands is one of the keys to business strategy and a key factor in the survival of the company. As a result, CSR policies and communication with the outside world are fundamentally important for maintaining and improving brand value, without which the company would not be able to compete.

## Organization level

| 2 – Organization |
|---|

**Level 2: Organization**
**Objective:** to provide a flexible environment, adapted to the different needs of the members of the organization
**Strategy:** an integrated corporate culture
**Instruments:** assessing work environment, human resources policies, internal communication, leadership commitment, training, development of interest group networks
**Results:** talent retention, variety in opinions, effective resonse to market demands, increase in resources, motivation and loyalty, cost savings, organizational flexibility, access to new markets
**Training strategy:** interactive training programs, shared organizational learning

Figure 6.3  **Levels of depth in diversity management: organization level**

### *Objectives*

Companies can only be effective globally if they can handle and benefit from their employees' various patterns of thought and action, and if they can adjust to the diversities of their respective markets.[17]

From the 1970s onward, the individual capacity began to be appreciated by companies as the key factor in being able to compete. Nevertheless, in order to be able to contribute the maximum, employees need to have their minimal levels of development catered for; in some cases they need flexibility to be able to balance their work and private lives, or they have certain special conditions caused by a disability they have. As a result, and so as to be able to retain the talent they need in order to be able to compete, from the 1980s onward, and in particular from the beginning of the 1990s, companies began to introduce a series of policies and programs aimed at providing a flexible environment that would be adaptable to the needs of the members of the organization.

### *Strategy*

The use of the term **organizational culture**, from which the terms corporate culture and corporate image derive, began to take on importance at the beginning of the 1970s. Nevertheless, since the beginning of business management, there has been a sense of something more or less ethereal that represented *the way of doing things* within an organization, as indicated by Professor Garralda;[18] these were values that were common within the organization, usually known as the company philosophy. This way of doing things was a reflection of the values of the company's senior management, and had a close relationship to the general expectations of society in the US at the time.

The philosophy of a company was considered to be something natural and intrinsic; it was perceived as a series of values that have emerged naturally in a homogeneous context, without thinking they could be modified in any way. From the 1970s onward, in the context of the changing business environment and the increasing difficulty of remaining competitive, companies began to understand the concept of **corporate culture** as something that could have an impact on the final outcome of strategy. Once the importance of corporate culture had been recognized, attempts were made to understand the term, and it became obvious that it was more complicated than had at first been imagined.[19]

The complexity of corporate culture resides in it not being one single culture that can be analyzed, taken apart and put back together again to your own specifications, but rather it is the result of a complex system based on a multitude of subcultures, which could include the culture of the country where the company had its head office, the culture of the different nationalities of the members of the subsidiaries in other countries, the subculture belonging to the business sector in which the company operates, the subcultures of the religious groups of the respective departments, or interest groups within the company. As Liz Mohn states, "Corporate culture can no longer be seen as the result of organic growth, but resembles instead a puzzle which needs to be solved in the right way."[20] The way in which senior managers resolve this jigsaw puzzle, and achieve the integration of the diverse elements in the company into the pursuit of a common objective, has become the main challenge for companies at the beginning of the 21st century.

The changes in the corporate world and society over recent decades have enabled a range of cultures and subcultures to survive side by side within a single organization and act simultaneously, and this makes it enormously difficult to have a single unique definition of all the different policies and concepts.[21]

A company needs to grow by taking advantage of the potential of the individual members who constitute it, but at the same time it needs to have at least a minimum level of corporate uniformity in order for it to function in a coordinated way in all its areas. As we saw in Part One, the success of management at the beginning of the 20th century was due to the establishment of a series of objective, scientific procedures to which all could subscribe. A basis of uniform procedures remains a base for company efficiency to this day, but something more is required too. In addition to efficiency, it is necessary to add value in some way, to offer something new or original, in short, to innovate. As a consequence of this need for innovation, it is necessary to allow individuals at least a minimum degree of freedom to be able to express themselves and to create something different.

This apparent contradiction forms the basis of today's corporate culture. It is a difficult equilibrium between the necessary flexibility for individuals to feel comfortable and the homogeneity that is necessary for the coherent functioning of the organization. This equilibrium between unity and diversity is the **integrated organizational culture** that companies today are demanding; they need everyone to work as though they were one but to be a multitude of unique individuals at the same time.

We will now look at some of the major tools that large companies have developed in order to achieve this integrated culture and find this difficult balance.

### Individual needs and group categories

In section 2, without wishing to ignore other types of diversity such as religious belief, age, sexual orientation and disability, all of which are still present, we identified three essential types of diversity: gender, culture and personality. However, at this stage it seems important to us to draw a basic distinction. All human beings by their nature have a personality, a culture (or several) and a gender, which form the basis for their way of thinking. At the same time, we all have personal experiences and circumstances in our lives which lead us to perceive reality in our own particular way, and these personal circumstances also in many cases lead to their own particular necessities. And it is here that we can distinguish other differences that make all of us, each in our own particular way, different – a particular physical disability, age, children, a mother to look after or a particular diet that we follow. These facts do not diminish us as people, quite the contrary; they enrich our personality and our perception of life. Nevertheless, these circumstances demand a certain degree of flexibility when it comes to doing our work. Javier Romañach said, in his writing defending the value of the disabled in our society:

> And that is why I am taking part in this social struggle, in a struggle for the acceptance of the dignity of diversity, in the conviction that we people with disabilities are a valuable resource for society, not a drain, as society would have us believe. In this conviction that disability, the loss of functioning that is always inherent in every human being and that becomes evident in the majority as they get older, is by its very nature natural and enriching.[22]

Gender, culture and personality form the axis of our basic thoughts. The different ways that different cultures have adopted to resolve problems enrich diversity and increase the possibilities for innovation and problem solving. As a result, learning the way that different cultures work, or learning the tendencies to masculine or feminine behavior, enrich us and enrich the company by offering different solutions to a problem. Nevertheless, learning from diversity of gender, culture or personality remains within the power of the person at the strictly individual level, as we will see later. The company can offer personal development programs for each individual, but, ultimately, it is always the individual who will decide whether to develop themselves or not.

On the other hand, what the company is able to do, and should do, is to provide sufficient flexibility in the work environment for the individual to feel that they have at least the minimum conditions necessary to be able to perform to the maximum of their potential; and give them sufficient confidence to continue growing and developing as individuals and as part of the organization of which they are members. In order to do this, companies are increasingly not taking measures aimed at specific groups by gender, culture or personality, but rather they are attempting to manage the individual circumstances of their employees and, with the intention of developing their talents, providing them with the environment they need in order to grow in their job.

## Instruments of best practices

There are no clear recipes in diversity policies, but rather a series of tools that, when combined, make the company a more flexible environment that is better adapted to a larger number of people. Not everybody needs to accept these policies, but everybody can adopt them if it seems appropriate to them. There is no need for the introduction of flexible working time to affect the whole workforce as many employees may prefer to receive a full salary for working the full number of hours. Nevertheless, all those who need this flexibility, independent of their gender, should be able to choose it if it meets the needs of their particular life circumstances.

The majority of large international companies have adopted a series of tools to manage diversity that we can break down into three categories: **assessing the work environment** and the needs of employees, **specific human resources policies** and **diversity supporting systems and structures**.

We will now look at each of these three categories in turn and see the different elements that have been adopted in concrete examples:

### Assessing the work environment[23]
The evaluation of the workplace atmosphere is the first step that organizations need to take if they wish to avoid possible resistance from their employees, who might see the new policies as an external element with

little relevance for the organization. The identification of the needs of the organization will help to justify the need for diversity and the necessity of developing a long-term plan for the organization. An appropriate environment will also help to establish reference measures for monitoring the progress that has been made.

This evaluation needs to incorporate some of the following elements:

- Gathering human resources data
- Mapping the data
- Collecting employees' perceptions
- Benchmarking against best practices.

We will now look at some examples of companies that have outstanding assessment policies.

---

**American Express**

American Express was one of the first companies to implement a strategy for assessing the work environment. Its analysis is based on an Annual Employee Survey which is the primary method of measuring employee satisfaction in twelve areas. Metrics linked to diversity were incorporated as early as 1993. The Annual Employee Survey results are published and communicated by the CEO to all employees worldwide. The survey has been repeated annually, which enables both senior managers and employees to see how the company is developing, in which areas the employees' perception of the company is improving, and what measures are necessary in other areas to improve the general level of satisfaction. American Express is one of the companies that has been recognized by the organization Catalyst for its work in favor of diversity; American Express won Catalyst's award for diversity in 2001.

*Source:* http://www.catalystwomen.org.

---

**Ford Motor Company**

Ford Motor Company has investigated the working environment within the company and the satisfaction of its employees at various levels in respect of different aspects related to their working lives, such as their satisfaction with the company in general and their job. In addition, it specifically included questions about the level of satisfaction regarding diversity in the company. In 2003, 72 percent of the company's employees took part in the survey, which showed a general level of satisfaction of 61 percent, whilst the level of satisfaction with regard to diversity was 71 percent.

*Source:* www.ford.com.

Human resource policies

Human resource policies normally recognize the need for flexibility on aspects such as working time or career development so that all the members of an organization can enjoy the benefits of a flexible environment.

Some of the principal policies are often referred to under the heading **work–life balance**. This normally includes measures related to flexibility of working conditions to meet the needs of employees, for example as parents, part of a couple where both partners are working, caring for elderly relatives, students, employees who are about to retire, single people and so on.

In addition to aiming to achieve this work–life balance, human resource policies help to establish wide criteria for the **recruitment and promotion** of personnel whilst meeting the criteria of diversity in a climate of equal opportunities.

Many companies try to offer guidance to their employees so that they can evaluate their own potential within the company and what they should do in order to progress. These policies are normally grouped together under the heading **career development programs**, and normally include such things as mentoring and coaching, which provide a form of personalized guidance and feedback and enable the person to be aware of their potential within the organization.

Many companies try to promote **employee networks** within the company; these networks could be based on the same religious or ethnic group, gay or lesbian groups and sports and so on. The objective of each of these groups is to create affinity between the members that allows discussion and sharing among the members and so promotes greater cohesion within the organization.

The final category that should be included in human resource policies is policies aimed at the **integration of disabled people**. Increasingly, companies are trying to develop programs that enable access for people with a disability with equality of conditions. These policies not only provide a dignified post to someone with difficulty of access, but, in many cases, they also provide the company with a highly motivated and talented person.

We will now look in greater detail at the policies implemented by some companies who are outstanding in this field.

**Work–life balance programs**

**JPMorgan Chase**

As a result of its merger in 1996, JPMorgan Chase adopted a new diversity strategy, one of the elements of which was the Flexible Solutions Toolkit, a

comprehensive instruction manual for creating flexible working arrangements. This manual enables senior managers and employees to look
together at the possibilities for flexible working patterns in specific job positions. Any request for a flexible working schedule that is turned down can be
looked at again with the human resources department. The company was
recognized by the Catalyst Diversity Award in 2001.

*Source:* www.catalystwomen.org.

---

**IBM España**

In order to enable its employees to try to achieve an appropriate work–life
balance, IBM España has adopted various measures, which have been
awarded the Premio Nacional Empresa Flexible 2004 (the 2004 National Flexible Company Prize by CVA (Comunicación de Valor Añadido)). IBM España has
also shown that such measures can be profitable, as there has been a substan-
tial increase in productivity in its employees following the introduction of teleworking, which enables workers to work from anywhere at any time.

IBM España has a system where employees work to obtain results, not to
complete a set number of hours, so it offers many options of **flexible
timetables**, possibilities for **leave permits** and the option of taking a
**sabbatical period**.

In addition, IBM España also provides its workers with information about
**nurseries** and **centers for the elderly** and makes available **transport, mobile
phones and many other services on its premises**.

*Sources:* "Companies fear that problems of achieving work–life balance are caused by
difficulties at work," *ABC*, 20th June 2004; "IBM and Coface win flexible company
awards" *Expansion y empleo*, 19th June 2004.

## Recruitment and promotion policies

---

**Grupo VIPS**

VIPS has expanded greatly in recent years, and this has made it difficult for
it to find the staff it needed to cover the positions that its expansion generated. "We are a growing company that has had shops that were ready to
open, but which we couldn't open for lack of employees," explained Miguel
Ángel García, VIPS's director of human resources.

The senior managers of the group understood that in order to promote the
incorporation of non-European Union citizens into its workforce, two distinct
advantages needed to be offered: a **personal life project** for the employees

through giving them permanent contracts and **professional development** through career plans, and a well-designed structure of internal promotion that would enable staff to become the manager of one of the shops within two years.

In 2004, 43 percent of the workforce of Grupo VIPS was made up of employees from 85 different nationalities, 60 percent of the employees were women, the average age of the workforce was 24 years old, and 23 percent occupied management positions. The company recruits professionals from Ecuador, Colombia, Dominican Republic and Morocco, it has also integrated professionals from Rwanda and Macao. Human resources managers travel regularly to those countries, and perform information sessions to potential candidates; giving information on the work and life expectations they could have by working for the group. As result of these policies, VIPS has achieved a model of labor integration that has been recognized by a number of institutions, including recognition by the Fundacion Universidad Empresa.

*Sources:* "From necessity to strategy," ABC Domingo, 3rd February 2004; http://www.grupovips.com.

---

### Caja Madrid

In 2000, in order to understand and meet the needs of an increasing population of immigrants, Caja Madrid began an active policy of recruiting non-Spanish professionals to work in its offices. It employed foreign nationals and trained them, which added to the diversity in its workforce and at the same time provided the company with a new tool for attracting new clients.

In 2003 Caja Madrid recruited 13 Moroccan professionals as part of this program. The new employees studied for a masters degree at the Francisco de Vitoria university and then spent six months gaining work experience in Caja Madrid branches. Once the training program was completed, the recruits joined the bank's branch network, with the objective of serving clients who came from their home country. By November 2004 Caja Madrid had 68 employees from 20 different nationalities.

For the bank, the challenge is to make diversity a factor that differentiates it from the competition and helps it to improve its attention to the customer. "It is about understanding cultural differences as a source of individual and business efficiency," says Rafael Fernández Cundes, director of Caja Madrid's personal development department.

*Sources:* "The multi-ethnic workforce is arriving" Actualidad Económica, January 2004; "From necessity to strategy" *ABC empleo*, Sunday, 8 February 2004; "Diversity: action to compete in global markets" *Expansión y empleo*, 6 November 2004.

## Career development programs

### Accenture

Accenture is a global company providing consultancy services on management, technological services and outsourcing. It is committed to the development of innovation and works with its clients to help them to convert their organizations into high yield businesses.

In 1994 Accenture developed its US Diversity Program which contained a section dedicated to the role of women, the US Women's Initiatives Program. The program produced very good results and as a result it was decided to expand this strategy to the rest of the company, which took place with the launch in 1999 of the Great Place to Work for Women program.

This initiative covered the whole company and aimed to create an inclusive culture in which all employees, irrespective of their geographical location, can achieve their professional aspirations.

Accenture has implemented innovative people management processes and monitored how well they have performed. These include measurement processes such as **geographic scorecards**, global **surveys** (the Global Leadership Survey and the Global People Survey) and **performance appraisals** and also include programs such as professional career guidance, mentoring programs for women and networking facilities.

This initiative is **fully supported by senior management**, and is co-sponsored by the chairman and the CEO of the company and managed globally by the chief leadership officer. These programs are available for all 75,000 of the company's employees, in 12 different geographical areas and in five operating groups. Although the programs are managed globally, the individual local offices are responsible for focussing on the aspects that most affect them. It is like a spider's web, where the center is the global leadership, which is linked to the different operational and regional groups through the interlinked strands of the web. The results are shared throughout the company by group and geographical unit.

The program focuses on four areas:

**Direction, global vision and coordination, adaptation, and local implementation.** Each operational group or geographical unit is responsible for creating a local action plan, adapted from the global initiative, and these are coordinated and reexamined every two years by Accenture's executive committee.

**Attracting women to the organization.** A number of measures were implemented to make the company more attractive to women. These ranged from strengthening relationships with universities and schools to recruitment campaigns, both for new graduates and for more experienced people, giving greater prominence in the media and on the corporate website to senior female executives, and keeping a close watch on trends that affect women by taking part in discussion forums such as the World Economic Forum and the Women Future Main Event on leadership.

**Development of women through their professional careers, and creating an inclusive working environment that will maximize commitment and company loyalty.** The intention is to address the issues that could lead women to move to another department or leave the company altogether by:

- Facilitating the adoption of flexible work arrangements such as working part time, flexible timetables, job sharing, intensive working weeks and teleworking.
- Sponsoring local forums on the development of women and promoting continuous learning through training and work experience.
- Including contributions to the development of others in the evaluation process in order to stress the importance the company gives to employees and senior management who help in the development of others as people developers, which requires the ability to work in a team, and to promote work–life balance.

**Helping to develop women in the organization.** The company provides careers advisors to guide the professional development process and create a visible career progression model, which is a report on the requirements of the steps to be taken by the person to develop their career within Accenture. It also established Global Leadership Development seminars which train the best female managers for posts in senior management.

The result was an increase in the number of women in Accenture. By 2002, 10 percent of the partners in the company were female, compared to only 5.8 percent in 1994. Overall, 14.1 percent of the new partners created in the company worldwide in 2002 were women, whereas in the US this rose to 19 percent; and 17 percent of the members of the highest management body, the management committee, were female. In addition, 41.4 percent of people promoted in 2001 were women, compared to 31.3 percent in 1994; 23.8 percent of total promotions were coloured women, whereas in 1994, coloured women had only represented 10.5 percent.

*Sources:* www.accenture.com; "Accenture: great place to work for women", Catalyst award winners 2003, http://www.catalystwomen.org.

**British Petroleum**

BP is one of the largest multinational companies operating in the energy sector; it made a profit of over $12,300 million in 2003 and employed more than 103,000 people.

BP has four main business areas: exploration and production, refining and marketing, petrochemicals and gas, and energy and renewables; the single biggest contribution to profits came from exploration and production.

BP has introduced policies that guarantee that the company is a **meritocracy** when it comes to professional development. The company defines merit as the ability to get the job done. As a result, it has refined its working practices and company culture in order to eliminate any barriers that impede the professional development of any member of staff.

BP has the following professional development programs, the first two aimed at executive level, whilst the third is for technical positions:

- **First level leaders (FLLs) development:** The FLLs is a global development program that is available to the 12,000 team leaders throughout the whole of BP; it is the single largest leadership development initiative ever undertaken by the company. The aim of the program is to help participants to develop their knowledge of supervision, their leadership skills and to form a network of employees who are at a similar stage of development. The program combines face-to-face meetings with senior leaders with online learning programs and a system of personal coaching. In 2003, more than 5,700 employees took part in the program, bringing the total who had taken part in the program up to the end of that year to 10,500 employees.

- **Senior level leaders (SLLs):** The SLLs is a development program aimed at senior BP executives using executive training programs developed in conjunction with the universities of Harvard, Stanford and Cambridge and external coaches. These programs deal with leadership styles, leveraging innovation, the new international business framework, social and environmental responsibilities, individual behavior and personal impact.

- **Professional recognition program:** This program aims to detect and develop specialists in key areas, such as finance or specialized engineering. The program aims to guarantee that recognition and promotion are available to the best specialists and their knowledge is made best use of by the company. These specialists do not follow the traditional career path of managers, who tend to be more generalists, but rather their role is to provide specialist advice, **mould company policies,** act as an example to others in the same field as them and lead the diffusion of best practices throughout the entire group.

In addition, special care has been taken to ensure that promotion procedures are free from any hint of bias, and mentoring programs have been set up, such as the mutual mentoring program for example, which associates junior employees with senior mentors with the aim of exchanging experiences and new ideas.

These policies resulted in an increase of 60 percent in the number of female executives in two years, five of the most senior 45 directors are now women, and there has been an increase of 38 percent in non-GB and non-USA employees. In 2003, 49 percent of people promoted to group leadership positions, the 609 most senior posts in the company, were women from outside the US or Great Britain, or were from minority groups in these countries; this percentage was higher than the target of 40 percent.

*Sources:* www.bp.com; "British Petroleum" *Annual Review*, 2003; BP *Sustainability Report*, 2003.

## Employee networks

**Ford Germany**

The Ford Motor Company diversity strategy promotes the formation of groups of employees, known as **employee resource groups**, throughout the company. These groups act as networks providing support to members of the community, facilitating their integration and the overcoming of barriers and enabling Ford to have a better understanding of and access to certain groups. An example of one of these groups, which has a presence in many countries, is the network of gay employees, known as **GLOBE** (Gay, Lesbian or Bisexual Employees).

Ford Germany was the first large company to support the formation of a network of gay employees, when GLOBE was formed in Cologne, Germany, thanks to the efforts of Roland Kayser in 1997.

Since then, the association has been highly active, helping the rights of the gay, lesbian and bisexual community to be recognized in Ford Germany and in wider society. Ford has become the main sponsor of the annual convention of gay and lesbian journalists in Germany, and has been involved in different initiatives such as painting a Galaxy in 2002 for the city's carnival to warn of the danger of AIDS. GLOBE also supplied a special rainbow-painted Ka as one of the Ford vehicles for the Christopher Street day parade.

In addition to these steps aimed at increasing awareness, GLOBE Germany has developed an 11-step plan for achieving equal rights for all homosexual employees, especially those living with their partner; since 2003 Ford has taken responsibility for widow's/widower's pensions for these partners.

In 2001 the GLOBE initiative in Germany received the annual diversity prize (CLAD) from the FMC and the Max-Spohr prize from the Association of Gay German Director's.

*Sources:* www.fordglobe.com; www.ford.com; "Managing Diversity" *Hernsteiner Magazine*, Issue 2, 2004, pp 33–6 quoted by Hans Jablonski, as interviewed by Peter Wagner; "Ford diversity brochure" Vielfalt als Stärke, *Diversity*, Issue 2002; Klingelschmitt, K. P. *Taz* newspaper, 6th April 2003.

---

**Kellogg African-American Resource Group**

This group of African-American Kellogg employees contributes to the company's objectives by ensuring the professional development of its members, enabling the construction of relationships between the members and serving as a resource to positively influence the Kellogg environment.

*Source:* http://www.kelloggs.com/careers/diversity/resource.shtml.

---

## Policies aimed at integrating the disabled

---

**Europcar**

Europcar is a car rental company that belongs to the Volkswagen group. The company has successfully implemented policies aimed at the integration of disabled people into its workforce. For example, in Catalonia in February 2004, 87 of the company's 625 employees had some form of disability; this represents 14 percent of the workforce, which compares to the 2 percent required by law. This policy of integration of disabled people is one of the company's permanent objectives, and has been part of its quality systems since the first of its centers was certified in 1997. Europcar has developed a series of measures aimed at integrating people with handicaps into its workforce, supported by agreements that it has with other bodies, such as the one it signed five years ago with Fundosa Social Consulting, the Fundación Española de Espina Bífida (the Spanish Spina Bifida Foundation) and Fundación Adecco.

In order to meet its objective of integrating disabled employees into its work-force, in some cases it has modified its premises and it has organized courses for colleagues to learn sign language and how to communicate with employees with listening or phonetic impairment.

*Source:* ABC domingo, 8 February 2004, "Europcar gana el premio Cermi de Integración laboral".

---

## FAMOVA-FORD ESPAÑA

One of the most important initiatives to come out of Ford's Almussafes factory in Valencia was the creation in May 2000 of **FAMOVA** (Fabricación Modular Valenciana – Modular Fabrication Valencia), a vehicle parts assembly work-force where most of the employees have a disability. It is "a project that aims to promote the incorporation of the physically and mentally disabled into the world of work and to give work to handicapped children of Ford employees." Fundación ONCE (the foundation for the blind) and the Generalitat Valenciana (the local government) also participated in the creation of FAMOVA with Ford.

FAMOVA works for Ford España, and its premises are within Ford's Almus-safes plant. Recruitment of personnel is undertaken by Fundosa Consulting, a company that specializes in employing and training disabled people, and is also responsible for organizing the training that is required for the workers to be hired. Once the training is complete, which lasts between two and three months and takes place in Ford's factory, the employees are hired; they are mostly between 20 and 30 years old and have a range of physical and mental disabilities.

The positions and tasks these workers have in the factory are determined by their disability, for example there are luminous signs for those with hearing difficulties, and those with physical difficulties are assigned tasks they are capable of undertaking, and are allowed to do so at their own pace.

The FAMOVA initiative received Ford's CLAD European prize, awarded to the best initiatives for promoting diversity within Ford in Europe, and in 2002 it received the Premio Inserta*. It has also received ISO 9.001 certification from AENOR, which recognizes the safety of the working environment and the rigor-ousness of the production processes and the quality of service to the client. In 2004 FAMOVA had 42 employees, of whom 40 had some form of disability.

*Sources:* La diversidad en Ford España; Programa ACCIÓN, number 2, Premios INSERTA.

* The Premio INSERTA is awarded by Fundación ONCE to companies that have done outstanding work to enable the integration of the disabled into the workplace.

**Organización Nacional de Ciegos Españoles (ONCE)**

ONCE is a non-profit making organization whose mission is to "improve the quality of life for blind people and the visually impaired throughout Spain." However, in addition to working with the blind and visually impaired in Spain, ONCE also works with people suffering from other disabilities (and the visually impaired) in other parts of the world, which has led to great diversification.

ONCE's principal activity is the management of a lottery, the tickets for which are sold by visually impaired people throughout Spain. In 1988 ONCE, working with other disabled groups, created the ONCE Foundation, the aim of which is the social integration of the disabled.

In 1993, seeking to find alternative sources of funding to the lottery and other forms of employment for the blind and visually impaired, ONCE created the ONCE Business Corporation (CEOSA).

The ONCE Foundation was created in 1988 in order to "integrate people with other disabilities into society through work and training and through the elimination of all barriers." Three percent of ONCE's gross revenue from the sale of lottery tickets is allocated to financing the Foundation; this is 20 percent of the overall operating margin of the organization.

## The ONCE Group

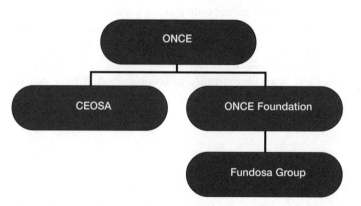

The promotion of employment for the disabled is the main priority of the ONCE Foundation. Between 1988 and December 2001, 42,800 new jobs and positions were created as a result of the Foundation's work.

In 1989 the Fundosa Group was established to aid the ONCE Foundation in meeting its objectives. Fundosa is "the operating arm of the ONCE Foundation for creating employment opportunities for the disabled." In 2004 Fundosa had equity capital of €162 million. The Fundosa group has five sectors of activity. More than 11,500 people are employed in the 70 companies either wholly or part owned or in which the group has a stake. More than 71 percent of the 11,500 employees had some form of disability.

*Sources:* www.once.es; http://www.ceosa.org; http://fundaciononce.es.

## Supporting systems and structures for managing diversity

All the experts agree that the key to success for any activity that aims to promote diversity is a clear leadership commitment. Firm and explicit commitment from senior managers and the existence of open and fluid communication at all levels is the best way of ensuring the success of diversity strategy within a company.

In order to carry this out in practice, many companies have developed systems for managing and monitoring the performance of their various diversity programs. It is not simply an issue of promoting diversity in the human resources department, but rather extending it to all areas of the company. In order to achieve this, many companies have created diversity positions, reporting directly to the general management of the company. Other companies have given responsibility for implementation and monitoring of the performance of diversity policies directly to a member of the board. The majority of companies have created diversity councils in their various branches and subsidiaries in order to organize their activities openly and coordinate the various policies.

In all these cases, and independent of the structure chosen, strong and clear leadership is essential to these policies working and being accepted by the members of the organization.

We will now look at some examples of companies that have outstanding best practices in the development of supporting systems for managing diversity.

### Shell

Shell understands **diversity** as being all the ways in which people are different, including both visible differences, such as age, gender, ethnic origins and physical aspect, and underlying aspects, such as ways of thinking, religious beliefs, nationality and educational background. For them, **inclusiveness** means a workplace in which diversity is valued, where all employees have the opportunity to develop their skills and talents, in line with their beliefs and the objectives of the company. The company's aim is to create a company in which all its individual members are involved, supported, respected and connected.

Shell regards diversity as a "complex process of change." In order to be successful, this process needs to be implemented in the same way as any other significant change in the way of thinking or behaving that is fundamental to the company achieving its key objectives and strategies.

The group's vision is to become a company that is recognized, both internally and externally, as one that values diversity, and to be a company that would be chosen by men and women from whatever cultural background. In this way the company will benefit from diversity by improving relationships with consumers, suppliers, partners, employees, governments and other stakeholders, and this will be reflected positively in the company's results.

In order to achieve this, the company has introduced what it calls its Global Diversity & Inclusiveness (D&I) Standard and its Group Diversity Framework, which, in addition to setting out the main criteria that should be applied, sets two specific targets:

- 20 percent of the most senior people in the company to be women by 2008.

- The country chair for each country to be filled by a national of that country in 100 percent of cases.

In order to achieve these objectives, Shell established a clearly defined structure for the framework for action, the procedures, assessment tools and the responsibility of each position affected, both in the normal chain of command and by the creation of specific groups to supervise and monitor the implementation of the diversity strategy.

- *Group Diversity Council (GDC):* the GDC is responsible for developing the vision of group diversity through recommendations from the Committee of Managing Directors (CMD) and the HR Council. The GDC also serves an audit and verification function, it monitors plans and processes in the group and its areas of business, establishes common strategic priorities and communication. The GDC is chaired by the CMD chairman.

| Conceptual framework | Implementation | |
|---|---|---|
| | Ordinary line | Specific line |
| Vision | Committee of Managing Directors (CMD) Regional Managing Directors (RMD) | Group Diversity Council (GDC) |
| Criteria and guidance | Business CEO Business Unit Executives Service Organizations | Diversity Business Focal Point |
| Implementation | Country Chair | Global Diversity Practice |

- *Diversity business focal points:* these work individually or as part of a team responsible for maintaining a diversity change process. They identify potential diversity issues and barriers. The diversity business focal point provides support on diversity planning by helping in the preparation, implementation and monitoring of plans and helping adapt them to local circumstances. They work directly with the people responsible for different business areas and teams.

- *Global diversity practice:* global diversity practice supports the group business leaders to develop their plans and objectives for diversity, influence the integration of diversity into human resources strategy, develop and provide tools, processes and advice and aids in the transfer of knowledge and the sharing of best practice.

*Sources:* www.shell.com; "Diversity and Inclusiveness at Shell. Foundation for the future," Shell, 2002; "Valuing and leveraging diversity to become a model of inclusiveness," Catalyst Award winner (www.catalystwomen.org), 2004.

---

**Fannie Mae**

Many companies have created **diversity councils,** such as Fannie Mae's Diversity Advisory Council (DAC). The DAC consists of the rotating office of the chairman's representative, senior management, and representatives from each Employee Networking Group. The DAC works as a team to identify and resolve questions related to diversity. The DAC format allows employees to speak directly with senior leadership about diversity issues. In addition to the DAC and in order to improve communication, the company also organizes "Java with Jamie" sessions, which give employees the opportunity to meet and talk in small groups with the vice-president, Jamie Gorelick.

*Source:* http://www.catalystswomen.org, winner of the Catalyst prize 2002.

---

## Results

These practices and tools lead to a flexible working environment in which employees can develop their full potential. They lead to an organization that has a greater degree of cohesion among its members and, as a result, achieves a series of results that have a direct result on the effectiveness of the company, including:

- **Talent retention:** many talented professionals leave an organization when they feel that it no longer meets their personal ambitions or provides an adequate work–life balance. In the competitive markets of the new century, companies will compete to attract and retain the best talent, which forms the company's most valuable asset.

- **Capitalization of corporate investment:** companies invest in their new employees, giving them training in the company and its business. Despite this, many women leave their careers between the ages of 30 and 40, feeling unable to achieve a balance between work and their private lives; this represents a real cost for the companies that do not manage to retain them.
- **Cost savings:** companies normally apply the same policies to all their employees. If they took diversity more into account, they would be able to offer suitable motivation based on the needs of all their employees, as some might be motivated by promotion, whilst others might be more motivated by a different type of incentive.
- **Access to new markets:** society is becoming more diverse, and many groups are becoming more influential as a result of their capacity as consumers or decision makers. The closer that the composition of employees reflects the composition of society, the more efficient will be the policies aimed at the market.
- **Adapting flexibly to changing environments:** the business world of the new century is undergoing rapid change. In order to change its objectives and strategies as rapidly as the background against which it operates changes, organizations need to consist of people who are capable of changing their perspectives rapidly.
- **Motivation and loyalty:** a company's most valuable asset is its human resources. Loyalty and motivation are the best ways of extracting the maximum potential from these resources.
- **An increase in resources:** people with different origins and different characters can bring new groups of clients and as a result increase the total resources of the company.

## Conclusion: levels and priorities

From the foregoing analysis, we can conclude that, in addition to fitting into its social background, the company in its diversity strategy needs to develop a flexible environment where all its employees can develop their work in accordance with their specific requirements.

We are not saying that this strategy is more important than the first level; quite the contrary, these strategies are equally important and need to be developed simultaneously. At the first level we were looking at society's demands, whilst at the second we have looked at retaining talent; both of these strategies help the company to grow, through access to new markets, improvements in brand image and the retention of the brightest talent, which is necessary in order for the company to be able to compete. For this reason, companies should take action at both levels simultaneously, although with specific tools and objectives for both, recognizing that the results will be achieved at different speeds and over different time scales.

## Individual level

| 3 – Individual |
| --- |

**Level 3: Individual**
**Objective:** support to the individual development of members of the organization
**Strategy:** awareness
**Instruments:** development of competencies and individual skills
**Results:** innovation, leadership, growth and adaptability to change. Harmonization of the members of the organization to the organization itself
**Training strategy:** personal development, trans-personal orientation

Figure 6.4 **Levels of depth in diversity strategy: individual level**

Finally we come to the individual, the heart of the company, with the thought that it is only if the individual can grow that the company can grow. Nevertheless, it is important to make clear that embarking on a path of personal growth is a matter of choice. Nobody can be forced to undertake personal development and it would be counterproductive to try to make them; organizations can create big problems for themselves if they are too aggressive about the promotion of personal development among their members. Peter Senge notes that there have been many cases in recent years of managers stubbornly insisting on development programs that their employees thought were in some cases contrary to their religious beliefs, and some of these resulted in legal action against the organization.[24]

For this reason, the third circle is about approaching "personal mastery" in Senge's terminology. Whilst the first circle deals with social relationships and the second deals with personal relationships ("persona" means "mask" in Greek), the third circle, in its very center "takes the mask away" to the transpersonal level. This is beyond external relationships and is where individuals search for themselves, discover themselves, come to know themselves and become self-aware, in the process that Jung calls "individualization"; individuals become aware of themselves, their resources and their development potential.

Following Maslow's terminology,[25] this is the space in which growth toward what he terms "self-realization" takes place, a state to which psychology gives a deep and subtle meaning. The route to transpersonal development begins beyond the person. According to Maslow's studies, people who have achieved self-realization are highly motivated, respect themselves and are more respectful of others, are highly empathetic, have high self-esteem, are less dependent on outside recognition and are generous. This is where the apparent contradiction arises; by going into an internal central space in which the subject transcends personal relationships and becomes deaf to the world, they return to the world strengthened, with greater charisma and conviction. Transpersonal motivation is largely values based; but it does not generate competition with those values (recognition, power, remuneration) that are the central and crucial ones for the majority.

It is important to remember that Maslow recognizes that the process of transpersonal development results in the person who has experienced the process possessing special charisma. This charisma is reflected in greater leadership skills, which is the treasure that the management of human resources is looking for. The person who seeks transpersonal development isolates themselves relatively and distances themselves partially from others, but returns with new weapons at their disposal that are to the benefit of the organizations that are capable of retaining this meta-talent. Still according to Maslow, those who focus their activity on this circle are those with the greatest capacity for work and leadership. Those who seek to overcome the barrier that the change of state to the third circle requires need a capacity for solitude; and only those who are capable of living through the special isolation that the final circle requires will, with time, develop the qualities of a warrior.

Very few people manage to get to the stage of being completely at home in this third state, but those who do make a qualitative change to the organizations they take part in. Heroes are required who are capable of natural leadership in organizations; people who are willing to give more than they receive, those who have transcended their own personality.

Whilst this level is the most important, it is also the one where companies have the most difficulty in promoting change: what they can do is promote personal development policies and the development of personal skills and competences where they find complementarity in the female and male models, and the different cultural and personality models in the personal development of each individual, as we saw in Part One. However, such personal development must be voluntary and must not be undertaken expecting the short-term results of earlier circles. In the first instance, the company can extend the first two concentric circles, those which allow the individual to be and breathe and, if they want to, to develop themselves and become conscious of their potential. Once they have discovered their potential, they are able to develop their capacity to learn other ways of doing things that are different to theirs, which will in turn lead to them developing new skills and resources for solving problems.

Another thing that companies can do in this third circle is to take full advantage of the drive and capacity for innovation of their most capable members. The creation of a learning organization, in which the organization is capable of capturing the knowledge of all its members, will be the most important tool for managing diversity. The programs that can be developed in this third circle, and the knowledge that can be generated from it, can easily be captured to the benefit of all areas of the organization. Today technology provides us with all we need to develop integrated learning platforms that are capable of acting in all three concentric circles simultaneously; there will be different objectives and rhythms, and different action groups, but all the knowledge generated can be collected into the same system in such a way that it can be of use to all the other members of the organization.

As a result, we would like to conclude this chapter with some notes on training and its importance at the different levels of action.

## Diversity and corporate training

In the 1970s companies in the US began to introduce training programs on diversity. In principle the idea behind this was to establish some simple rules that all employees would be able to follow with regard to the conduct demanded or forbidden by the law at that time. This type of training normally focussed on issues such as sexual harassment or respect for the disabled. From the middle of the 1980s and throughout the 1990s, the majority of training developed to give a more complete perspective on diversity. A survey conducted in 1995 of 50 large American companies showed that 70 percent of them had formal training programs covering the topic of diversity.[26]

Another study into diversity training programs has shown that the majority of such programs focus on individual attitudes, whilst others, which are more complete, incorporate aspects such as individual behavior and human resources policies and systems; however, the most complete of all consist of an effort by all the organization to change the culture in the workplace by using models of organizational development.[27]

---

**Bayer Corporation**

By way of example, we can look at the strategy of the Bayer Corporation, which has implemented a series of training programs on diversity, including:

- **Diversity training programs:** mandatory for all managers, and attendance for nonsupervisory employees varies by division. The executive committee was the first group to attend the two-day training program.

- **A biannual Bayer Diversity Conference on best practices in internal diversity:** best practice is analyzed and shared internally and new strategies are developed for promoting diversity.

- **The sales hiring initiative:** aims to convince managers of the importance of the sales team reflecting the diversity of their clients.

*Source:* http://catalyswomen.org, winner of the Catalyst Prize 2002.

---

The efficiency of training programs and related tools and policies will be much greater if they are applied in a way that is focussed on the level they are aimed at and the objective they are designed to achieve.

At the first social level, the aim is fundamentally to make all personnel sensitive to the vision and mission of the company in the area of diversity. There are currently some interesting developments in internal electronic communication systems that make this type of sensitization campaign much easier to organize. For example, the majority of companies now include company policy statements on social responsibility and news relevant to this sector on their intranet; in addition, they may also include a relevant speech by the company president, news about an award that has been received in this area or a suggestion box for communicating with senior management. This first level of training action is aimed initially at all the members of the organization.

At the second level, that of the organization itself, it is important to bring together the different visions and diversity policies within the company. The aim is to develop training programs that feature interaction and discussion. They are not aimed at the organization as a whole, but only those who are closely affected by a particular issue (diversity councils, work groups and so on). Training courses aimed at the people with the greatest responsibility in the field are especially useful in companies that work in different cultural environments, as in this way it can be observed which diversity policies work in a particular context and which do not and which ideas have been generated about a particular area.

Finally, at the individual level, the aim is to develop training courses for leadership skills and abilities, and, at the deepest level, personal development programs. This latter group of personal development will be the smallest, as it will only benefit those who are really determined to take the development path; these courses will be highly ineffective if attendance is compulsory.

Many types of training have been developed to enable participants to focus on themselves, know their abilities, understand the value of differences and try to apply different ways of understanding reality. The integration of different ways of acting when faced with the same problem enables individuals to have a wider variety of solutions and resources at their disposal to do their job, thus making them more complete and more effective.

## Conclusions

In recent years, companies have developed useful policies for managing diversity. These policies differ, in the same way that the objectives of the different companies differ. The priority for some companies is to establish a good reputation for themselves and so position themselves in the market; in such cases CSR policies are likely to be among their priorities. Other companies, on the other hand, need policies that will enable them to hold on to their brightest talents, particularly at difficult times such as reductions in employment, when it is likely that policies of flexible working patterns will be adopted to help them to meet the needs of their employees. Some companies need to innovate, and in this case they need to develop the individual capacity of employees with the best development potential.

There is no single correct recipe, nor an implementation guide; as needs and opportunities arise, these policies are gradually implemented. The rhythms might be different, as might the visibility of the results. It is not a case of setting out a plan of action with rigid targets to achieve radical change at the three levels of action; rather, it is about beginning a step-by-step journey affecting the three levels, with greater or lesser emphasis on each, which in the long term will lead to the creation of an integrated, continuous learning organization that can act as a whole but made up of well-developed individuals who are capable of creating and innovating.

Society is changing rapidly; the business world gets more global by the day, new groups come into the market and the climate is becoming more competitive. Diversity at all levels of the organization is an imperative that is recognized by the majority of International companies. But at the same time, the ever increasing diversity of the workforce brings with it a whole new set of problems and conflicts that managers in the future will have to be able to solve if they want to create flexible, diversified organizations capable of creating and innovating within a single vision and unique strategy. The challenge for the 21st century manager is to find a balance between diversity and the unity of aims and objectives of the company.

# Section 4

# CASE STUDIES

# Case 1
## JPMorgan Chase & Co in Latin America: The Management of Diversity as a Tool for Developing Human Capital

*JPMorgan Chase has seen first-hand the benefits gained with a corporate culture that's actively inclusive, where colleagues are recognized based on their talent and skills, and where diversity is used as a competitive advantage to benefit from the broadest possible pool of employee talent, experiences and perspectives.*[1]

William B. Harrison Jr., chairman and chief
executive officer, JPMorgan Chase & Co

JPMorgan Chase (JPMC) is among the world's leading financial services companies; it is a Fortune 50 company that focusses on commercial and investment banking. Following the merger of JPMorgan Chase with Bank One in July 2004, the company now has assets of $1.1 billion and operations in more than 50 countries in all the continents and employs over 100,000 people. The company has over 32 million clients in the US. JPMC's headquarters are in New York, whilst its retail and commercial banking head offices are located in Chicago.

Chase Manhattan Corporation's merger with JPMorgan in September 2000 presented the challenge of integrating two gigantic financial operators with very differing cultures. Chase focussed on attracting and retaining a diverse group of people and taking advantage of their experiences, perception and skills. This focus had proved effective when Chase merged with Chemical Bank in 1996, and it was decided to adopt a similar strategy in the merger with JPMorgan, using diversity as a tool for facilitating the integration of the two groups. As a result, diversity has become one of the key strengths of the group.

## JPMC's diversity strategy in the US

JPMC has developed its diversity strategy based on the following definition:

> It's a belief of JPMorgan Chase that everything that makes us unique as individuals makes the firm all that much stronger. Our commitment is to create a working environment for each of us where we can do our best work and that means building a company in which differences are respected and valued.[2]

The company has implemented a range of strategies that affect a large number of areas within the company, including human resources strategy, training, assessment and communication.

## Nondiscrimination policy

The nondiscrimination policy has the objective of creating an inclusive and nondiscriminatory working environment in which all employees are valued and supported:

> An employee or qualified applicant will not be discriminated against because of his or her race, color, national origin or citizenship status, creed, religion, religious affiliation, age, sex, marital status, sexual orientation, gender identity, disability, veteran status or any other protected status.[3]

## Human resources policies

### Recruitment policies

JPMC recruits university and business school students through its entry-level programs. In order to promote diversity in the organization and increase the range of talent available to it, JPMC has established agreements with various colleges and universities, such as those belonging to the HBCU (Historical Black Colleges and Universities), Florida A&M University (Tallahassee), Howard University (Washington DC), Morehouse College (Atlanta), Spelman College (Atlanta) and Chicago State University (Chicago). In this way it is guaranteed access to students from diverse groups.

JPMC has a team dedicated to maintaining a visible presence on each campus to develop strong links with students interested in a career in business.

JPMC also works with other associations, such as the Consortium for Graduate Study in Management[4] and the Robert A. Toigo Foundation,[5] which aim to provide opportunities in the business world to minority groups.

## Internship programs

JPMC makes available various internship programs especially for candidates from ethnic minorities, such as INROADS, which offers students the opportunity to undertake paid internships during the summer. Students also have the opportunity to take part in the Sponsors for Educational Opportunity (SEO)[6] program in the US and Great Britain, which offers the opportunity of work during the summer.

## Workplace life

The objective of these policies is to create a comfortable workplace for all. It is based on three principles: a harassment-free workplace, flexibility and engagement:

- **Harassment-free workplace:** JPMC has a policy of not tolerating harassment, whether it is sexual or any other form of discriminatory harassment.
- **Flexibility:** the company has developed a range of options to increase flexibility in the working day for its employees, which is known as the "flexible solutions toolkit." This packet of options allows employees and managers to examine together the possibilities for making the work schedule flexible in certain posts. Should the request for flexibility be denied, the employee can discuss the request with the human resources department.
- **Engagement:** the engagement of employees is fundamental to JPMC being able to develop these diversity initiatives; but in addition to the engagement from employees, there also needs to be commitment from management, through the Corporate Diversity Council and local diversity councils.

## Employee networking group

Employee networking groups are groups of employees which enable employees to meet and exchange ideas; they enable professional development, the creation of relationships throughout the organization and the strengthening of the culture of diversity within the company. There are 90 groups which represent more than 18,000 employees all over the world. Of the many groups, there are ones for administrative professionals, African-Americans, the disabled, gays, lesbians, bisexuals and transsexuals, Hispanics, Italian-Americans, women and so on.

*Career management*

In its endeavors to get the best from each of its employees, the company has developed programs to guide and develop their professional careers. These include:

- **Mentoring:** there are formal programs developed and implemented by the individual line of business and the company also supports the development of informal mentoring relationships. The objective is to build relationships that will enable all employees to acquire and develop the skills and competences needed to compete in the current business world.
- **Mobility assessment program (MAP):** the MAP is a succession planning system, which enables managers to evaluate and develop their employees, creating an environment where all employees have the same opportunities. The MAP process begins with a group of managers discussing the "promotability" and the level of experience of each employee. The managers inform the employees and they then discuss their objectives and interests.

*Training*

All the company's employees participate in mandatory training courses on diversity. In these training courses the company employs a new technique, known as "learning rooms," where the participants choose between a series of short discussions on a range of topics, such as generational diversity, sexual orientation or religion in the workplace.

The company also provides specific training programs for women, such as the executive leadership program at Smith College, for women with high potential, or the Center for Creative Leadership's "women's leadership program," as well as programs for junior executives such as the Aspen Institute's young executive seminars.

Communication policies

Communication can be studied at two levels, internal and external:

- **Internal:** internal communication takes place through such media as conferences, news bulletins, the intranet and email. The aim is to communicate those behaviors and values that are acceptable and form a part of corporate culture and those which do not.

- **External:** JPMC promotes three awards: the Harlem YMCA-Black Achievers in Industry Award, the National Hispanic Corporate Achievers in Industry Award and the YWCA Salute to Women Achievers Award, all of which promote the development of their relative communities.

## Implementation and assessment

JPMC's diversity strategy is designed by the Corporate Diversity Council, which consists of employees from business areas all over the world and is presided over by the company's CEO. The implementation of strategies is then the responsibility of the local diversity councils. There are three phases to the implementation process (Figure CS1.1).

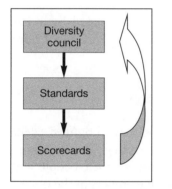

Figure CS1.1 **Diversity management at JPMC**

1. **Diversity councils:** there are more than 60 local diversity councils all over the world. Through these councils, JPMC defines specific diversity issues that are relevant to their workplace and then implements programs and solutions to address those needs.
2. **Standards:** the Corporate Diversity Council sets out criteria and annual objectives on diversity issues, which are collected together into the standards set for each year.
3. **Diversity scorecards:** each of JPMC's business units develops an annual plan to achieve the diversity objectives that have been set. This process leads to the development of a diversity scorecard (DS), which is used to ensure a results-oriented focus. The DS measures the critical points that reflect progress in the area of diversity, such as the opinion of the employees, demographics or leadership activities. The DS gives JPMC a simple means of measuring the results of their initiatives.

Results

The company's experience with this strategy in the US was satisfactory; it survived subsequent mergers and has led to a noticeable increase in the representation of women in the company.[7] As a result, the group decided to expand the program to other regions and in 2002 developed a strategy for Latin America.

# JPMC in Latin America

JPMC has a widespread presence throughout Latin America. In addition to its offices in New York, where it has a team dedicated to Latin America, the company has offices in six countries: Argentina (Buenos Aires), Brazil (São Paulo), Chile (Santiago), Mexico (Mexico City and Monterrey), Peru (Lima) and Venezuela (Caracas).

The company has more than 700 employees, managed by a 19-person human resources team, of whom 6 are in New York and 13 are in the region.

## The design of the strategy for Latin America (2002)

The strategy for Latin America aimed to incorporate the brightest talent into the organization. In order to do this, the strategy defined three major themes: attracting talented people, developing their people and adopting a company culture that would enable all members of the organization to contribute to their full extent.

The objective of the Latin American strategy designed in 2002 was to attract and retain the brightest possible talent, by creating an environment that encouraged innovation, promoted leadership, exceptional performance and guaranteed a meritocracy at all levels.

**Table CS1.1**  JPMorgan Chase diversity strategy in Latin America

| | |
|---|---|
| • **Objective:** to attract and retain best talent | • Themes: |
| | • Attraction |
| | • Development/retention |
| | • Culture/integration |
| • Responsible bodies: | • Priorities: |
| • Regional Leadership Board | • Gender |
| • Country Diversity Councils | • Ethnicity (socio-economic and educational background) |
| | • Work–life balance |
| | • Diversity training and communication |

The strategy focussed on three themes:

1. **Attraction:** implementing recruitment strategies that ensured the inclusion of diversity through agreements with various universities, and the development of procedures to ensure equal opportunity in recruiting.
2. **Development and retention:** monitoring and assessment of inclusive access to professional development programs, such as training, mentoring, coaching and leadership. The development of procedures to ensure inclusive promotion processes such as talent reviews, succession planning as well as engagement with the intermediate levels of management.
3. **Culture/integration:** ensuring the support of senior management for the commitment to diversity through leadership training, work–life balance, quality at work and relations with the community.

Specific **priority areas** were defined for the region:

- **Gender:** the objective was to bring more women into JPMC's structure in Latin America, ensure that they were retained and were geographically mobile. This meant identifying the employees with the highest potential in each business unit and agreeing a development timetable with them and their managers that would meet the employee's aspirations and career objectives, a personal development plan defining their role and responsibilities, assigning them a sponsor and monitoring their progress.

  The intention was to increase the number of women at all levels in the company, establish a pipeline for them to develop their career and ensure their continuous development through career planning and development for each individual.
- **Ethnicity (social/economic/educational background):** the strategy identified four areas: training, recruitment, INROADS and a program of grants:
  - Training – developing a diversity training program for more than 300 employees in the region
  - Recruitment – developing a recruitment process so that in 2003 50 percent of new employees would be recruited from local schools
  - INROADS – a summer internship program in Mexico
  - Providing grants for the neediest students.
- **Work–life balance:** an action plan was developed for 2003–4 based on the data collected in the region from focus groups, surveys and

polls in specific countries and evaluation of the results of the flexibility policies already introduced. In order to promote and diffuse best
practices, a training and development director was appointed to take
advantage of the experience gained in the US and other regions.
• **Diversity training and education:** development of customized diversity training program to be delivered throughout the region. The program developed was designed to inform, increase awareness and provide an opportunity for skill building to all employees.

Country diversity councils in each country and a regional leadership
council were established to pilot the process.

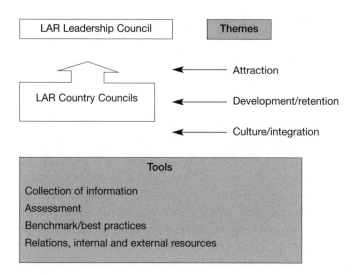

Figure CS1.2 **Diversity management in Latin America**

The regional management committee is chaired by the manager
responsible for the Latin American region (LAR), and consists of the
chairperson of each of the national committees, together with other key
diversity champions in the region.

The country diversity councils consist of managers and employees and
their role is to develop diversity plans for each country, supervise their
implementation, monitor their progress using scorecards and inform the
regional committee of progress.

# Perspectives

JPMC considers its diversity policies to be crucial to the company's performance in the longer term and so accords them a central place in their strategy. As William B. Harrison, the chairman and CEO, said in the 2002 Annual Report:

> Our main resource is the depth and breadth of our intellectual capital in the form of the people who work at JPMorgan Chase.
>
> In the long term, therefore our success rests squarely on their ability to execute-making full and effective use of the tremendous capabilities and talents within the firm.

## Sources:

JPMorgan Chase
- JPMC Annual Report 2002
- JPMC Annual Report 2003
- www.jpmorganchase.com
Interviews with JPMC staff
JPMorgan Chase and Co, Using diversity to forge a new culture: the Chase-
    Chemical merger experience, Catalyst. http://www.catalystwomen.org
UNCF. United Negro College Fund: UNCF Scholars Program, www.uncf.org
SEO. Sponsors for Educational Opportunity, www.seo-ny.org

# Case 2
## Corporate Social Responsibility at Grupo Santander

Jaume Pages, deputy director of Universia, writes this in the introduction to its Annual Report for 2004:

> Universia has received more than 68 million visits to its webpage every month, and has 3.5 million registered users. These figures mean that we are the biggest channel of information for university students in Spanish and Portuguese, in addition to being the best way for our university students to answer their questions about training portals, grants, getting their first job, studying in other countries and so on. We are very pleased with the results for 2004 as they show the important role of collaboration with universities and the support of the Grupo Santander in the project. It is important to highlight the addition of another country to our network; the universities of Uruguay have now joined the significantly increased number of partner universities in the other ten countries.[1]

This Annual Report showed how the launch of Universia was not simply an isolated piece in Grupo Santander's CSR policy, but rather the culmination of committed activity that the company had been involved in practically since it was founded. Emilio Botín, the company's president, had outlined the plan in a speech whilst presenting 70 grants to Latin American students a year earlier:

> Companies should take on a commitment to society that goes further than the search for short term profits ... and by doing so they contribute to the development of the societies that we work in and strengthen our image with investors, employees and clients, all of which will have an impact on the bank's results.[2]

In his speech, Botín justified the bank's social actions as a strategic investment that would benefit the bank in three ways:

- attracting investment capital from investors who use social responsibility criteria in their investment decisions
- attracting clients who are more and more concerned about the social responsibility of the companies with which they work
- attracting and motivating employees who are sensitive to the social impact of the companies where they work.

The Grupo Santander has taken note of all these interest groups and has become an active social agent, meeting the needs and the concerns that exist in society and in the company through a commitment to society and a commitment to diversity.

Grupo Santander is a financial services group built around Spain's Santander Central Hispano bank. As at 31 December 2004, the group's market capitalization was €57,101 million, an increase of 43.6 percent over its value in 2003; it is the fourth most successful bank in the world at creating value for its shareholders.[3] The group has 126,488 employees in around 9,300 offices. It manages the funds of more than 44 million clients, principally in Spain, Great Britain (through its acquisition of the Abbey National bank), Europe and Latin America (where it controls the main banks in Brazil, Mexico, Chile, Puerto Rico and Venezuela, and has a market share of around 10 percent with 23 million clients).

## Grupo Santander's social action programs

Botín's thinking represented a qualitative leap in the traditional under-standing of patronage and social action; involvement in social projects would no longer be considered as a cost, but would become an "invest-ment," and as such decisions should be taken based on strategic consid-erations and be coordinated at the highest executive level. As a result, Botín delegated the creation of a new unit that would be responsible for coordinating the bank's social responsibility plans to Juan Manuel Cendoya, the bank's director general of communication and research. Cendoya was also charged with reporting to the bank's executive committee every three months on progress made by the unit.

Within the communication and research division, José Casas, the group's director of institutional relations, put the project in place and appointed Borja Baselga, who had previously dedicated his career to the business side of the bank's activities, as the director of the new CSR department. Baselga interpreted his new responsibilities as trying to create value through what the group was returning to society through its various initiatives.

## Grupo Santander and corporate social responsibility

The group presented its Strategic Corporate Social Responsibility Plan (Plan Estratégico de Responsabilidad Social Corporativa) in 2002, and since then has accumulated experience that has enabled it to implement and expand its commitments from an overall perspective of sustainabil-ity, as reflected in the following pyramid:[4]

CORPORATE SOCIAL RESPONSIBILITY

ECONOMIC – SOCIAL – ENVIRONMENTAL DIMENSION

CORPORATE GOVERNANCE – TRANSPARENCY – INTANGIBLES

CLIENTS – SHAREHOLDERS – EMPLOYEES – SUPPLIERS – SOCIETY

Grupo Santander's Strategic Corporate Social Responsibility Plan focussed in 2003 on the following measures, which are shown in Table CS2.1:

**Table CS2.1** CSR at SCH

| Santander Universities | Performance 2003 |
| --- | --- |
| Cooperation agreements | Cooperation with 320 academic institutions (universities, associated centers, institutions) in Spain, Portugal and Latin America. |
| | €35.8 million invested in 2003. |
| Universia portal | Brings together 736 Spanish, Portuguese and Latin American universities and institutions. |
| | Connects 8 million students. |
| | €13.1 million invested in 2003. |
| Miguel de Cervantes virtual library | Open access portal featuring more than 12,000 works in Spanish Catalan, Valencian and Galician and Portuguese. |
| **The nine measures** | |
| Adherence to the UN's Global Compact | Internal and external dissemination. |
| | Promoting membership to other companies (291 large companies became members). |
| | Active participation in the United Nations Environment Program Finance Initiative. |
| | Adherence of Chile and Peru. |
| Corporate social responsibility department | Publication of the CSR Plan – awards received from experts. |
| | Inclusion of the SAN share in the FTSE4Good index. |
| | The SAN share continues to be listed in the Dow Jones Sustainability Index. |
| Work/life balance | Optima Program in Spain. |
| | Work and family program, "Working better" in Chile. |
| | Subsidies for nursery schools in Argentina. |
| | Human development program and creation of value in Argentina. |

*cont'd*

| Co-participation of employees | Support for volunteers – Junior Achievement Program (Spain, Brazil, Peru). |
| --- | --- |
| | Creation of the Social Responsibility Fund: Aid for Galicia. |
| | One Roof Program for Chile. |
| Corporate social responsibility training | Initial training: Spain, Portugal and Latin America. |
| Environmental risk analysis | Initial training of managers and analysts. |
| | Analysis of the loan portfolio. |
| Environmental certification at work | ISO certification 14.001 for the headquarters in Chile. |
| Limiting the environmental impact | Approval of the Group's environmental policy. |
| | 3Rs Plan: reduce, reutilize and recycle. |
| Development of social marketing | Contribution in Mexico of one peso per ATM transaction to UNICEF. |
| | One Roof Program for Chile. |

## Commitment to diversity

One highlight among all these actions is the commitment that Grupo Santander has to its almost 127,000 employees to enable, develop and improve their relationship by promoting the balance of professional and family life and active and reciprocal communication. The gender profile of its workforce is almost in balance, with 56.4 percent being men and 43.5 percent being women. It pays particular attention to regulations on discrimination and the protection of ethnic minorities, and it has never been the subject of complaints in these areas. The efforts the company has made to promote equal opportunity have been recognized and endorsed by the Instituto de la Mujer (the Women's Institute).

The Group actively promotes the integration of women into its workforce and the achievement of a work–life balance. As a result, it is participating in the Work and Social Affairs Ministry's Optima Program, which requires the implementation of 29 measures to encourage the integration of women into the workforce. The Group decided to build a nursery (the largest in Spain) at the new Grupo Santander city development in Boadilla del Monte, Madrid, which has space for more than 400 children. It has included other social facilities in its new headquarters development to facilitate the personal development of its employees, for example sports facilities, canteens which have been carefully designed to accommodate diversity and to be welcoming, shops to meet all everyday needs, transport to all parts of the city, accommodation for use during training programs and so on.

This policy is repeated by the Group in all the countries where it operates. In addition, Grupo Santander has developed a program for the inclusion of people with disabilities, and in Puerto Rico it complies with legislation that requires the development of an affirmative action program.

## Clients, shareholders, employees, suppliers and society

Grupo Santander is also aware of the importance of its attitude to clients, shareholders, employees, suppliers and society as providing the fundamental base not only of its business, but also its corporate image with all those who have any relation with it. The Group has clear policies toward these groups, which are summarized in Table CS2.2.

**Table CS2.2**  Stakeholders' policies at SCH

| | |
|---|---|
| Clients (59 million) | A quality plan involving more than 65,000 surveys. |
| | Adhesion to the CNMV's guide to procedures for marketing financial investment products. |
| | Renewal of ISO 9001 global certification for Totta in Portugal. |
| | Santander Banespa Solutions Center in Brazil to centralize all communication with clients. |
| | Santander Santiago's SAC customer service system in Chile. |
| Shareholders (2.26 million) | A 43.6% increase in share price. |
| | The fourth most successful bank in the world in creation of shareholder value. |
| | A dividend of €0.3029 per share, 5 percent higher than the year before. |
| | Strengthening of the communication channels with shareholders. |
| | A letter from the president to the shareholders, and implementation of the action set out in the letter. |
| | Elimination of the requirement to own at least 100 shares in order to attend the AGM. |
| | Adaptation of the corporate website to new guidelines on transparency. |
| | An increase in contact and meetings with shareholders and investors. |
| | New options for exercising rights by telephone or electronically. |
| Employees (103,038) | A letter from the president to all employees. |

| cont'd | |
|---|---|
| | Centralization of personnel administration processes in Spain. |
| | Improvements in assessment of the management group. |
| | Adhesion to the Optima Program in Spain. |
| | Review of evaluation procedures. |
| | Development of the Group executive development plan. |
| | Launch of the International Training City in Grupo Santander City. |
| Suppliers | Incorporation of electronic bidding systems into the purchasing process. |
| | All purchases to be paid in accordance with terms and conditions. |
| | Adherence to the UN's Global Compact reaches 50% of suppliers in Columbia and 75% in Puerto Rico. |
| Society | Santander Universities is the most important and symbolic corporate social responsibility program. |
| | The Group continues to cooperate in cultural, educational and social projects in areas where it operates, such as the Santander Cultural Center in Porto Alegre, Brazil and the cooperation campaigns with the Red Cross and Unicef. |
| | The Group is taking advantage of the move to Grupo Santander City to transform itself into a reference point for CSR. |
| | Dialogue is maintained with key interest groups. |
| The environment | Measurement and control of consumption. |
| | ISO 14001 certification for the headquarters in Chile. |
| | Development of an environmental risk control system. |
| | Publication of the Group's environmental policy. |

Through these actions, Grupo Santander has defined its commitment to diversity and social responsibility and good corporate governance clearly and specifically, integrating it into the development of the organization in a way that from now on will be considered strategic.

## Pending questions

Grupo Santander's decision to integrate and coordinate its CSR programs has created a series of unprecedented management challenges for Cendoya, Casas, Baselga and the rest of the management team. One of these challenges relates to the limits to the group's social actions. The simple announcement of the formation of the CSR department had increased the number of requests for sponsorship by more than 100 percent from social bodies in a wide range of fields. And this led to the question, what indicators should the bank use to assess the profitability of these social investments?

Another important question was related to the way in which the commitment to CSR should be presented. Cendoya and his team were aware that if it was used aggressively in marketing the bank it would be seen as opportunistic and might even be counterproductive. But at the same time, it would be no use to the company if these large investments in social projects were to go unnoticed by public opinion. At the beginning of March 2003, the Group published a full page advert in the national press communicating the success of its Prestige campaign. In November 2004, the Group launched a press, radio and TV campaign in which the organization communicated its support of education and the universities, which led to an extraordinary improvement in its image.

The final issue is internal management. Nearly all CSR projects have implications that have an impact across many functional areas. With around 127,000 employees, any change in the attitudes of the company's workforce represents a major challenge to the introduction of change to the corporate culture. How should initiatives that would affect the internal operations of the bank be planned and managed? How can momentum be maintained to involve the whole of the workforce in internalizing CSR in the value systems of the corporate culture?

# Case 3
## Diversity in Ford Almussafes – An Example of Adaptation

### The vehicle sector – a global industry

The motor vehicle sector has been most affected by globalization. It is a mature industry, with fierce competition and narrow margins that have led companies to search for economies of scale, which has in turn led to a process of concentration such that the industry is now dominated by only a handful of large groups.

According to ANFAC[1], there is global excess of manufacturing capacity in the industry equal to around 20 million vehicles. In North American and Europe, the two regions that generate the majority of revenue and profits in the sector, excess capacity in 2003 was 14 and 17 percent respectively. This excess capacity, together with greater commercial flows, has resulted in strong and persistent pressure on prices, which has had a negative effect on margins and profitability.

As in the rest of Europe, the industry in Spain is faced with strict regulations, heavy taxation, high labor costs, strong pressure from outside competitors, especially Asian countries, and the threat of delocation, which has become particularly strong following the expansion of the EU in May 2004.

Operating in this competitive environment and under great pressure to reduce costs, can diversity management be used to obtain highly necessary competitive advantage?

### Ford Motor Company

Ford Motor Company (FMC) was founded in June 1903 in the US by Henry Ford and eleven partners. Ford's development goes hand in hand with industrial development during the 20th century; Ford introduced a new production model, which came to be known as "Fordist," with the development of the moving production line, which enabled the worker to stay in one position performing the same task over and over on the vehicles that passed them on the production line. This led to enormous increases in productivity which allowed Ford to far surpass the productive capacity and levels of production of its rivals. Henry Ford's initial dream of making the car into a product available to everyone became a reality in 1908 when FMC launched the legendary Model T, which, 19 years on and 15 million cars sold, was to be Ford's most popular car and the highest selling car of all time.[2]

In 2004, FMC was responsible for the following brands: Ford, Lincoln, Mercury, Mazda, Volvo, Jaguar, Land Rover, Aston Martin, Ford Credit, Genuine Parts and Service, Motorcraft and Hertz.

Ford was at this time the second largest producer of cars in the world, being responsible for around 13 percent of total worldwide production, with over 20 percent of the market in the US and around 11 percent of the European market. It had 105 production plants in 38 countries and its products were on sale in more than 200 markets; it had a turnover of more than $160 billion and employed more than 350,000 people.

As Bill Ford, the chairman and CEO, says, FMC's objectives and challenges for the future are to build great products, a strong company and a better world.[3]

FMC's ties to Europe are almost as old as the company itself. In 2004, FMC was the fourth largest vehicle producer in Europe (Table CS3.1).

**Table CS3.1** Principal European motor manufacturers, 2003

| 1 | Volkswagen | 3,498,530 |
|---|---|---|
| 2 | PSA | 3,057,345 |
| 3 | Renault/Nissan | 2,604,742 |
| 4 | Ford | 2,169,173 |
| 5 | General Motors | 1,862,358 |
| 6 | DaimlerChrysler | 1,350,193 |
| 7 | Fiat | 1,327,496 |
| 8 | BMW | 890,927 |
| | Others | 2,268,245 |
| | Total Europe | 19,029,009 |

With its Ford 2000 initiative, FMC merged its American and European operations totally, creating a single global management team, although Ford Europe maintained its own strong identity and personality, designing, developing and manufacturing its own range of vehicles for the 42 markets that it serves.

## Diversity in Ford

## A long "historical legacy"

In 1914 Henry Ford introduced an innovative policy of $5 a day pay for everyone capable of doing the job. Over time, FMC became one of the main employers of choice for African-Americans and immigrants arriving to work in the US, as a result becoming one of the first companies to have a workforce that accurately represented the community that it served.[4]

In recent years Ford has continued to play a leading role in corporate diversity, and has received many prizes as a result.[5] Ford defines diversity as follows:

> Diversity embodies all the differences that make us unique individuals. Not limited to physical aspects of race, ethnicity, gender, age, disability, and sexual orientation, it includes culture, religion, education, experience, opinions, beliefs, language, nationality and more.[6]

The defining characteristic of Ford's diversity policy is its "positive vision." Ford values diversity as:

> we recognize that diversity is not only a reality of our global nature, it's a distinct advantage, and one that we value and embrace. We also know that we can only leverage the benefits of diversity by understanding and respecting the differences among all employees.[7]

## Diversity strategy

FMC designs its diversity policies from a global perspective through its Global Diversity Council, and then filters this through regional and local diversity councils to enable the policies to be adapted to the specific needs of each community.

The diversity councils have the chief responsibility for ensuring communication, awareness raising and transmitting management's commitment to the employees, for example European management produce the monthly *diversity@ford* bulletin.

Ford's diversity strategy has various levels of "adaptation," which feed into each other and which try to mould the general message of the group to local needs and situations.

The final link in the chain consists of the national diversity committees, the function of which, in the words of a member of the diversity committee from the Almussafes plant, is "to create an environment in which everyone feels comfortable and accepted. It aims to create unity, not uniformity."

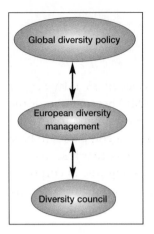

Figure CS3.1 **Diversity management at Ford**

In addition, the diversity committees are responsible for keeping **diversity scorecards** to measure to what extent objectives have been met, to set timetables and evaluate and monitor the initiatives that have been implemented.

FMC has a well-established policy of being an equal opportunity employer; its human resources, monitoring, evaluation and communication policies all aim to promote diversity at the heart of the company.

The human resource policies include the support of the formation of employee resource groups (ERGs), which consist of employees with a shared interest who provide the company with viewpoints from their perspective, enabling the company to understand its consumers better. In addition, by giving its support to the members of a community, aiding their integration and helping to eliminate any barriers that might still remain, they contribute to the professional development of their employees.

The company has also adopted policies aimed at helping employees achieve a balance between professional and private life, such as flexible timetables, teleworking and help with caring for children and elderly relatives. The objective of these policies is to attract and retain the best professionals, increase commitment inside and outside the company, increase productivity and make balance a valuable part of the company culture.

## Assessment systems

FMC monitors and assess the objectives that have been set by using diversity scorecards. It also produces an annual report, the Corporate Citizenship Report, following the criteria and the parameters established in the Global Report Initiative (GRI). These reports include, in addition to quality, safety and environmental parameters, other aspects specific to working conditions, such as respect for human rights, job conditions and satisfaction surveys on the working environment.

## Exporting diversity

Ford tries to export its vision of diversity to other areas in which it works, such as suppliers, distributors and community.

- **Distributors**: Ford has various programs aimed at helping minority groups to manage (minority dealer operations), access to credit (Ford Credit Minority Dealer Programs) and training (Automotive Dealership Education Program for Minorities and the National Automobile Dealers Association Training Program). In addition, it holds seminars for its distributors to analyze how the diversity dimension can influence marketing operations and sales. Ford USA has more than 360 minority distributors, 7 percent of its total number of distributors.
- **Suppliers**: Ford uses its Supplier Diversity Development Office to develop business opportunities for women and minority groups. In 2003 it spent $3,400 million with suppliers belonging to women or minority groups.
- **The community**: Ford uses initiatives such as Mi Negocio (My Business), its portal for Latin American businesspeople, and BEST[8] (Best Business Plan Contest) to try to promote development in the communities where it is based.

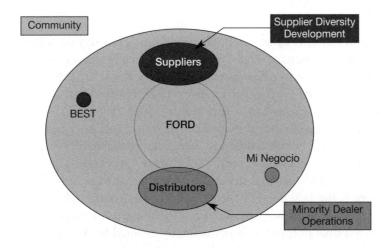

Figure CS3.2 **Stakeholders' policies in Ford's diversity strategy**

# The Ford factory in Valencia, Spain

Ford's factory in Almussafes, Spain is over 30 years old and is one of the most advanced manufacturing plants in Europe. It is capable of the high volume production of four models (the 5-door Fiesta, the 4- and 5-door versions of the Focus, the Ka and the Mazda2) simultaneously, which is the highest number of different models of any Ford plant.

The plant's impact on the economy of the Valencia region has been enormous; it accounts for around 11 percent of the region's GNP, 20 percent of its total exports and around 7 percent of total employment.

The plant's workforce is around 10,000 people, comprising both permanent and temporary workers. The majority of the workforce is permanent, providing a stable workforce with low turnover; in October 2004, more than 6,200 of the plant's employees were permanent. The plant's temporary personnel are employed to cover production needs at specific moments; on average 2,500 people are employed on a temporary basis, although this rises to 3–4,000 at peak periods.

# The Valencian perspective on diversity: different realities, different policies

Ford España's vision of diversity is:

> Diversity is a continuous and participative process at all levels of the organization, which respects, values and promotes the effective use of all the differences, both visible and invisible, of all the women and men who constitute Ford España.[9]

The actions and initiatives that are implemented in Spain should reflect the demographic and social reality of the factory, which in many cases are very different from those in other parts of Europe or the US. As Amparo Rodríguez, president of Ford España's diversity committee states, "it is not about creating problems where they don't exist."

The main challenge of diversity faced by the Valencia factory today is the historic distinction between different categories of employees – those who belong to the "workforce" and "temporary" workers. This is a legacy of the company's original structure, which needs to be solved.

The factory is the base for Ford España's diversity committee, which consists of around 15 members and is chaired by Amparo Rodríguez. The committee has a dual purpose; it is permanently attuned to the opinions of the workforce and communicates these to management, and at the same time it links the company's theorizing about diversity to the reality of the factory, trying to translate Ford's theory into action. As such, it serves as a two-way transmission mechanism between the employees and management (Figure CS3.3).

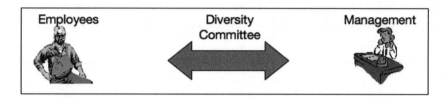

Figure CS3.3 **Diversity dialogue at Ford Almussafes**

The committee consists of employees from all departments of the company who volunteer to take part. It holds monthly meetings to examine the day-to-day operations of the factory and any particular problems or issues that might arise, for example special menus for diabetics.

The committee's objectives are:

1. To develop and maintain a "diversity website" on the company intranet, dedicated to the communication and monitoring of initiatives that have been implemented.
2. To carry out diversity and work–life surveys.
3. To hold focus groups and refreshment sessions.
4. To train group heads and managers in the issues of diversity.
5. To hold regular workshops and give presentations for minority associations.
6. To develop social activities and encourage work–life balance.

In addition to these regular activities, the diversity committee manages the following:

- **European Diversity Week:** a week dedicated to raising awareness of the workforce to diversity issues throughout Ford Europe. During the week, there are conferences, discussions, meetings and other activities aimed at promoting diversity, knowledge and respect for other realities.
- **Ford ¡Ahora! (Ford now!):** an internal communication tool for communicating the initiatives that are taking place.
- **Fund raising:** campaigns aimed at raising money for worthy causes from time to time.
- **Other activities:** for example organizing a wheelchair tennis championship.

All these activities are planned and monitored according to a master schedule for the year, which sets out objectives, results and responsibility.

The work of Ford España's diversity committee has been recognized on many occasions. It has been a candidate for Ford Europe's prize for the best initiative for promoting diversity on several occasions, and came third in 2002. In addition, the company has also received recognition for the work of its employees in the Valencia factory on an individual basis.[10]

# Epilogue

## Ten Concrete Questions for Global Reflection

1      Gracia Cardador, director of *Actualidad Económica* (Economic News), Spain

2      Amparo Moraleda, general manager, IBM Spain, Portugal, Greece, Israel and Turkey

3      Rachid Slimi, president of the ONA Foundation and director of general affairs and corporate relations for ONA Group, Morocco

4      Marianne C. Toldalagi, vice-president of the IE Fund, New York

5      Luiza Helena Trajano Inàcio, general director *Magazine Luiza* Network, São Paulo, Brazil

6      Arpad von Lazar, member of the International Advisory Board of the Instituto de Empresa, Madrid, and emeritus professor at the Fletcher School of Law and Diplomacy, Boston, USA

# 1

# Gracia Cardador

## Director of *Actualidad Económica* (Economic News), Spain

Gracia Cardador has a degree in Journalism from Madrid's Complutense University and a Masters in Management Development from the IESE Business School in Madrid, Spain. She began her career working for the Televisión Española TV company and joined the Grupo Recoletos media company in 1989 as a journalist for *Actualidad Económica*. In 1996 she joined the editorial team of the *Expansión* daily business newspaper and since then has undertaken various roles within the group. In 2000 she was appointed as director of contents of the Argentinean daily business newspaper *El Cronista*, which also belongs to the Recoletos group, and she was actively involved in overhauling its design and relaunching it. She also took on responsibility for the magazines *Apertura* and *Information Technology*. Since January 2003, she has been editor-in-chief of *Expansión,* with additional responsibilities for overseeing the process of editorial coordination and integration of all the Recoletos group's business information services: the daily newspaper *Expansión*, Expansion.com, Expansion TV and *Actualidad Económica*. Since 2004 she has been editor of *Actualidad Económica*.

## 1 ¿Qué entiende por diversidad?

Enriquecimiento. Intercambio de culturas, razas, religiones y géneros. Caracteres que tienen distintas opiniones y visiones del entorno. El futuro.

## 2 ¿Cree que la diversidad es uno de los rasgos que mejor define nuestra sociedad actual?

El crecimiento de la sociedad española en los últimos años ha venido de la mano de la diversidad. Sin embargo, esa realidad social no se ha reflejado en las empresas ni en las instituciones. Queda un largo camino por recorrer, pero se están dando algunos pasos. En los últimos años se ha producido una apertura de la sociedad motivada por la globalización y el intercambio informativo en tiempo real de acontecimientos acaecidos en cualquier lugar del mundo. Pero esto no se manifiesta en nuestro comportamiento diario. Todavía estamos a años luz de incorporar con naturalidad a los inmigrantes en nuestro entorno social y a las mujeres, en los puestos directivos. Por no hablar de la intolerancia ante ciertas religiones o razas y de la escasa sensibilidad hacia las personas con discapacidades físicas o mentales.

*3 ¿Cuáles son las principales barreras de nuestro tiempo para poder aprovechar la diversidad?*

Toda clase de ismos: machismo, feminismo, clasismo, racismo e inmovilismo. Las barreras se producen por el miedo a lo desconocido, la comodidad (es más fácil entenderte con los que piensan como tú), los prejuicios, la concentración de poder, las normas anticuadas, la falta de estímulos de las empresas y las administraciones. Y sobre todo por rutina, siempre se han hecho las cosas de una manera que ha funcionado. Entonces, surge la pregunta de siempre: ¿para qué cambiar?

*4 ¿Deben revisarse las grandes cuestiones de gestión empresarial en razón de la diversidad?*

Rotundamente sí. Estamos desaprovechando el talento y perdiendo oportunidades para ser más competitivos. No podemos olvidar que compartimos un mundo globalizado con rivales y mercados muy diversos. Lo lógico sería que se organizaran las estructuras y se eligieran a los gestores empresariales de acuerdo con su capacidad de respuesta a las singularidades de cada producto y cada mercado.

*5 ¿Cuáles son las principales aportaciones de la diversidad?*

La diversidad aporta creatividad. Otros estilos y otras formas de comprender la realidad y actuar sobre ella.

*6 ¿Empresas e instituciones están aprovechando esas aportaciones?*

Creo que en nuestra sociedad se ha instalado una cierta inquietud por analizar las ventajas que la diversidad de gentes puede aportar. No obstante, las empresas y las instituciones se encuentran muy lejos de sacar partido de ello.

Nos encontramos ante la generación de directivos más preparados y cosmopolitas de la historia. Considero que esta circunstancia permitirá en poco tiempo cambiar la cultura y el funcionamiento de las empresas.

*7 ¿Qué políticas deberían hacer empresas e instituciones para poder rentabilizar esas aportaciones que propone la diversidad?*

En los procesos de selección o de ascenso premiar el talento y los resultados por encima de cualquier condición física o ideológica. A veces, y para acelerar los procesos, las empresas podrían implantar medidas que favorezcan el flujo e intercambio del conocimiento de todas las filiales y mercados en los que está presente.

También habría que fomentar la responsabilidad social corporativa para que las empresas y las instituciones impulsen el desarrollo social y protejan a los más desfavorecidos, como la incorporación al trabajo a los disminuidos psíquicos y físicos.

*8 ¿Cuáles son los principales desafíos y retos a los que se enfrentan en la aplicación de las políticas de diversidad?*

Aprender a gestionar esa diversidad para lo que se necesitan líderes convencidos y con capacidad para superar las dificultades de estos cambios sociales. Premiar el talento sin caer en demagogias que en lugar de ayudar, retrasan estos procesos.

Establecer un marco político que anime a las empresas a fomentar la variedad de sus integrantes y la riqueza cultural e ideológica.

*9 ¿Cuál es la tendencia que considera va a seguir su empresa en gestión de la diversidad?*

Una compañía especializada en comunicación tiene que estar atenta a todos los cambios que se producen en la sociedad. Con las ventajas que ofrece la globalización como telón de fondo, nuestra vocación es estar atentos a la diversidad y enriquecimiento social que se produzca en España y fuera de nuestras fronteras. Aprovecharemos las oportunidades que ofrece un medio de comunicación para fomentar y divulgar las bondades del buen entendimiento de las diferentes razas, culturas y religiones, con el fin de impulsar el desarrollo de nuestras empresas y nuestro entorno.

*10 ¿Cómo serán las empresas del futuro?*

Sobrevivirán aquellas que hagan de la diversidad una ventaja competitiva que les permita crecer tanto geográficamente como mediante la gestión del conocimiento. El proceso globalizador es imparable. La sociedad es cada vez más plural. Sólo aquellas empresas que acepten y reflejen esa pluralidad en sus estructuras estarán preparadas para satisfacer a sus clientes y favorecer el desarrollo social.

# 2
# Amparo Moraleda

## General manager, IBM Spain, Portugal, Greece, Israel and Turkey

Amparo Moraleda Martínez studied Industrial Engineering at the ICAI (Universidad Pontificia de Comillas) University in Madrid and then took a Masters in Business Administration at the IESE business school.

Amparo Moraleda's career has been linked to IBM since 1988, when she joined the company as a systems engineer. Subsequently, she went on to undertake various management roles within the company in Spain and Europe, including being responsible for corporate development for the IBM group in Spain, the management of human resources for the service division IBM Global Services in Europe, the Middle East and Africa.

In 1997 she was named general manager, INSA, Ingeniería de Software Avanzado SA (Advanced Software Engineering PLC), of which IBM owns a 49 percent share and which specializes in providing professional IT services.

Prior to her current position, which she took in July 2001, Amparo Moraleda was worldwide vice-president of technological integration services, based in the US, and before that she was executive assistant to Louis V. Gerstner, the president of IBM Corporation at the time; from this time on she has been involved in the company's strategic decision making, with particular focus on Europe, Latin America and the Asia-Pacific area.

Ms. Moraleda is a member of various committees, which include:

- Vice-president of the Círculo de Empresarios (Businesspeople's forum)
- Member of the Advisory Council of the Confederación Española de Organizaciones Empresariales (Spanish Federation of Business Organizations)
- Member of the board of trustees of the La Caixa Bank Foundation
- Member of the managing body of the Fundación Real Academia Española (the Spanish Royal Academy Foundation)
- Member of the managing body of Madrid's Autónoma University
- Member of the advisory council of Catalyst, the nonprofit making body designed to promote the advancement of women in business and professional spheres.

Among the prizes and awards she has won, there are the 2002 prize for excellence from the Federación Expañola de Mujeres Directivas, Ejecutivas, Profesionales y Empresarias (Fedepe – the Spanish Federation of Women Directors, Executives, Professional and Businesspeople); the Golden Master from the Forum de Alta Dirección (the Senior Managers' Forum) in 2003, and the ninth Javier Benjumea prize, awarded every year by the ICAI Association of Engineers, which recognizes engineering professionals who are outstanding as a result of their prestige or career profile.

In 2005, Amparo Moraleda was inducted to the Women in Technology International Hall of Fame, considered one of the most prestigious award honoring women in the science and technology fields.

## 1 ¿Qué entiende por diversidad?

Dentro del ámbito de la empresa, diversidad implica crear un entorno en el que todas las sensibilidades y diferencias sean no sólo respetadas, sino bienvenidas (desde la convicción de que aportan valor a la empresa, a sus clientes y a la sociedad) y donde los únicos factores que cuentan para valorar a un profesional tienen exclusiva relación con su rendimiento en el trabajo, su talento y su aportación al proyecto de la empresa.

## 2 ¿Cree que la diversidad es uno de los rasgos que mejor define nuestra sociedad actual?

Es evidente que vivimos en un mundo cada vez más abierto, global e interrelacionado. Como todo proceso de esta magnitud y complejidad, en la globalización conviven fuerzas aparentemente contrapuestas y, por eso, lejos de ser un triunfo de la homogeneización y de la visión única del mundo, estamos en un tiempo que se está construyendo más como un mosaico de sensibilidades y desde la convergencia de perspectivas de diferentes grupos y comunidades. En ese mundo, la diversidad, en todas sus dimensiones, describe y explica mucho mejor la realidad en la que estamos.

## 3 ¿Cuáles son las principales barreras de nuestro tiempo para poder aprovechar la diversidad?

Sin duda, las que no se pueden derribar únicamente mediante normas. Entender la diversidad (no ya sólo como algo a respetar, sino como algo a fomentar y valorar), exige, sobre todo, actitudes y posiciones culturales y emocionales abiertas y positivas frente a lo diferente. Cuando se analiza, por ejemplo, las principales barreras al avance de la mujer dentro de la empresa, los obstáculos más persistentes y difíciles de vencer tienen que ver con el ámbito de los prejuicios, las falsas ideas preconcebidas y el inmovilismo de determinados "estados de opinión" dominantes.

## 4 ¿Deben revisarse las grandes cuestiones de gestión empresarial en razón de la diversidad?

Creo que las empresas que quieran prosperar y tener futuro deben estar en un permanente proceso de revisión de sí mismas, incluyendo a las "grandes cuestiones" y que la diversidad debe ser un factor muy importante en la conformación de la cultura de una organización. Las empresas sólidas deben basar esa continua revisión de su modo de hacer en una razonable estabilidad de su modo de ser, para que los cambios no sean circunstanciales, sino que arraiguen con la profundidad necesaria. La promoción de la diversidad en una empresa como IBM, por ejemplo, sería impensable en su nivel actual sin una coherencia con unos valores lo suficientemente consolidados dentro de la organización y sin estar fundamentada en una evolución histórica claramente favorable a la inclusión.

## 5 ¿Cuáles son las principales aportaciones de la diversidad?

Además de los evidentes valores de equidad, inclusión e igualdad de oportunidades que aporta a una organización, creo que la diversidad ayuda a la empresa a algo tan importante como dotarse de la variedad de talento y de perspectivas necesarias para ponerse en sintonía con la realidad del mundo al que se dirige y entender mejor la realidad, expectativas y formas de ser de los diferentes colectivos con los que interactúa. Una empresa que promueve la diversidad va a estar mucho más cerca de los clientes a los que atiende, de los potenciales profesionales a lo que quiere atraer y, en definitiva, de la sociedad en la que opera. Siempre es más fácil relacionarte y hacer negocios con alguien con el que te sientes más identificado y próximo. Es un poderoso caso de coherencia entre sensibilidad y responsabilidad empresarial, por un lado, y valor de negocio, por otro.

## 6 ¿Empresas e instituciones están aprovechando esas aportaciones?

Cada vez hay más conciencia del sentido que tiene ponerse del lado de la diversidad y creo que es un valor en alza, que se está incorporando en unos casos y reforzándose en otros dentro de las agendas de las organizaciones más avanzadas.

**7 ¿Qué políticas deberían hacer empresas e instituciones para poder rentabilizar esas aportaciones que propone la diversidad?**

En mi opinión, más allá de las políticas concretas, lo más importante es la coherencia entre lo que se dice y lo que se hace, la constancia en llevar a la práctica las iniciativas favorecedoras de la diversidad y poner las condiciones necesarias para que la inclusión acabe convirtiéndose en una actitud connatural a la organización y no en algo forzado. Como he dicho anteriormente, la clave para que la diversidad se convierta no sólo en algo razonable y "políticamente correcto," sino en algo verdaderamente enriquecedor para la organización y la sociedad es pasar del respeto pasivo por lo diferente a su potenciación activa como fuente generadora de valor.

**8 ¿Cuáles son los principales desafíos y retos a los que se enfrentan en la aplicación de las políticas de diversidad?**

Al final la diversidad tiene que ver, fundamentalmente, con la relación cotidiana entre personas y, como tal, contiene toda la complejidad y variedad de matices que caracterizan a todo lo esencialmente humano. Por eso insisto en que lo más difícil es conseguir dentro de la organización la mentalidad adecuada, deshacer los prejuicios y construir el tipo de cultura necesaria para que la diversidad se asiente.

**9 ¿Cuál es la tendencia que considera va a seguir su empresa en gestión de la diversidad?**

Para una empresa con la tradición, los valores y la dimensión global de IBM, posiblemente el reto más importante es mantenernos alerta, activos y en continua revitalización de lo que significa e implica la diversidad. Nuestra política, por ejemplo, de pagar un mismo salario por un mismo trabajo, sin discriminaciones por razones de sexo, raza o religión, data de 1935; es decir, 28 años antes de que se promulgara una ley en Estados Unidos en ese mismo sentido. Pretendemos seguir siendo capaces de entender las realidades sociales de cada momento y darles respuesta dentro de nuestro ámbito de actuación con la mayor anticipación, intensidad y celeridad posibles.

**10 ¿Cómo serán las empresas del futuro?**

Creo que las empresas que quieran tener futuro deberán reflejar y responder a las expectativas y realidades de la sociedad del futuro, estar a la altura de las circunstancias de su tiempo. Estoy entre quienes piensan que las empresas juegan un lugar cada vez más importante en la conformación de los valores de una sociedad y que su responsabilidad en ese sentido aumenta día a día. De manera recíproca, creo que la sociedad (los clientes, los socios comerciales, los ciudadanos, los empleados) van a valorar de manera creciente a las empresas en función de sus comportamientos, actitudes y compromisos, como ámbitos indisociables de la operativa del negocio. En ese sentido, estoy convencida de que la diversidad va a ser un rasgo característico de las empresas del futuro.

# 3
# Rachid Slimi

## President of the ONA Foundation and director of general affairs and corporate relations for ONA Group, Morocco

Rachid Slimi graduated from the Public Management Institute of George Washington University, Washington DC, has a Masters in Political Science and Public Finance from Mohamed V University in Rabat. Mr. Slimi has developed his career in finance and management in different roles, including equity analyst for La Banque Commerciale du Maroc, advisor to the minister of finance in Rabat, head of the cabinet of the minister of education in Rabat, director of the OCP (Office Chérifien des Phosphates) in Casablanca, vice-president of development and communication of the Al Akhawayn University in Ifrane and executive director for strategy and development of the CDG (Caisse de Dépôt et de Gestion).

Rachid Slimi serves on the management boards of several Moroccan and international companies. He is an advisor to the World Bank Institute, was appointed a member of the official jury in the "Nature's Wisdom Award" in Aichi, Japan in 2005, is a member of the Denmark-Canada initiative for security regional cooperation and has been nominated as "Young Global Leader" at the World Economic Forum of Davos.

### 1 Qu'entendez-vous par diversité?

La diversité réfère aux différences des individus, que ce soit dans leurs systèmes de valeurs, leurs styles de vie, leurs origines culturelles, leurs traditions ou leurs croyances. C'est cette pluralité qui constitue la réalité sociale d'un monde hétérogène. Toutefois, la diversité doit permettre l'adhésion à un ensemble de valeurs communes qui peuvent être approchées de différentes façons et à partir d'angles différents.

J'ai une vision très pragmatique de la diversité dans le sens où plusieurs idées interagissent, convergent, complètent les unes les autres et viennent constituer ou compléter un puzzle.

*2 Pensez-vous que la diversité est devenue un principe caractéristique de la société d'aujourd'hui?*

Certainement oui et l'histoire elle-même l'a démontré à travers les courants culturels et sociétaux. Depuis la fin de la guerre froide, nous avons pu être témoin de l'émergence d'identités et de cultures spécifiques, dès lors réduisant l'impact du monde bipolaire. Aujourd'hui, les sociétés adhèrent de plus en plus au libéralisme, qu'il soit économique, culturel ou encore social. La diversité est devenue aujourd'hui une réalité qui a besoin d'être prise en considération et les tendances actuelles évoluent vers des dimensions économiques, culturelles, sociales et religieuses encore plus diversifiées.

Aujourd'hui, de nouveaux sujets de débat voient le jour, notamment celui de l'égalité des sexes ; un sujet qui anime les débats les plus polémiques. La composition des ressources humaines continuera à évoluer puisque nous voyons de plus en plus de représentation des femmes à tous les niveaux des organizations et une composition plus diverse de l'effectif du personnel dans le cadre professionnel.

*3 Quels sont selon vous les obstacles majeurs qui nous empêchent de mettre à profit les avantages de la diversité?*

Je pense que c'est principalement l'appréhension des différences entre les individus qui constitue un obstacle majeur. Des efforts doivent être faits dans ce sens partant de l'éducation. L'éducation devrait être plus orientée vers l'ouverture d'esprit, le cosmopolitanisme et l'acceptation des différences. Même en terme de religion, son évolution, son interprétation et ses pratiques, l'acceptation des différences est cruciale pour son accomplissement.

*4 Les pratiques du management en entreprise devraient-elles être repensées en raison de la diversité culturelle qui existe?*

C'est un impératif aujourd'hui dans le monde du travail et des affaires. La globalization et ses conséquences en termes de profitabilité économique et financière, et de développement sociétal dans son acceptation la plus grande, incitera les entreprises à intégrer la diversité dans leurs activités, leurs marchés et leur capital humain. Nous pouvons également voir l'impact de la diversité à travers les processus de négociation. Pour opérer au-delà des frontières nationales, il est devenu fondamental de comprendre la culture et les pratiques du pays dans lequel l'entreprise entend opérer.

## 5 Quels sont selon vous les avantages majeurs qu'apporte la diversité?

C'est avant tout de comprendre et accepter les autres pour pouvoir avancer ensemble. Dans un environnement où l'individualisme triomphe, nous avons besoin de la dynamique de l'intelligence collective à travers ses particularités et sa diversité pour avancer positivement. La diversité dans les styles et les approches du management est devenue essentielle pour être compétitif sur le marché international.

La richesse dans les processus décisionnels ne peut provenir que dans un contexte où sont réunis des talents diversifiés. C'est en travaillant avec un personnel diversifié que l'on peut rechercher des solutions constructives qui maintiennent l'organization en mouvement et contribuent à son développement. Chaque culture possède ses spécificités et ses richesses, mais qui sont bien souvent mal interprétées par les autres. A ce propos, la diversité représente justement l'opportunité pour donner lieu à des interactions et exposer ces richesses et les comprendre.

## 6 Les entreprises et les institutions mettent-elles ces avantages à profit?

Non parce que le processus n'est pas complet; c'est encore en progrès, cela s'explique notamment par la disparition de certaines barrières comme la langue dans certains pays exotiques tel que le Japon. Nous pouvons le voir également à travers les séminaires qui sont organizés à travers le monde. Par exemple, celui de Davos dont l'organization se tenait régulièrement en Suisse, et qui est aujourd'hui organizé à un niveau régional.

## 7 Quelles mesures les entreprises et institutions devraient-elles adopter pour capitaliser les avantages qu'apporte la diversité?

D'une part, du point de vue de la gestion des ressources humaines, les entreprises devraient témoigner d'une ouverture croissante vis-à-vis du recrutement de compétences et de talents d'origine étrangère. La condition de base d'une politique de diversité est le recrutement et l'évaluation des compétences, non plus sur la base de critères tels que l'âge, la couleur de peau, la nationalité, la religion, ou le sexe, mais plutôt sur la base d'aptitudes, de qualifications, de mérite et de potentiel des individus à créer de la valeur ajoutée en entreprise.

D'autre part, les entreprises doivent effectuer des benchmarkings et particulièrement pour celles qui opèrent à l'international. Cela permettrait aux entreprises d'adopter des pratiques reconnues (« world class business practices »).

Par ailleurs, la diversité concerne tous les niveaux hiérarchiques. Ainsi, même la composition des conseils d'administration des institutions doit être représentative et diversifiée.

**8 Quels sont selon vous les défis auxquels les entreprises devraient faire face en inscrivant la diversité dans leur politique de ressources humaines?**

C'est principalement en recherchant la croissance et en donnant un sens concret à la globalization qui est souvent répétée et galvanisée. Le défi est d'intégrer et aligner les cultures pour faire en sorte que les différents talents œuvrent pour l'intérêt de l'entreprise. C'est la même logique pour les activités et les opérations d'une entreprise. C'est aussi le cas dans le cadre des risques entrepris lors d'une capitalization dans les marchés boursiers étrangers.

**9 Quelle approche de la diversité ferait votre entreprise?**

Notre approche s'inscrirait dans la même logique citée précédemment.

**10 Comment seraient selon vous les entreprises de demain?**

Le monde des entreprises continuera à évoluer à un rythme de croisière et le concept du « global village » se répandra davantage. Le courant des entreprises virtuelles se multiplie mais je ne dirais pas que les entreprises de demain deviendraient complètement virtuelles. L'aspect humain est crucial et très important. J'imaginerais bien les entreprises futures adopter une politique de gestion du capital humain basé sur le mérite et exploiter les différences comme une source de créativité et une plus-value économique; simplement de la même manière que les synergies génèrent la croissance et les opérations se délocalisent. C'est devenu la pratique dans le monde des affaires: diversifier vos ressources, diversifier vos activités et vos opérations, le tout étant basé sur le concept de l'avantage compétitif.

# 4

# Marianne C. Toldalagi

Vice-president of the IE Fund, New York.
Former senior vice-president and general
manager of consumer travel for American
Express in the US

Marianne C. Toldalagi was a senior executive at some of the top international travel companies. At American Express from 1994 through 1998, she was senior vice-president and general manager of the consumer travel division. At Thomas Cook Travel from 1989 to 1994, she was senior vice-president and executive vice-president. In her previous tenure in the travel industry, she was an executive at Crimson Travel, a founding member of the Travel Business Round-table, where she chaired its policy committee in 1998, and served on the board of Thomas Cook Travel, USA.

She is now an independent investor, board member and senior advisor in new ventures.

She was on the board of directors of Tripadvisor, Inc., a highly successful travel internet venture. At Kidrobot, Inc., a company that specializes in developing, manufacturing and distributing unique toys and characters, she was an investor, active advisor and board member. She is now partnering in the launch of a new venture in the financial services area, Business Technology Associates.

She has been a member of the Instituto de Empresa's International Advisory Board since 1993 and is vice-president of the IE Fund in the US.

*1 What do you understand by diversity?*

Successfully managing a workforce that integrates different value systems, cultures, communication styles, and operating modes.

*2 Do you think that diversity is one of the most defining characteristics of today's society?*

No, I personally don't relate to a single-issue approach to problems. I believe that the challenges and opportunities presented by a diverse workforce are just one small layer in the fundamental issues that impact society and our direction for the future.

### 3 What are the main obstacles in our times that prevent us from taking full advantage of diversity?

The issues that affect the outcomes for the initiatives that are commonly labelled as "diversity" are extremely complex. There are no common accepted methods of measuring success and consequently, no understanding of which path to go down.

Rather than looking at it as an "obstacle," we have to understand the issues first and define what outcomes we are trying to create.

Some of the issues to look at include our values as a society as a whole, leadership styles and skills, business structure and success measurements, and individual choices of what it means to succeed.

If we look at the issues for women, huge progress was made by changing the laws and regulations. Through the incredible effort and determination of many very courageous people, the playing field was levelled from the legal and structural point of view.

This foundation led to many groundbreaking initiatives in corporations with an incredible focus on "diversity." Many value statements were written underscoring corporate commitment; new policies and procedures were written and implemented.

What is the outcome? Should these policies be labeled as failures or are we in fact seeing slow, almost evolutionary progress that needs the span of more time to be evaluated?

I like to look at things from the perspective of results.

One outcome certainly should be more women in top leadership roles. Has it happened in a significant way? While there are some important exceptions, my impression is that women are not in the top power positions in corporate America. I don't see a strong pipeline of future leaders, either.

Do we really understand why this is happening and what can or should be done to measurably change the landscape? My point is that we cannot address this situation simply by defining it as a diversity issue. If that were enough, than we should have seen better results already in the US.

While a great deal has been said about how that balance of leadership styles – the broadly accepted "feminine" and "masculine" traits – add value to the fabric of an organization, I believe that strong leaders in an organization have many more common leadership traits. To succeed and thrive in today's business culture, successful leaders – male or female – need to be aggressive, determined, risk takers, visionaries and driven by a strong sense of purpose.

In fact, quite often, women who have fought their way to the top tiers are not interested in being identified with "women's issues." It denigrates their accomplishment and certainly the perception of their power.

So why aren't more women willing to play in these ranks, even when they have the opportunity? Of course, we also have to consider that despite all the window dressing of diversity focus, a large number of women do not have the opportunity for lots of reasons that go beyond the corporate structure to be effective players.

### 4 Should major business management issues be rethought because of diversity?

Business management issues are most likely to succeed if they are market-driven. While to the credit of the leadership in many corporations in which there is a focus on the "right thing to do," ultimately a corporation's success or failure is measured by a tangible set of success criteria, foremost by financial performance. Therefore, if new initiatives support these goals and are in alignment with the measures of success, those initiatives have a much greater chance to be fully integrated into the fabric of the organization.

### 5 What are the main advantages of diversity?

A diverse workforce brings different skills sets to bear, which fosters a more creative approach to creating new products or solving problems. It should also translate into a much broader sensitivity to marketplace needs. Companies can tap the advantages of a broader, potentially more talented workforce.

### 6 Are companies and institutions reaping the full benefits of these advantages?

The question for me is to understand whether the already existing initiatives have led to greater success. Are the results measurable in terms of the performance of the company? Is the employee population more satisfied? Do the employees take greater pride in their workplace?

I don't believe that we have a really diverse workplace, so I don't really see measurable results.

*7 What policies should companies and institutions adopt to*
*leverage the advantages that diversity brings?*

I am very negative about more rules and regulations as the avenue to
leverage diversity.

I think institutions and business should continually assess and challenge the underlying causes and foster initiatives that can impact on a
more fundamental level – education, leadership skills, understanding the
work/family conflict and so on.

*8 What are the main challenges that companies face when applying*
*diversity policies?*

Some of the challenges include the following:

Leadership skills – many leaders don't understand the conflicts some
of their employees might be experiencing and can't help mentor or
counsel effectively.

Conflicts among employee groups – sometimes policies are not
"bought into" by the broader population and thus can be undermined
in many subtle ways.

Comfort zone – many management people like to surround themselves with people with whom they are comfortable. They make choices
that reflect their own values and ways of approaching situations. It
requires an extremely sophisticated management skill to effectively integrate a diverse workforce and make it work as a coherent team. I don't
see business schools or leadership training programs creating a new
generation of leaders with the requisite skills or sophistication.

Costs – are the diversity initiatives viewed as costly? If so, policies
might be only half-heartedly implemented as soon as there are financial
or marketplace pressures.

Frustration of employees – many employees don't see opportunities
for themselves. What is the success for an individual and how can an
environment be fostered in which more people share in the sense of
success? Not everyone can be CEO – the definition of success needs to
be broader. Companies need to reinforce the message and substantiate it
in real ways so that all employees have dignity and a full sense of their
own worth and contribution.

*9 What trend do you think your company will follow where diversity*
*is concerned?*

Not applicable.

Sheffield Hallam University
Adsetts Centre (2)

Issue receipt

Title: Managing the flexible workforce / Richard
Pettinger.
ID: 1017120811
**Due: 14-03-11**

Title: Diversity at work / edited by Arthur P.
Brief.
ID: 1018944923
**Due: 14-03-11**

Title: Managing diversity in the global
organisation : creating new business values /
Celia De Anca and Ant
ID: 1018225528
**Due: 14-03-11**

Total items: 3
05/03/2011 04:42 PM

Don't forget to renew items online at
http://catalogue.shu.ac.uk/patroninfo or
telephone 0114 225 2116

*10 What will the business corporations of the future be like?*

I believe that there are no signs at this juncture to indicate any fundamental changes. I don't see huge changes in how business is structured or how it operates. I think it would be more effective to think of solutions in different terms. Let us accept the fact that business structures aren't going to change. Now, what do we do?

# 5

# Luiza Helena Trajano Inàcio

General director *Magazine Luiza* Network, São Paulo, Brazil

Luiza Helena Trajano was born in Franca, São Paulo; she is married and a mother of three. She began working for *Magazine Luiza* at the age of 12, when she decided to give up her holidays to work. As she enjoyed the experience, she repeated it in subsequent years, and within a few years began to work full time for the company, progressing through all the departments of the group, including accountancy, management, sales and sales management; in 1991, when a holding company was created, she was appointed director general. She is trained in law and business administration and has been responsible for the rapid growth of the company; under her management, the company has grown from a network of 37 outlets in 1991 to 175 outlets, with revenue of 920 million Brazilian reales in 2003.

*Magazine Luiza* has been operating since 1957 and currently employs 4,400 people in 234 locations; it is considered one of the best business networks in the country. The company was chosen as the "Best place to work in Brazil" in 2003 and 2004, and has also won an award for being the "Most admired" company in the e-commerce sector in a survey undertaken jointly by *Carta-Capital* and *Interscience* magazines.

Among the numerous awards she has received, Luiza Helena Trajano was awarded the Antônio Proost Rodovalho prize in November 2001 by the Federation of Sales Associations of the State of São Paulo, and was the first woman to receive this prize. In 2003 she received the "Award for Executive Value", which recognizes executives who obtain the best results in their sector in a particular year. She won the Claudia Award 2003 in the business category and was named "Sectorial Business Leader" at the Gaceta Mercantil leaders' forum in the same year.

In 2003, peers paid homage to her at the International Women's Day held by the city of Franca'a Chamber of Commerce, where she was awarded the title of "Citizen Emeritus"; and in March of that year she won the "Businesswoman of the Year" prize and in 2004 the "Business Merit" prize, which is considered to be the Oscar of Brazilian business life. In April 2004 she was awarded the "Emeritus Adminitrator 2003" prize by the São Paulo Regional Administration Council, again being the first woman to win this award, which recognizes the ethical behavior, leadership capabilities and contribution to business excellence of the winner. She is one of the founders of the citizens' group "NGO – Franca Viva" in her hometown of Franca.

## 1 O que entende por diversidade?

Entendo por diversidade as diferentes características das culturas, povos, etnias, sexo, indivíduos, que compõem nossa sociedade. O próprio nome "sociedade" já é uma junção de muitas características, e engloba o conceito de diversidade. Somos uma miscigenação de costumes, credos e hábitos, que vão se mesclando e criando novas culturas, sempre resultantes da integração das diferenças.

## 2 Você pensa que a diversidade é um dos rasgos que melhor descrevem a nossa sociedade atual?

No meu entendimento a diversidade sempre foi característica forte em todos os tempos, e é ainda mais forte no mundo contemporâneo. É o retrato de nossa sociedade. Mesmo assim, penso que ainda estamos aprendendo a descobrir as vantagens da diversidade, a ter abertura para o novo, e uma curiosidade autêntica diante do outro.

## 3 Quais são as principais barreiras do nosso tempo para poder aproveitar a diversidade?

Acredito que seja o nosso modelo mental ainda muito individualista, nossa pouca capacidade para aprender com o outro. Precisamos entender a grande sabedoria que está em saber aproveitar as diferenças e o melhor de cada um. Não olhamos para o outro da forma como ele é, mas da forma que nos projetamos nele, e isto atrapalha perceber a beleza da diversidade.

## 4 Devem-se rever as grandes questões de gestão empresarial em relação com a diversidade?

Não creio que se trata de rever, mas sim de aumentar o nível de consciência para entender a riqueza que a diversidade pode gerar de benefícios para as empresas e conseqüentemente para a própria sociedade, porque à medida que a empresa se abre muda o paradigma da sociedade.

Quando pessoas diferentes são valorizadas pelas empresas, esta empresa modifica a cultura da sociedade. Para isto é preciso uma mudança de paradigmas para que se aceite melhor e se agregue valor às diferenças.

*5 Quais são as principais contribuições da diversidade?*

O ser humano é muito complexo. A partir do momento que conseguimos entender cada um dentro de seu universo, passaremos a ter um mundo muito mais interligado, uma visão melhor do todo, e conseguiremos atender os anseios do coletivo e não apenas de alguns segmentos da sociedade.

*6 Como as empresas e instituições estão aproveitando estas contribuições?*

As empresas estão começando a romper as barreiras do modelo mental coletivo de extrema competitividade e individualismo. No Magazine Luiza, além de não termos restrições quanto à idade, gênero, etnia e pessoas com deficiência, também adotamos várias políticas que estimulam o processo participativo e integrador destas pessoas. Considero fundamental ter claras as políticas de não discriminação, o código de ética e conduta, para que todos conheçam o compromisso formal da empresa com estas propostas.

*7 Que políticas deveriam fazer empresas e instituições para capitalizar estas contribuições que propõe a diversidade?*

O Magazine Luiza deixa explícito este comprometimento em sua missão, valores e princípios, na postura de seus acionistas e diretores, incorporado em seus processos cotidianos, o seu respeito profundo pelo Ser Humano. Este respeito está evidenciado em sua MISSÃO: "Ser uma empresa de competitividade, inovadora e ousada que visa sempre o bem-estar comum"; em seus VALORES: "As pessoas são a força e a vitalidade da nossa organização" e "O comprometimento com a evolução do ser humano através da postura ética e do investimento no processo educativo"; e nos seus princípios: "Respeite o Ser Humano na sua globalidade," "Invista na Aprendizagem Coletiva através da troca de experiências em equipe," "Faça aos outros aquilo que gostaria que fizessem a você," "Participe no planejamento e nas ações para atingir as metas e os objetivos individuais e globais das unidades, preservando o crescimento mútuo," "Seja honesto, verdadeiro e transparente nas relações para que elas sejam benéficas a todos."

*8 Quais são os principais desafios enfrentados pelas empresas e instituições na aplicação das políticas de diversidade?*

O principal desafio é assumir e identificar as manifestações do preconceito arragaido e subliminar, impregnado na cultura das organizações, nas pequenas atitudes discriminatórias. Para isto, acredito que o caminho que as empresas podem seguir é o do incentivo à cooperação, ao trabalho em equipe, às metas coletivas, da aceitação das diferenças.

## 9 Qual é a tendência que pensa que sua empresa vai seguir na gestão da diversidade?

Acredito que nossa tendência é continuar sendo exemplo de democracia nas relações, de participação, de fomento das oportunidades de contribuição, buscando incentivar que as pessoas sejam mais felizes e que seu sucesso seja o sucesso de todos.

Além das políticas, pretendemos ter sempre canais abertos para participação, criando condições e meios para definição conjunta dos objetivos, comemorar juntos os resultados e rever as estratégias de forma participativa, mesmo no momento de grande expansão que estamos vivendo agora.

## 10 Como serão as empresas do futuro?

As empresas do futuro terão que investir na felicidade das pessoas. Terão que fazer de cada colaborador autor da sua história e da história da empresa, respeitando suas contribuições. Cada pessoa deverá sentir-se considerada em suas particularidades, e integradas ao todo que é a empresa e a sociedade.

# 6
# Arpad von Lazar

**Member of the International Advisory Board of the Instituto de Empresa, Madrid, and emeritus professor at the Fletcher School of Law and Diplomacy, Boston, USA**

Dr von Lazar is a member of the International Advisory Board of the Instituto de Empresa in Madrid and emeritus professor in international relations at the Fletcher School of Law and Diplomacy in Boston (USA). He has been responsible for the development of academic programs in international development, energy and environmental studies. During his academic career, Professor von Lazar has worked as a consultant for some of the largest American and international oil companies, in addition to numerous financial institutions, foundations and various governments, including that of the US.

Since leaving Fletcher in 1998, he has acted as an investment consultant for numerous European and American banks and various financial institutions. He is a member of the Hungarian Academy of Science, the Rome Club and the Hungary 2000 Committee, in addition to being on the board of many companies and consultative committees.

## 1 What do you understand by diversity?

The ability to think, organize and carry out policies in order to accommodate and make use of various human resources capital; also to be able to integrate values and principles with decisions. Diversity is both a way of thinking and legitimizing them through action, that is, decisions and policies.

## 2 Do you think diversity is one of the most defining characteristics of today's society?

Yes, but unfortunately much misinterpreted and misunderstood. Still, the world, especially the business world, is every day becoming more international and globally interconnected, especially the labor force at all levels, hence the reality of diversity is every day more and more apparent. Of course, cultural resistance is prevalent, especially in terms of denying the need for changed attitudes and behavior.

### 3 What are the main obstacles in our times that prevent us from taking full advantage of diversity?

In secular/modern societies, it is primary stereotyping that is most damaging ("women are bad drivers") along with class, strata and group-based prejudices in terms of perceptions. In more traditional societies, it is cultural and often religious conceptions of reality, which act as an obstacle to taking advantage of diversity. Tradition, culture and fear of change are a powerful mix!

### 4 Should major business management issues be rethought because of diversity?

Either all management issues and practices will have to be rethought or the entire exercise is worthless. While change might be slow and incremental, the approach has to be all-encompassing. Changes and adjustments on the margin are at best useless, at worst counterproductive.

### 5 What are the main advantages of diversity?

A capacity to improve, what I would call a "lateral vision," to be able to detect, analyze and evaluate policies that do not seem to appear in the focus of day-to-day activities; develop a more diversified and swifter market adjustment and response; surprise competitors with one's flexibility and vitality.

### 6 Are companies and institutions reaping the full benefits of these advantages?

Most of them don't, because they pay only lip service to diversity and take a "mechanical" approach to solving diversity problems.

### 7 What policies should companies and institutions adopt to leverage the advantages that diversity brings?

First of all to make sure that within the corporation there is a consensus about the importance of the issue and the need to carry out policies, second to realize that diversity is an ongoing process, that is, leveraging demand continually! Improving continually intercultural communications within the firms and outside is imperative.

*8 What are the main challenges that companies face when applying
   diversity policies?*

First, the inherent rigidities of hierarchies and, second, the strength of
traditional structures and patterns of policy making and execution.
Change is often only "pro forma," a new way of dressing up all patterns
of thinking and doing!

*9 What trend do you think your company will follow where diversity
   is concerned*

Not applicable.

*10 What will the business corporations of the future be like?*

More flexible in terms of organization of its management and the structure of its labor force; more diverse labor force and a better educated
one, with higher mobility level.

Faster market response, with a better balance between "leading"
consumer demand and "following" it.

Corporations will be totally globally integrated, including the inter-
nationalization of the supply chain. Corporations will be longer in structure, but more "local" and "smaller" in terms of market response and
internal staffing, decision making and ability to adjust. They will be more
humane and more fun to spend the work day at.

# Appendix: List of Organizations

# Notes

## Initial Reflections

1. Ibarra, H. *Estrategias poco convencionales para reinventar su carrera profesional*, Ediciones Deusto, Barcelona, 2004.

## Introduction to Part One

1. Ridderstråle, J. and Nordström, K. *Funky Business: Talent Makes Capital Dance*, Pearson Education, London, 2000, p. 94.
2. European Commission, *La gestión de la diversidad: ¿Qué gana la empresa?*, Brussels, 2004, www.stop-discrimination.info.
3. Mayo, M. *La gestión de la diversidad*, Expansión y Empleo, 30 August 2002.
4. Jung, C. G. *Arquetipos e inconsciente colectivo*, Paidós, Barcelona, 1970.
5. Micklethwait, J. and Wooldridge, A. *The Company; A Short History of a Revolutionary Idea*, Weidenfeld & Nicholson, London, 2003, p. 166.

## Chapter 1

1. Ridderstråle, J. and Nordström, K. *Funky Business: Talent Makes Capital Dance*, 2nd edn, Pearson Education, Harlow, 2001.
2. Ridderstråle, J. and Nordström, K. ibid., p. 85.
3. Drucker, Peter, *Managing in the Next Society*, St Martin's Press, New York, 2002.
4. Llano, A. *La nueva sensibilidad*, Espasa Universidad, Madrid, 1988, p. 154.
5. Friedman, M. The social responsibility of business is to increase its profits, *New York Times Magazine*, 13 September 1970.
6. Sotelo, C. Reputación corporativa: al mayor activo de las compañías, *Ideas de PricewaterhouseCoopers*, 1, 2003, Madrid, p. 14.
7. Greenspan quoted in Sotelo, C. ibid.
8. Ridderstråle, J. and Nordström, K. op. cit., p. 87.
9. Ridderstråle, J. and Nordström, K. op. cit., p. 136.
10. Stein, G. *El arte de gobernar según Peter Drucker*, Editorial Gestión, 2000, p. 125.
11. Maslow, A. *El hombre Autorealizado*, Kairos, 1993.

12. Llano, C. *El empresario y su mundo*, McGraw-Hill, Mexico, 1990.
13. Ridderstråle, J. and Nordström, K. op. cit., p. 88.
14. "Lo que el management se llevó, Alejandro Llano. Asociación Mexicana en Dirección de Recursos Humanos, AC, 20 September 2004, *www.amerdirh.com.mx.*
15. Ridderstråle, J. and Nordström, K. op. cit., p. 100.
16. Etayo, C. *Un modelo en gestión del conocimiento*, Ideas de PricewaterhouseCoopers, 1, 2003, Madrid, pp. 51–3.
17. Delgado Planas, C. *Mucho más que salario: La compensación total flexible*, ed. McGraw-Hill/Interamericana de España SAU, Madrid, 2002.
18. Delgado Planas, C. Compensación total flexible orientada a los objetivos de la empresa y del profesional, *Ideas de PricewaterhouseCoopers*, 1, 2003, Madrid, p. 30.
19. Muñoz-Najar, J. A. Una compañía innovadora de valor, *Ideas de PricewaterhouseCoopers*, 1, 2003, Madrid, p. 54.
20. The author's research.
21. Drucker, P., *The Effective Executive*, Harper Perennial, New York, 1993.
22. PricewaterhouseCoopers, *Responsibilidad social corporativa: tendencias empresariales en España*, 2003, p. 4.

## Chapter 2

1. Rosemberg, N. and Birdzell Jr., L. E. *How the West Grew Rich*, Basic Books, New York, 1986, pp. 113–43.
2. Micklethwait, J. and Wooldridge, A. *The Company; A Short History of a Revolutionary Idea*, Weidenfeld & Nicholson, London, 2003, pp. 13–15.
3. Warner, M. (ed.) *The Concise International Encyclopaedia of Business Management*, Thomson International Business Press, London, 1997, p. 2.
4. Oldcorn, R. *Company Accounts*, Macmillan Business Masters, Bristol, 1996, pp. 37–8.
5. Rosemberg, N. and Birdzell Jr, L. E. op. cit., p. 68.
6. De Anca, C. *Economía islámica y economía étnica: convergencias en la diversidad cultural: fondos islámicos de inversión y fondos de inversión ética en el mercado de Londres*, UAM Ediciones, Madrid, 2003, p. 48.
7. Weber, M. *La ética protestante y el espíritu del capitalismo*, Ediciones Península, Barcelona, 1979, p. 248.
8. Weber, M. ibid., p. 248.
9. Rothbard, M. *Historia del pensamiento económico*, vol I, *El pensamiento económico hasta Adam Smith*, Union Editorial, Madrid, 1999, p. 173.
10. For an extensive analysis of Max Weber's theory and the influence of religion in the emergence of capitalism, see Tawney, R. H. *Religion and the Rise of Capitalism*, New York, New American Library, 1954.
11. Schluchter, W., Max Weber, economy and society, in *Max Weber and Islam*, Huff, T. and Schluchter, W. (eds), Transaction Publishers, New Brunswick, 1999, pp. 79–80.
12. Crone, P., Weber, Islamic law and the rise of capitalism, in *Max Weber and Islam*, ibid.
13. Rothbard, M., op. cit., pp. 340–2.

14. Rosemberg, N. and Birdzell Jr., L. E. op. cit., pp. 22–36.
15. Micklethwait, J. and Wooldridge, A., op. cit., pp. 45–60.
16. Micklethwait, J. and Wooldridge, A., op. cit., p. 63.
17. Chandler, A. *The Visible Hand: the Managerial Revolution in American Business*, Harvard University Press, 1993, pp. 287–9.
18. Micklethwait, J. and Wooldridge, A., op. cit., p. 68.
19. Rosemberg, N. and Birdzell, Jr., L. E., op. cit., p. 243.
20. Chandler, A. op. cit.
21. Drucker, *Management Challenges for the 21st Century.* HarperCollins, New York, 1999, p. 24.
22. White, W. and Nocera, J. *The Organization Man*, University of Pennsylvania Press, 2002 (first published 1956).
23. Micklethwait, J. and Wooldridge, A., op. cit., p. 118.
24. Sirvan Schreiber, J. J., *Le defi américain*, DENOEL, Paris, 1967.
25. Micklethwait, J. and Wooldridge, A., op. cit., p. 119.
26. For more information on the major management models, see Goharriz, K. K., *Sistemas de organización de la empresa*, in *Organización empresarial*, Harper & Lynch, 1993, special edition, *La gaceta de los negocios* (serie optimización empresarial), pp. 19–25.
27. Drucker, P., *The Concept of Corporation*, Mentor, New York, 1983.
28. Goharriz, K. K., op. cit., pp 19–25.
29. Drucker, P., op. cit., 1999, p. 16
30. McGregor, D. *The Human Side of Enterprise*, McGraw-Hill, New York, 1960.
31. Drucker, P., 1999, op. cit., pp. 15–19.
32. Emmering, M., *Inventing Reason, Reflections on Knowledge and Understanding with a View to Innovation*, Universal Press, Veenendal, 2004.
33. Shultz, T. W. quoted in Davenport, T.O., *Capital humano, creando ventajas competitivas a través de las personas*, Ediciones Gestión, Barcelona, 2000, p. 39.
34. Davenport, T. O., *Human Capital. What it is and Why People Invest it.* Jossey-Bass, San Francisco, 1999.
35. Drucker, P., op. cit., 1999, pp. 233–5.
36. Senge, P. M., *The Fifth Discipline.* Doubleday, New York, 1990.
37. For more information on systems theory, see Fischer, H. R., Retzer, A. and Schweizer, J., *El final de los grandes proyectos*, Gedisa, Barcelona, 1997.
38. To understand more on the theory of mental models, see Argyris, C., *Reasoning, Learning and Action: Individual and Organizational*, Jossey Bass, San Francisco, 1982.
39. Baets, W., *The Hybrid Business School: Developing Knowledge Management through Management Learning*, Prentice Hall, Englewood Cliffs, NJ, 2000.
40. Baets, W., *Organizational Learning and Knowledge Technologies in a Dynamic Environment*, Kluwer Academic Publishers, Norwell, MA, 1998.
41. Mostyn Bird, M., *Women at Work: A Study of the Different Ways of Earning a Living Open to Women*, Chapman & Hall, London, 1911.
42. Roosevelt, T., *Elements of a Successful "Diversity" Process, Part I*, American Institute for Managing Diversity, Atlanta, 2001.

43. Thomas, D. A. and Ely, R. J., Making differences matter: a new paradigm for managing diversity, *Harvard Business Review on Managing Diversity*, Boston, 2002, pp. 33–66.
44. Thomas D. A. and Ely, R. J. ibid, p. 60.
45. Drucker, P., op. cit., 1999, p. 12.

## Chapter 3

1. Torazno, G. *La presencia de la mujer en la vida social*, Nuestro Tiempo number 123, p. 331.
2. Chinchilla, N. and Leon, C., *La ambición femenina*, Editorial Aguilar, Madrid, 2004, p. 25.
3. Naisbitt, J. and Aburdene, P. *Megatendencias de la mujer*, Editorial Dorma, Buenos Aires, 1991, p.27.
4. De Miguel, A. *La sociedad española 1994–1995*, Editorial Complutense, Madrid, 1995, p. 165.
5. Romano, A. Mujeres en la cima: ellas Mandan, http://www.pymesdigital.com.ar.
6. Peters, T. *Ponencia Expomanagement 2004*, http://winred.com/EP/ideas/n/0060000600102381.html.
7. International Labour Office (ILO), *Breaking through the Glass Ceiling. Women in Management*, Geneva, Switzerland, 2004.
8. International Labour Office (ILO), *Time for Equality at Work*, Global report under the follow-up to the ILO declaration on fundamental principles and rights at work, Geneva, Switzerland, 2003.
9. ILO, ibid., p. 41.
10. Eurostat, most recent update, 27 September 2004.
11. Randstat, *Workpocket 2004*, guide to work for employers and workers, 2004.
12. Catalyst, *Catalyst Census of Women Board Directors 2003*, New York.
13. "There are only 115 women on the boards of the 300 largest companies" *Expansion*, 30 December 2002.
14. Singh, V. and Vinnicombe, S. *The 2004 Female FTSE Report*, Cranfield Centre for Developing Women Business Leaders, November 2004.
15. Singh, V. and Vinnicombe, S. *The 2002 Female FTSE Report*, Cranfield Centre for Developing Women Business Leaders, November 2002.
16. Morrison, A. M. White, R. P. and Van Velsor, E. *Breaking the Glass Ceiling: Can Women Reach the Top of America's Largest Corporations?*, Center of Creative Leadership, 1987 (The term "glass ceiling" was made popular by this book).
17. Meyerson, D. E. and Fletcher, J. K. *A Modest Manifesto for Shattering the Glass Ceiling*, HBR, 2001, pp. 67–93, p. 88.
18. *Women in Leadership. A European Business Imperative*, Catlyst – The Conference Board, www.catalystwomen.org, 2002.
19. Data from Ranking MBAs, *Financial Times*, 2003.
20. ILO, op cit., 2003.
21. Institute for Women's Policy Research, *The Status of Women in the States*, Washington, DC, November 2004.

22. Nurmi, K. *Gender and the Labour Market in the EU*, Ministry of Social Affairs and Health, 1999. A third of the difference between the salary of men and women is due to occupational segregation, whilst between 10–30 percent remains "unexplained."

23. Manpower Labour Index, *La desigualdad salarial por razones de sexo*, January 2005.

24. Moir, A. and Jessel, D., *Brain Sex: The Real Differences Between Men and Women*, Dell, New York, 1991.

25. www.soloellas.com/diferenciashombresmujeres04.html.

26. www.diariomedico.com/geriatria/n250101.html.

27. *Nature* magazine, 1995, J. Shaywitz.

28. Jung, C. G., *Arquetipos e inconsciente colectivo*, Paidos, Barcelona, 1970.

29. Bird, B. and Brush, C. A gender perspective on organizational creation, *Entrepreneurship, Theory and Practice*, **26**(3), Spring 2002, p. 4.

30. www.mujeresdeempresa.com/management/mangement020302.shtml.

31. Séller, L. *Women Business Leaders in Latin America*, Center for Gender in Organizations, Simmon School of Management, Boston, 7 November 2002.

32. Naisbitt, J. and Aburdene, P., op. cit., p. 215.

33. Barbera, E. *Rompiendo el techo de cristal: los beneficios de la diversidad de género en los equipos de dirección* www.uv.es/~iued/investigacion/techo-cristal.htm.

34. Naisbitt, J. and Aburdene, P., op. cit., p. 121.

## Chapter 4

1. Baur, M. and Ziegler, G., *La aventura del hombre*, Maeva Ediciones, 2003, p. 5.

2. Tylor, E. B., *Primitive Culture*, abridged edn, Harper, New York, (1871/1958).

3. Schein, E. H., *Organizational Psychology*, Prentice Hall, Englewood Cliffs, NJ, 1982.

4. Katan, D., *Translating Cultures: an Introduction for Translators, Interpreters and Mediators* (2nd edn), St Jerome Publishing, Manchester, 2004.

5. Hoecklin, L., *Managing Cultural Differences: Strategies for Competitive Advantage*, Economist Intelligence Unit (EIU), 1994–95, p. 8.

6. Hoecklin, L., op. cit., pp. 1–15.

7. For more information, see Katan, D., op cit., pp. 24–37.

8. Trompenaars, F., *Riding the Wave of Culture*, Irwin, Chicago, 1994.

9. Hofstede, G., *Cultures and Organizations: Software of the Mind*, McGraw-Hill, London, 1991.

10. Hall, E. T., *The Silent Language* Doubleday, New York, 1990 (originally published 1952).

11. Trompenaars, F., op cit.

12. The dimensions described in this section are based on Storti, C. *La cultura sí importa*, manual transcultural del cuerpo de paz, Peace Corps Information Collection and Exchange (ICE) T0087.

13. Hall, E. T. and Hall, M. R., *Understanding Cultural Differences: Germans, French and Americans*, Yarmouth, ME, Intercultural Press, 1990, pp. 14–15.
14. Hofstede, G., *Culture's Consequences: International Differences in Work-related Values*, Sage, Beverly Hills, 1980.
15. Hofstede, G., Organizational Culture, *The Concise International Encyclopaedia of Business Management*, Malcolm Warner (ed.), Thomson Business Press, London, 1997, pp. 543–5.
16. Sackmann, S. A., *Cultural Complexity in Organizations: Inherent Contrast and Contradictions*, Sage, California, 1997.
17. Smith, K. and Berg, D. N., Cross-cultural groups at work, *European Management Journal*, **15**(1) 1997, pp. 8–15.
18. www.nlpuniversitypress.com.
19. Dilts, R. and Judith, D. *Encyclopaedia of Systemic Neurolinguistic Programming and NLP New Coding*, www.nlpu.com.
20. Bennett, M., *Towards Ethnorelativisim: A Developmental Model of Intercultural Sensitivity*. Michael R. Paige (ed.), Yarmouth, ME, Intercultural Press, 1993, pp. 22–73.

## Chapter 5

1. Naranjo, C., *El eneagrama de la sociedad*, Temas de Hoy, Barcelona, 1995, p. 175.
2. Jung, C. (ed.) *Man and his Symbols*, Macmillan – now Palgrave Macmillan, London, 1964.
3. Campbell, J., *El héroe de las mil caras*, Fondo de Cultura Económica, México, 1959; Mascetti, M. D., *Diosas; el renacimiento del culto a lo femenino*, Robinbook/Circulo de lectores, Barcelona, 1990.
4. See, for example, some applications developed by Y&R at www.emea.yr.com/Icon.pdf.
5. *Suplemento Formación y Empleo*, ABC Domingo, 5 December 2004, p. 36.
6. Naranjo, C. op. cit.
7. The original Sufi conception is that all human beings have something of the divine in them and this is reflected in their characters and personalities. However, no one is aware of this divinity until, through human love, they see not only the greatness of the personality of the loved one, but also their own divinity reflected in the other as though they were a mirror. The unity of all human characters constitutes the unity of the divine. For more information about the Sufi view of unity, see Lings, M., *Sufism, Religion in the Middle East*, Cambridge University Press, 1969, pp. 253–69 and Pareja, P., *Islamología*, Razón y Fe, 1954, p. 646.
8. Naranjo, C., *El eneagrama de la sociedad*, Temas de Hoy, Barcelona, 1995, p. 22. These authors add the sins of fear and vanity to the seven traditional Christian sins.
9. Jung, C. (ed.) op. cit., pp. 49–50.
10. www.humanmetrics.com.
11. There are many books that give more information about the enneagram. In addition to Claudio Naranjo, see also Riso, D. R. and Hudson, R. *La sabiduria del eneagrama*, Urano, Barcelona, 2000.

12. Crosby, L. A., Bitner, M. J. and Gill, J. D., Organizational structure of values, *Journal of Business Research*, **20** 1990, pp. 123–34.
13. Shwartz, S. H. and Sagiv, L., Identifying culture-specifics in the content and structure of values, *Journal of Cross-cultural Psychology*, **26**(1), 1995, pp. 91–116.
14. Sully de Luque, M. F. and Sommer, S. M., The impact of culture on feedback-seeking behavior: An integrated model and propositions, *Academy of Management Review 2000*, **25**(4) pp 829–49.

## Conclusion to Part One

1. Ridderstråle, J. and Nordström, K., *Funky Business*, Pearson Education, Madrid, 2000.
2. Ridderstråle, J. and Nordström, K. ibid.
3. Goleman, D., *Emotional Intelligence*, 1995.

## Chapter 6

1. www.stop-discrimination.info/fileadmin/pdfs/costsbenefexsum_es.pdf.
2. Micklethwait, J. and Wooldridge, A., *The Company: A Short History of a Revolutionary Idea*, Weidenfeld & Nicholson, London, 2003, p. 181.
3. Porter, M. E. and Kramer, M. R., *The Competitive Advantage of Corporate Philanthropy*, Harvard Business School Publishing, Boston, 2002.
4. Friedman, M., *Capitalism and Freedom*, University of Chicago Press, Chicago, 1962/1982.
5. European Commission, 2 July 2002, http://europa.es.int.
6. Other international initiatives include OIT 1977/2000, OECD Guidelines for multinational enterprises 2000 UN and OECD Principles of corporate governance 1999.
7. www.unglobalcompact.org.
8. www.unglobalcompact.org.
9. www.globalreporting.org.
10. www.globalreporting.org.
11. *Los nuevos líderes*, Actualidad Económica, number 2403, 8 July.
12. www.ftse.com/ftse4good.
13. www.dowjones.com.
14. www.eiris.org.
15. www.greatplacetowork.com. The Great Place to Work Institute Inc is a research and management consultancy based in the USA with affiliated offices throughout the world (Diversityinc, www.diversityinc.com). Their mission is to provide education and clarification of the benefits of diversity in business.
16. http://europa.es.int/comm/employment_social/equal/index_en.cfm.
17. Sackmann, S., Cultural Complexity as a Challenge in the Management Global Context, in *A Cultural Forum: Corporate Culture in Global Interaction*, vol III, Bertelsmann Foundation, Guetersloh, 2003, pp. 58–80.

18. Garralda, J., *Cultura de empresa,* IE working paper.
19. Garralda, J., op. cit.
20. Mohn, L., *A Cultural Forum: Corporate Culture in Global Interaction,* vol III, Bertelsmann Foundation, Guetersloh, 2003, p. 9.
21. Sackmann, op. cit., p. 61.
22. Cabrero Romañach, *Los errores sutiles del caso San Pedro,* Cuenta y Razón del Pensamiento Actual, num 135, January, 2005.
23. Catalyst, *Assessing your Work Environment,* The catalyst making change series, Catalyst, New York, 2002.
24. Senge, P. M., *The Fifth Discipline,* ed. Granica, Barcelona, 1992, p. 220.
25. Maslow, A., *El hombre autorealizado,* Kairos, 1993.
26. Lynch, F., *The Diversity Machine: The Drive to Change the White Male Workplace,* Free Press, New York, 1997.
27. Bendick, M., Egan, M. L. and Lofhjelm, S. M., Workforce Diversity Training: from Anti-discrimination Compliance to Organizational Development, *Human Resource Planning,* **24**(2) 2001, pp. 10–15. The Human Resources Planning Society, New York.

## Case 1

1. Diversity, www.jpmorganchase.com.
2. www.jpmorganchase.com.
3. Nondiscrimination policy, www.jpmorganchase.com.
4. The Consortium is a group of 15 business schools that provide management training opportunities to African-American, Hispanic and Native American students.
5. The Robert A. Toigo Foundation provides support to African-Americans, Hispanics and Asian-Americans in the finance sector, through financial help, mentoring, internship programs and job placement. JPMC works with the Toigo Foundation by providing mentors and career opportunities.
6. SEO is an organization that prepares young coloured people for leadership roles in their families, communities and careers (SEO Mission statement).
7. Before the merger with JPMorgan, 20 percent of the corporate officers and 3 of the 17 board members of Chase Manhattan were women. Promotion has been particularly rapid at senior management level, where the percentage of women rose from 19 percent in 1996 to 24 percent.

## Case 2

1. *Informe 2003,* Universia, p. 9.
2. Speech by Emilio Botín, University of Salamanca, Spain.
3. www.gruposantander.com, 22 February 2005.
4. *Corporate Social Responsibility Memorandum,* Grupo Santander, 2003, p. 8.

## Case 3

1. Asociación Nacional de Fabricantes de Automóviles y Camiones.
2. In 1921, 56.6 percent of all the vehicles registered in the world were Model T Fords (*FMC 100 years*).
3. www.ford.com.
4. The Middle Eastern community in Dearborn, Michigan, established for the main part by workers at Ford between 1900 and 1910, built the first mosque in the USA in 1919.
5. Prizes in the USA: Number 1 in the ranking of the top 50 companies for diversity by Diversityinc 2003; Urban Wheels prize for its commitment to diversity in the automobile industry; the Gay & Lesbian Alliance Against Defamation's Fairness prize. In Germany: the Media Capital award for diversity in 2004. In the UK: the Opportunity Now award for commitment to equal rights.
6. FMC: *On the team*. www.ford.com.
7. FMC: *Valuing diversity*.
8. www.ford.com/go/best with DiversityInc and Score.
9. Amparo Rodriguez interview by Jose Luis Silvestre. Ford Almussafes, June 2004.
10. For example, the awards received by Cristobal Aguilar and other volunteers for their efforts in the campaign to clean up an oil spill on the Galician coast; Maite Arnáiz of the Finance Department in Valencia, for the development of a web forum for cultural exchange aimed at promoting community services for minorities; and Ignacio Sáinz (posthumously) for his work in FAMOVAL, an initiative for creating employment for disabled children of factory workers.

# Bibliography

## Books

Aburdene, Patricia and Naisbitt, John *Megatrends for Women*. Ballantine Books, USA, reprinted November 1993.

Argyris, C. *Reasoning Learning and Action: Individual & Organizational*. Jossey-Bass, San Francisco, 1982.

Baets, Walter *Organizational Learning and Knowledge Technologies in a Dynamic Environment*. Kluwer Academic Publishers, Dordrecht, Netherlands, 1998.

Baets, Walter *The Hybrid Business School: Developing Knowledge Management through Management Learning*. Pearson Education, Uitgeverij, BV, Holland 2000.

Baur, Manfred and Ziegler, Gudrun *La aventura del Hombre*. Maeva Ediciones, Madrid, 2003.

Bird, Mostyn *Women at Work: a Study of the Different Ways of Earning a Living Open to Women*. Chapman & Hall. London, 1911.

Campbell, Joseph *The Hero with a Thousand Faces*. Bollingen, New York, 1949, reprinted 1972.

Chandler, Alfred *The Visible Hand: The Managerial Revolution in American Business*, Harvard University Press, Boston, MA, 1993.

Chinchilla, N. and Leon, C. *La ambición femenina*, Editorial Aguilar, Madrid, 2004.

Davenport, Thomas O. *Human Capital. What It Is and Why People Invest In It*. Jossey-Bass, San Francisco, 1999.

De Anca, Celia *Economía Islámica y economía ética: convergencias en la diversidad cultural: fondos Islámicos de inversión y Fondos de inversión ética en el mercado de Londres*. UAM Ediciones, Madrid, 2003.

Delgado Planas, Carlos *Mucho más que salario. La compensación total flexible*. McGraw-Hill/Interamericana de España, S.A.U. Madrid, 2002.

Dilts, Robert and Delozier, Judith *Encyclopedia of Systemic Neurolinguistic Programming and NLP New Coding*. www.nlpu.com.

Drucker, Peter F. *The Concept of Corporation*. Mentor, New York, 1983.

Drucker, Peter F. *The Effective Executive*. HarperBusiness, New York, 1996.

Drucker, Peter F. *The Age of Discontinuity*. Harper & Row, New York, 2000.

Drucker, Peter F. *Management Challenges for the 21st Century*. HarperCollins, New York, 2001.

Emmering, Machiel *Inventing Reason: Reflections on Knowledge and Understanding, with a View to Innovation*. Universal Press, Veenendal, 2004.

Fischer, H.R., Retzer, A. and Schweizer, J. *El final de los grandes proyectos.* Gedisa, Barcelona, 1997.

Friedman, Milton *Capitalism and Freedom.* University of Chicago Press, Chicago, 1962/1982.

Goharriz, Karl K. "Sistemas de organización de la Empresa" in: *Organización Empresarial,* Harper & Lynch 1993, special edition of *La Gaceta de los Negocios,* Madrid (business organization series).

Goleman, D. *Emotional Intelligence. Why it can matter more than IQ.* Bantam, New York, 1995, reprinted 1997.

Hall, Edward T. *The Silent Language.* Doubleday, New York, 1990 (orginally published 1952).

Hall, Edward T. and Hall, Mildred Reed *Understanding Cultural Differences, German, French and Americans.* Intercultural Press, Boston, MA, 1990.

Hoecklin, Lisa *Managing Cultural Differences, Strategies for Competitive Advantages.* EIU Economist Intelligence Unit, Cambridge University Press, Cambridge, 1994/1995.

Hofstede, Geert *Culture's Consequences: International Differences in Work Related Values.* Sage, Beverly Hills, CA, 1980.

Hofstede, Geert *Cultures and Oganizations: Software of the Mind.* McGraw-Hill, London, 1991.

Huff, Toby and Schluchter, Wolfgang (eds) *Max Weber and Islam.* New Brunswick/London, 1999.

Ibarra, Herminia *Estrategias poco convencionales para reinventar su carrera profesional.* Ediciones Deusto, Barcelona, 2004.

Jung, Carl *Man and his Symbols.* Macmillan – now Palgrave Macmillan, London, 1964.

Jung, Carl G. *Arquetipos e inconsciente colectivo.* Paidós, Barcelona, 1970.

Katan, David *Translating Cultures, An Introduction for Translators Interpreters and Mediators.* St Jerome Publishing, Manchester, UK, (1999), 2004.

Lings, Martín *What is Sufism?* Islamic Texts Society, Cambridge, 1993.

Llano, Alejandro *La nueva sensibilidad.* Espasa Universidad, Espasa-Calpe, Madrid, 1988.

Llano, Carlos *El empresario y su mundo.* McGraw-Hill, México, 1990.

Lynch, F. *The Diversity Machine: the Drive to Change the White Male Workplace.* Free Press, New York, 1997.

Mascetti, Manuela Dunn *Diosas, el renacimiento del culto a lo femenino.* Robinbook/Circulo de lectores, Barcelona, 1990.

Maslow, Abraham *El hombre autorrealizado.* KAIROS, Barcelona, 1993.

McGregor, Douglas *The Human Side of Enterprise.* McGraw-Hill, New York, 1960.

Micklethwait, John and Wooldridge, Adrian *The Company: A Short History of a Revolutionary Idea.* Weidenfeld & Nicolson, London, 2003.

Moir, Anne and Jessel, David *El sexo en el cerebro, la verdadera diferencia entre hombre y mujer.* Planeta, Madrid, 1991.

Morrison, A. M., White, R. P. and Van Velsor, E. and the Center for Creative Leadership. *Breaking the Glass Ceiling: Can Women Reach the Top of America's Largest Corporations?* Addison Wesley, Reading, MA, 1987.

Naranjo, Claudio *El eneagrama de la sociedad.* Temas de Hoy, Barcelona, 1995.

Oldcorn, Roger *Company Accounts.* Macmillian Business Masters, Bristol, UK, 1996.

Pareja, P. *Islamología.* Razón y Fe, Madrid, 1954.

Peters, T. and Waterman, R. *In Search of Excellence: Lessons from America's Best Run Companies.* Warner Books, New York, 1984.

Porter, Michael E. and Kramer, Mark R. *The Competitive Advantage of Corporate Philanthropy.* Harvard Business School Publishing Corporation, Boston, 2002.

Ridderstråle, Jonas and Nordström, Kjell *Funky Business,* Pearson Education, London, 2000.

Riso, D.R. and Hudson, R. *La Sabiduria del Eneagrama.* Urano, Barcelona, 2000.

Rosemberg, Nathan and Birdzell, Jr L.E. *How the West Grew Rich.* Basic Books, USA, 1986.

Rothbard, Murray *Historia del pensamiento Económico. Vol I: El pensamiento económico hasta Adam Smith.* Unión Editorial, Madrid, 1999.

Sackmann, Sonja A. *Cultural Complexity in Organizations: Inherent Contrast and Contradictions.* Sage, Thousand Oaks, CA, 1997.

Schein, Edgard H. *Organizational Psychology.* Prentice Hall, Madrid, 1982.

Senge, Peter M. *The Fifth Discipline.* Currency Doubleday, New York, 1994.

Sirvan Schreiber, Jean Jacques *Le Défi Américain.* Denoel, Paris, 1967.

Stein, Guido *El arte de gobernar según Peter Drucker.* Editorial Gestión, Chile, 2000.

Tawney, Richard H. *Religion and the Rise of Capitalism.* New American Library, New York, 1954.

Taylor, Frederick *The Principles of Scientific Management.* Harper & Brothers, New York, 1919, reprinted Dover, 1998.

Trompenaars, Fons *Riding the Waves of Culture.* Irwin, Chicago, 1994.

Tylor, Edward Barnett *Primitive Culture.* Abridged edition, Harper, New York, 1871/1958.

Weber, Max *La ética protestante y el espíritu del Capitalismo.* Ediciones Península, Barcelona, 1979.

White, William H. and Nocera, Joseph *The Organization Man.* University of Pensylvania Press, Philadelphia, 2002 (originally published 1956).

Studies and reports

A Cultural Forum. Volume III. *Corporate cultures in global interaction.* Bertelsmann Foundation, Guetersloh, 2002.

Arnáiz, Maite in Diversity@Ford, June 2004.

Accenture "Great Place to Work for Women" program. Catalyst Award Winner 2003.

Barbera, E. "Rompiendo el techo de cristal: los beneficios de la diversidad de género en los equipos de dirección". Valencia University.

Bennett, M.J. "Towards Ethnorelativism: A developmental model of intercultural sensitivity", *Education for Intercultural Experience*, Michael R. Paige (ed.) Intercultural Press, Yarmouth, ME, 1993.

Bird, Barbara and Brush, Candida "A gender perspective on organizational creation", *Entrepreneurship: Theory and Practice*, spring 2002, **26**(3): 4.

Catalyst *Assessing Your Work Environment*, The Catalyst Making Change Series, New York, 2002.

Catalyst *Catalyst Census of Women Board Directors of Canada*, New York, 2003.

Catalyst *Women in Leadership: A European Business Imperative*, Catalyst – The Conference Board, 2003.

Comisión Europea, "La gestión de la diversidad: ¿Qué gana la empresa?", *Hojas informativas*, Brussels, Belgium, 2004.

Crosby, L. A., Gill, J. D. and Bitner, M. "The organizational structure of values", *Journal of Business Research*, **20**, 1990, 123–34.

De Miguel, A. "La sociedad Española 1994–1995". Editorial Complutense, Madrid, 1995, p. 165.

Delgado Planas, Carlos "Compensación total flexible, orientada a los objetivos de la empresa y del profesional", *Ideas de PricewaterhouseCoopers*, p. 27.

Etayo, Cristina "Un modelo en gestión del conocimiento", *Ideas de PricewaterhouseCoopers*, pp. 51–3.

EU Employment, Social Affairs and Equal Opportunities Directorate, "Costes y beneficios de la diversidad", 2003.

Ford, "Valuing Diversity", www.ford.com.

Ford Diversity brochure, "Vielfalt als Stärke, *Diversity*, 2002.

Ford España, "La diversidad en Ford España".

Garralda, Joaquin "Cultura de empresa", IE working paper.

Hofstede, Geert "Organizational culture", *The Concise International Encyclopaedia of Business Management*, directed by Malcom Warner, Thomson Business Press, London, 1997, pp. 543–5.

Institute for Women's Policy Research. Washington, "The status of women in the States", November 2004.

International Labour Office (ILO), "Time for equality at work", Global report under the follow-up to the ILO Declaration on Fundamental Principles and Rights at Work, Geneva, 2003.

International Labour Office (ILO), "Breaking through the glass ceiling. Women in management", Geneva, 2004.

JPMorgan Chase & Co "Using Diversity to Forge a New Culture: the Chase-Chemical Merger Experience." Catalyst Award Winner 2001.

Manpower "La desigualdad salarial por razones de sexo". Manpower Workforce Survey, Spain, January 2005.

Meyerson, Debra E. and Fletcher, Joyce K. "A modest manifesto for shattering the glass ceiling", *Harvard Business Review on Managing Diversity*, HBR, 2001, pp. 67–93, 88.

Muñoz-Najar, José Antonio "Una compañía innovadora de valor", *Ideas de PricewaterhouseCoopers*, Madrid, 2003, p. 54.

Nurmi, K. "Gender and labour market in the EU", Ministry of Social Affairs and Health, Helsinki, 1999.

*OECD Principles of Corporate Governance 1999*, www.oecd.org.

OIT 1977/2000, www.ilo.org.

"Premios INSERTA" in Programa ACCION, **2**.

PricewaterhouseCoopers "Responsibilidad social corporativa: tendencias empresariales en España" 2003, p. 4.

Randstat "workpocket 2004", 2004.

Romañach, Javier "Los errores sutiles del caso San Pedro", *Cuenta y Razón del Pensamiento*, **135**, January 2005.

Roosevelt, Thomas R. "Elements of a successful diversity process: Part I", *American Institute for Managing Diversity*. Atlanta, 2001.

Sackman, Sonja "Cultural Complexity as a Challenge in the Management Global Context", Corporate Cultures in Global Interaction. A cultural Forum Vol III Bertelsmann Foundation. Guetersloh 2003, pp. 58–80.

Schwartz, Shalom H. "Individualism–Collectivism", *Journal of Cross-cultural Psychology*, **21**(2): 139–57, June 1990, Western Washington University.

Schwartz, Shalom H. and Sagiv, Lilach "Identifying culture-specifics in the content and structure of values", *Journal of Cross-cultural Psychology*, **26**(1): 91–116, January 1995, Western Washington University.

Séller, Lidia "Women business leaders in Latin America", Center for Gender in Organizations, Simmon School of Management, Boston, 7 November 2002.

Shell "Diversity and inclusiveness at Shell", *Foundation for the Future*. 2002.

Shell Oil Company US "Valuing and Leveraging Diversity to Become a Model of Inclusiveness", Catalyst Award Winner 2004.

Singh, Val and Vinnicombe, Susan "The 2002 Female FTSE Report: Women directors moving forward". Cranfield Centre for Developing Women Business Leaders, November 2002.

Singh, Val and Vinnicombe, Susan "The 2004 Female FTSE Report". Cranfield Centre for Developing Women Business Leaders, November 2004.

Smith, Kenwyn and Berg, David "Cross-cultural groups at work", *European Management Journal*, **15**(1): 8–15, 1997.

Sotelo, Carlos "Reputación corporativa: el mayor activo de las compañías", *Ideas de PricewaterhouseCoopers*, Madrid, **1**: 14, 2003.

Storti, Craig "La cultura sí importa", *Manual Transcultural del Cuerpo de Paz*. Peace corps Information Collection and Exchange (ICE) T0087.

Thomas, David A. and Ely, Robin J. "Making differences matter: A new paradigm for managing diversity", *Harvard Business Review on Managing Diversity*, HBR, Boston, MA, 2002, pp. 33–66.

Toranzo, Gloria "La presencia de la mujer en la vida social". *Nuestro Tiempo*, **123**: 331.

Universia, *Informe 2003*, p. 9, www.universia.es.

## Press articles

*ABC*, 5 December 2004, Formación y Empleo supplement, p. 36.

Bendick, Mac, Egan, Mary Lou and Lofhjelm, Suzanne M. "Workforce diversity training: from antidiscrimination compliance to organizational development", *Human Resource Planning*, **24**(2), 2000, pp. 10–15. The Human Resources Planning Society, New York.

"De la Necesidad a la estrategia", *ABC*, 8 February 2004, p. 200.

"Diversidad: Acciones para competir en mercados globales", *Expansión y Empleo*, 6 November 2004.

"El Mundialito de las naciones". www.nostresport.com. Thursday 15 July 2004.

"Europcar gana el premio Cermi de Integración laboral", *ABC*, 8 February 2004.

Friedman, Milton "The social responsibility of business is to increase its profits", *New York Times Magazine*, 13 September 1970, p. 29.

"IBM y Coface ganan los premios a la empresa flexible", *Expansión y Empleo*, 19 June 2004.

Klingelschmitt, Klaus-Peter in *Taz* newspaper, 6 April 2001, p. 8.

"Las empresas temen que los problemas de conciliación familiar deriven en dificultades laborales", *ABC*, 20 June 2004.

"Llega la plantilla multiétnica", *Actualidad Económica*, January 2004.

"Los nuevos líderes", *Actualidad Económica*, 8 July 2004.

"Managing Diversity", *Hernsteiner Magazine*, Issue 2/2004, pp. 33–6.

Mayo, Margarita "La gestión de la diversidad", *Expansión y Empleo*, 30 August 2002, p. 15.

Shaywitz, J. *Revista Nature*, 1995, p. 103.

## Legislation

The Amsterdam Treaty:

Council Decision of 27 November 2000 which establish a community action programme to combat discrimination (2001–2006).

Directive 76/207, 9 February 1976, on the implementation of the principle of equal treatment for men and women as regards to access to employment, vocational training, and working conditions.

Directive 92/85/EEC, 19 October 1992, on the introduction of measures to encourage improvements in the safety and health at work of pregnant workers and workers who have recently given birth or are breastfeeding.

Directive 96/34/EC, 3 June 1996, modified by Council Directive 97/75/EC, 15 December 1997, relating to the framework agreement on parental leave.

Directive 2000/43 EC, 29 June 2000, implementing the principle of equal treatment between persons irrespective of racial or ethnic origin.

Directive 2000/78 EC, 27 November 2000, establishing a general framework for equal treatment in employment and occupation.

## Websites

Accenture: www.accenture.com
Asociación Mexicana en Dirección de Recursos Humanos:
    www.amedirh.com.mx
BP: www.bp.com
Catalyst: www.catalystwomen.org
CEOSA: http://www.ceosa.org
Diario Médico: www.diariomedico.com
Diversityinc: www.diversityinc.com
Dow Jones: www.dowjones.com
Eiris: www.eiris.org
European Union: http://europa.eu.int
Eurostat: http://epp.eurostat.cec.eu.int
Ford Globe: www.fordglobe.com
Ford Motor Company: www.ford.com
FTSE: www.ftse.com/ftse4good
Fundación Once: http://www.fundaciononce.es
Global Compact: www.unglobalcompact.org
Global Reporting Index (GRI): www.globalreporting.org
Grupo Santander: www.gruposantander.com
Grupo Vips: www.grupovips.com
http://nlpuniversitypress.com
Human Metrics: www.humanmetrics.com
Instituto Nacional de Estadística (INE): www.ine.es
JPMC: www.jpmorganchase.com
Kellog: www.kelloggs.com/careers/diversity/resource.shtml
Mi negocio: www.ford.com/go/best
Mujeres de Empresa: www.mujeresdeempresa.com
Nostresport: www.nostresport.com
Once: www.once.es
Programa EQUAL:
    http://europa.eu.int/comm/employment_social/equal/index_en.cfm
SEO: www.seo-ny.org
Shell: www.shell.com
Solo Ellas: www.soloellas.com
Stop Discrimination: http://www.stop-discrimination.info
The Great Place to Work Institute, Inc: www.greatplacetowork.com
UNCF: www.uncf.org
Universia: www.unversia.net
www.stop-discrimination.info
www.expansionyempleo.es

# Index